CYCLING INTO YOUR SOUL

A journey out into the
world and down into
the soul.

A triumphant return
with newfound
wisdom.

CYCLING INTO YOUR SOUL

Published by:
The Monday Communications Group Ltd
212 Hawkwood Drive NW
Calgary Alberta Canada T3G 3M9
Fax: (403) 283-5983
Email: monday@nucleus.com

CANADIAN CATALOGUING
IN PUBLICATION DATA

Archibald, Marg, 1946 -
    Cycling into your soul

Includes bibliographical references.
ISBN 0-9682100-4-X

    1. Archibald, Marg, 1946 — Journeys. 2. Spiritual biography. 3. Voyages
and travels — Reigious aspects. 4. Self-realization — Religous aspects. 5. Bicycle
touring. I. Monday Communications Group. II. Title.

G465.A731999   291.4'092 C99-900121-3

The creation of this book was nurtured by Linda and Ian Dallas.
The cover and pages were designed with loving care by Lynne Rennie.

Dedicated, with love,
to my Spirit Guide
Renee Josephine Archibald,
a world Traveler,
an independent woman,
my Grandmother.

CONTENTS

THE OTHER TRAVELER

Two travelers set out on a journey. One deals with all the practical details – and on a journey there are plenty of those, the reservations, accommodations, timing, boat versus train versus bus, places to eat, language complications, customs, packing and unpacking, finding bathrooms, finding water, finding maps. All of it.

The Other Traveler starts the trip quietly. Watching. Probably unknown. And may still be unknown at the end, for that matter. But on a magic journey, the Other Traveler flourishes and grows. Day by day, the Other Traveler starts — well — calling the shots. It's the best thing that can happen to any Traveler. First Nations People call it finding one's Spirit Guide.

This is a story of how The Other Traveler became strong, proud and the leader. This is the story of how the Other Traveler became The Spirit Guide.

RIDING INTO THE VOID

Russians are nervous about Russians. They see Mafia and thugs and gangs everywhere. They all know someone who has been killed by the Mafia. They came into his apartment and shot him. They shot him and his mother. He was selling black market videos. He was nineteen.

They see money and goods disappear. Anyone with a business, even a little kiosk, pays protection money. Huge, multinational conglomerates pay out of their Russian offices. "We just pay once a week and have no problems." Mikhail expressed concern about the Mafia bothering me if I rode my bicycle.

"They are ruthless. They will get you. "

"Why?"

Shrug.

"Why would they be interested in getting me?"

"Because that is what they do."

Acquaintances, strangers, strangers' grandmothers, all stopped what they were doing, to talk me out of cycling in Russia. I would be sideswiped by trucks, I would have problems with no-one speaking English, I would be lost, robbed, killed, raped, murdered. Their conviction was scary.

"Travel around by bus. Get on a tour. Do not ride your bicycle here."

I found a television crew standing in the street in — Pereslovl Zullisky. I asked them if they knew the right road to get out of town and get to Yuri Polskei. They interviewed me and asked, "What do you do for protection? Do you have a gun?"

I reconnected with Maxim who I had met while training in Calgary. We had tea at the Radisson Stanislayovskia Hotel in Moscow before I headed out on my bicycle. He said, "Do not do this. Do not ride your bike in Russia. You don't realize what you are up against. You don't know how poor and desperate these people are. You will not last an hour. You are foreign. You have money. American money. You have things. They will know as soon as they see you that you have things they want. They will kill you for your camera. They will kill you for twenty dollars."

Even levelheaded Canadian men who had cycled extensively in Canada and had worked in Moscow for years said, "I wouldn't."

Oh dear. It was unanimous: dangerous and foolhardy beyond description. Never have so many well-meaning people tried to stop me from doing something.

But somewhere in me I was sure that I would be fine. This felt like the start of a mythical journey. This was the testing part. There would be barriers in my way. And here was the first one. Go back. Danger lies here. Do Not do this. But if I were somehow pure of heart (how corny! how sanctimonious! What did I mean?) I would emerge victorious. Burnished. Older, wiser and richer. I had the choice. Want to back down? Want to stay safe? Or want to take on life?

What I wanted to do was to reclaim my independence. My generous hosts in both St Petersburg and Moscow, had insisted on being my protectors, guides, translators and historians. They had taken over my life. They had dissempowered me as they opened doors and looked after my interests. They wouldn't let me step outside without coming along. I was ready to face the uncertainty of my own adventures. Now I would spin away on a bicycle, alone in Mother Russia. If this was the way I was meant to die, it sure beat dropping dead at my desk. Anyway, I knew the coming days would be an amazing adventure. And that my most serious dangers would probably be insects, getting my bike up stairs and gross toilets.

As they say in adventure movies: "I'm going in."

INTO RUSSIAN ON A BICYCLE

I would get up early in the morning and cycle out of Jaroslavl, northeast of Moscow. Thank goodness I had all of my support team from home with me, the people who encouraged me to take this on. Tomorrow – the road. Sonia, do you remember that feeling of excitement and trepidation when we got up at 5AM to beat morning traffic out of Tours, France? Anxiety, exhilaration, the heady thrill of approaching the unknown? It's time to ride. It was like that.

I'M ARMED

It mattered to Russians that I like Russia. They had a child-like eagerness to be seen in a good light. In North American, self-help-speak we would say that they suffer from low self-esteem. They all asked what I thought of Russia with hopeful, open faces. They loved their birch forests, their history, their old churches, their music. They loved the way Russia could be if only it weren't the way it is. They grieved for Russia and ached for things to be better.

And they held out hope that a traveler would see some of the loveliness, would enjoy some of the people, would like the food, would hear the music, would admire the wasting architecture, would be dazzled by the awesome Hermitage art collection, would relish the late sunsets, the wild mushrooms, would be amazed by the Mafia limousines and their cluster of outriders, would see the beauty in the old churches and kremlins — would be touched by the Russian soul.

So they asked. "What do you think of Russia?" Hopefully, expectantly. They wanted to be re-assured.

This provided the clue I needed on how to look after myself. I am a communicator. Why not use my natural strength to protect myself? On the river cruise-boat up to Jaroslavl, I asked a school psychologist to teach me to say: Ya goste vashee-ay stran-ee-a. It means, "I am a guest in your country". Except for the most hardened Mafia hit man, against which no one has a defense, Russians hearing this sentence would rise to the occasion. It turned them into hosts. Their job was then to make Russia wonderful. Any ill intent would be swept away by their sense of responsibility. Mother Russia was counting on them. They couldn't stop themselves.

Armed with that, I felt thoroughly protected. A friend at home mused wryly; "Most people wouldn't consider that armed, Marg."

HIGHWAYS AND BYWAYS

I started riding the Golden Ring highway by heading southwest from Jaroslavl. This kept me away from the intensely thick Moscow traffic but I soon learned I hadn't escaped it altogether. Traffic is fast on the Golden Ring Road. It was common to see a vehicle passing a vehicle that was passing. Riding down the middle of the road was common. It was noisy and alarming. There was no paved shoulder so I followed the example of the locals who cycled serenely between villages on old cruisers. Like them, I often cycled along the packed sand on the shoulder. It was mercifully firm.

After two days of the highway, I turned into the isolated roads that laced through the middle of the Golden Ring. This step caused a whole new wave of alarm.

STEPPING INTO THE PICTURE

You take the right fork off the Golden Ring to get into Rostov. The fork road has a row of trees on each side. It reminded me of the black and white photograph on one of my farewell cards: a flat field with a road winding through it, bordered by tall Lombardy Poplars. Somewhere in France maybe.

There are no people in it. It feels timeless. It seems to say, "The road beckons".

Pondering that picture, the explorer wants to see what is down there; the cyclist wants to feel the trees gliding by. Why does it feel so good to ride between two rows of trees? It duplicates the movie sensation of flying between buildings or rushing through space.

Now, here I was, at that road between rows of beckoning trees. Like a grand driveway. Suddenly quiet. I felt happy. I was riding into my well wishes from others. I was answering the call of the beckoning road. I was suspended in its timelessness, which felt liberating and peaceful. My body felt a shuddery tingle. I had put myself in the picture. Now I was outside of my body watching. The journey and hopes for the journey had become one.

IT ALL STARTED WITH...

It hadn't looked good when, two years before, I saw fifty crouched beside the road ahead. Single woman, aging, losing value. A few tattle tale wrinkles beyond laugh lines. A few body parts dropping or at least drooping. And spreading. My market value on the singles scene was about to plummet. As a single, female, ballroom dancer I looked ahead and saw myself replaced by the new, fresh, younger women. The tiny waists and long legs. The lithe ones. Me, a has-been. Half my life left and I was a has-been.

The advertising agency I owned was losing money. Losing momentum. Losing clients. Losing the edge. A losing proposition.

The only way I could imagine transforming the big five-oh into a positive gesture was to do something grand and outrageous — like going around the world. With my bicycle. Yeah. Why not?!? That's how the idea was born.

Don't get me wrong. I'm no athlete. I'm not fast and I'm not strong. I'm no hero. I just like exploring places on a bicycle. No toe clips. No drop handlebars. No personal best. Just pedal, pedal, look at the scenery, listen to the trees, watch the world, explore out there and inside myself. If I can do that around Southern Alberta, or Ireland, or France, then why not — anywhere?

The idea nearly went off the rails as money got scarce. It took my nephew, Andrew, to suggest that I re-mortgage my house. He said, "Use the money to clear your debts. Rent out the house to cover its costs. Then take the rest of the money and go."

Later, it was my daughter, Sonia, who restored my confidence in the enterprise. After a particularly rough day at work I wailed to her, "Maybe this trip is just another step toward becoming a lonely old woman. And poor. Maybe this is self-deceived folly." She said, "I don't know Mom. All I know is that every single one of my friends wishes it was them. Maybe the question is: "At your next high school reunion do you want to be the person who is telling about this trip or the one listening to someone else telling about this trip?"

Well yes, that's one way to look at it.

STARTING WHERE?

People asked "Where will you start?" That was everyone's first question. I kept saying, "I don't know." But I was asking the same question. Going all the way around was important to me. Fifty called for circumnavigating the globe. But starting, hmmm, where?

When a friend recounted that "We took the overnight train from Moscow to St Petersburg," I knew my answer. Yes. St Petersburg. That's the place to start. The beautiful, exotic, Russian city, rich with architecture and art and a window between east and west. Venice of the north. How appropriate to begin this journey at the crossroads of the world.

Where did that come from? The knowing that that's where I would enter the world? Patty said the words St Petersburg and my heart leapt. There was the missing piece. Aha. I said, "St Petersburg! Yes. I've always wanted to go there. That's where I'll go first."

The decision was made. I never questioned it. Then, when people asked me where I was starting my trip I said, "St Petersburg." They said, "Russia?" They said it like Rush-ahhh?!? I guess there is a St Petersburg in the United States. Yeah, St. Petersburg Russia. *

"NOW YOU'RE READY."

A month before leaving I edited a newsletter for a new client, a psychiatrist. He held several prestigious positions and was clearly trusted and respected by his medical colleagues. Oddly enough, in spite of his years of disciplined medical training, he was working on the body/mind/spirit connection. Leading edge, non-traditional work. So I asked him to prepare me for my journey rather than pay me for my services. For three weeks he was my advisor. He taught me several useful skills:

- protecting my body from disease by drinking copious amounts of water;
- connecting with a wise travel guide within myself;
- nurturing myself with a visualization of light within and
- creating good will with strangers by sending them peaceful thoughts.

You will see how these traveling companions unfolded on the road.

Running down the sidewalk, late for my last appointment with him, I glimpsed headlines of a 747 crash, killing most of the passengers. Suddenly it seemed significant for me. My plane could crash. I could be annihilated before getting off the runway in Calgary. Shit.

Next thought: what the hell — at least I'd finally be on my trip. While still on the Calgary runway I would already be gone. The trip would have begun. Heck the trip had begun now. I was in countdown. I was finally free and doing what I wanted. What better time to cease to exist than when I was on the brink of flying? It didn't matter if my plane crashed.

I was still breathless from running when I sat down with my advisor. I told him of the headline and my reaction to it.

He said, "You are ready to go"

(*Note: For the itinerary, see "Journey at a Glance" and a route map on page 184.)

GOODBYE

Clustered at the departure gate I felt no urge to cry. Tears welled up in my friend Pat's eyes. My daughter, Sonia was her usual level self. My nephew, Andrew, beamed with pride. His traveling protégé was achieving liftoff. I had pulled it off. Goodbye goodbye, take care, wave wave, further and further away, through security, last wave over the shoulder. On my own.

This was it. I was walking, alone to the boarding lounge. I was leaving. Leaving all of it. My affairs were in order.

A friend was moving into my sunny house to look after my beloved calico cat, Brenda, until the house got rented. My house had been a source of joy, a place where I entertained, worked, enjoyed my garden, played my piano and heard guests exclaim: "I love this house!" The renter would get a house with food, table linen, CDs, plants and piano music. I had boxed my clothes and toiletries and walked away. The renter got the rest.

Including my cat, Brenda. She and I had a mutually doting, gently nurturing relationship. She loved to sit on my desk and push the top of her head into my chin. I loved that she did that. At the end of the day, lying in bed with Brenda on my chest felt like the perfect transition into oblivion. She was my buddy. Now I was trusting her to the care of others, knowing that she perceived me as the source of All.

My advertising agency was suspended. Several people were completing the work in progress. My mortgage was life insured. My insurance and my will were current. My accountant, lawyer and bank manager were ready to work as a team, helping Sonia with the transition if I died. I had my shots. Sonia had signing authority and was ready to move the mortgage advance from savings into chequing as I traveled. Bills would get paid. I had said goodbye to my ballroom dancing friends. I had trekked up to Mom's for a goodbye visit. I had cut ties. I was as ready to die as I ever have been. And ready to start living. Now was the moment that my whole life had trained me for. Others have said that. Other's have felt their history and experience suddenly re-sort and go click. All of life up to now was apprenticeship. Now, real life was beginning. I was fifty years, three months and fourteen days old.

Whatever the adventure is, it is now.

SLEEP WRITING

It was afternoon of the "next" day - in airline talk - when I landed in Frankfurt. The airport was full of travelers from all over the world waiting for onward flights. I had four hours to wait for mine.

Experiencing my first time-zone leap and the results of trying to sleep "overnight" on an airplane, I was a sleepwalker. I had traveled through space and time. I had been dropped down in an airport with the familiarity of the new generation of international airports and all the newness of the foreign. And my prior life was left behind. And ahead? I hadn't the foggiest idea. I was in a half-way house, waiting to be airlifted to the next place in my life. The next timescape, lifescape.

I repeatedly fell asleep as I wrote in my journal. Actually I never did catch myself falling to sleep, I caught myself jolting awake. I was convinced that I was getting important insights as I dropped off — then I would wake up. The handwriting was wobbly and hard to decipher. Dropping off, gravity dragged the writing down below the lines. Then I jolted awake mid-word. The insights just eluded me as I woke, but so close. I let myself drift back so I could try again to capture what was rising up from my primeval fog. Just let me grab it, it's right there.

The writing of a sleeping person. Would I learn amazing things if I were able to keep writing while asleep?

INTO THE WORLD
THROUGH RUSSIA

AEROFLOT

They have the worst record in the aviation industry. Western business travelers won't get on an Aeroflot plane under any circumstances. For some reason that didn't phase me. I could hardly wait to start on the Russian part of my experience. Flying KLM into St Petersburg would have felt like cheating.

Close-up, Aeroflot was like an airline twenty years ago. A wide-bodied plane with frayed orange and pink décor. The stewardesses had stewardess outfits — dated, but real. The no-crease, A-line skirts, serviceable pumps with low heels, white blouses and identical, colourful scarves. They also had the same brusque public relations skill, that veneer of almost-friendliness that masks their people-management. Where do stewardesses go to learn that?

I could see it fall apart back in Smoking. Thick smoke hung in the air. The air was smoke. Three guys in the middle section had managed to fold down the chair backs of a row of seats and were sitting facing each other around this improvised coffee table. They looked like they are playing cards but Johnny Walker Red and cigarettes were all that was visible. They were talking loudly and acted like the nearly empty cabin was theirs.

After all the dreadful things I had heard about Aeroflot I felt sorry for the crew. They didn't quite have control of the plane and its passengers, but they were trying.

THE PLAN

I needed a Russian visa to get into Russia and I needed two things to get a Russian visa: a return ticket and an "invitation" to go there. So I bought a return ticket even though I didn't intend to use the second portion and I booked four nights at the St Petersburg Youth Hostel. They generated an invitation, which is a letter written in Russian Cyrillic stating that the St Petersburg Hostel has invited me to come and stay with them. It specified the date I would be there. This invitation was stapled to my visa application and sent to the Russian embassy in Ottawa. After the necessary four days at the Hostel, I would move to Elena's apartment, which I had found through my International Marketing Course.

I would take my bicycle along but I didn't intend to ride in the cities. I would fly into St Petersburg with my bike. At some point I would ride. At some point I would go to Moscow. At some point I would leave Russia for someplace else. That was the plan. That's as far as it went.

PARTING THE IRON CURTAIN

This was serious. This was men without a sense of humour. Men and women, who have had the power of life and death over intrepid travelers crossing the dreaded iron curtain. This was the scene of foreign intrigue, where terrified citizens acted performances for all their lives were worth and spies became the identity that matched their papers. This dark room that felt like a basement was for real, not a movie set, not an it-was-like. This was Russian customs.

And I was there. Bicycle, panniers, passport, Russian visa typed in Cyrillic, that I couldn't understand, and an airplane ticket back out of Russia in a month that I didn't plan to use. My fellow passengers were intent on getting to the front of the line and getting through. What were they thinking behind those blank, bored faces? Had they crossed here in fear before? Were they conscious that this room has been the scene of danger? life crises?

Maybe the officials had found out I wasn't going to use my return ticket. Maybe they would decide I was a spy. Maybe I looked the same as a notorious international criminal. They would snatch me out of the shuffling line and away from my bike and panniers. They would shove me into a windowless room and leave me there without food or water. Then ugly men with no necks and mean mouths would come and shout questions at me in Russian. They would grab me by the hair and shout in my face. They would hit me. They would twist my arms behind my back. What an adventure. I was thrilled by the prospect that I was unprotected out in the world. Nothing but my common sense and my credit cards.

Stamp. Slap. The dead-faced woman slid my stamped visa across the counter back to me and turned to the next in line. I'm in. I'm in Russia. It was a bit disappointing that I wasn't interrogated.

THE TWITCH

I first noticed the eye twitch in the taxi from the airport to the St Petersburg Hostel. My right eyelid dropped a bit and kind of fluttered. There it was again. Well I guess after 24 hours of diurnal chaos and sitting in daylight when my body expected night and the weird air in airplanes — I guess it was to be expected that my body was twitchy.

THE BODY SPEAKS

My initial four days — or more appropriately nights — of jet lag, were in the Hostel in St. Petersburg. For someone who cannot go to sleep with any light or noise, it felt like I was in a different body. Uncontrollable sleeping. Seemed quite odd. Lying on my bed in the evening, surrounded by four other women, light on, chatting people coming and going, I kept falling asleep. First dreaming, then just gone. I'd surface and then sink. Sometimes I would even rejoin the conversation for a brief time before sinking away again. The sleep was bigger than all of us.

How can a woman who has lived self-indulgently alone for ten years suddenly be happy sleeping in a room with four other people? I felt pleased with my fellow travelers — women on the move — and drifted off.

TRANSCENDING EFFICIENCY

I headed out on foot thinking about my route and my plan for the day. I was thinking of what I wanted to do in this as-yet-unexplored part of St Petersburg. I wanted to check out a monastery with famous people in the graveyard — people like Dostoyevsky — find a park to sit and write in my journal; eventually get lunch; maybe have a walk along the river — all without retracing my steps so that I could explore new places along the way. I heard myself thinking that I'd like to figure out the most efficient combination of tasks and routes.

Then, FLASH: Why? Why do I need the most efficient? Efficiency would screen out possibility and creativity. It would preclude whimsy. How could I follow my instincts while I was following a plan? How could I change my mind when something wonderful came along?

Suddenly I saw the drive for efficient as a problem. The source of many problems. To be efficient is to manage opportunities out of our lives. We are efficient at the expense of natural flow. It is fair enough to be capable of efficiency. But to run our lives by the golden rule of efficient is to live in harness.

I was good at efficiency. I did a minimum of two things at once. Often three. I was fast. Onlookers were dazzled by my ability to juggle effectively, work efficiently and fit it all in.

Now I had six months not to be efficient — to be something else. In-efficient. I could savour, dawdle, be aimless, repeat, backtrack, stare into space, dither and waste time. What a luxury. Had I arrived at the land of don't push the river?

I sat on a park bench and wrote in my journal: It is liberating to not be whizzing along doing three things at once as fast as possible. The rebellious thrill of in-efficiency. Whee!

THE ST. PETERSBURG BUILDINGS SPEAK

In St Petersburg I saw amazing splendour. Only a Czar could create St Petersburg. It had been a swamp buzzing with disease-laden insects. Hundreds of thousands of slaves died building it. An edict from Peter the Great dragged Moscow nobility, kicking and screaming, to live there. And here it stands. Buildings of peach, yellow, pale green, robin's egg blue, salmon orange and pearly grey with curved walls and ornate carvings and moldings. A network of canals with sculpted bridges bordered by stunning architecture and parks.

The word rococo comes to mind. What does rococo mean? Who knows. This is rococo. Now these beauties were terribly run down. Faded, peeling, crumbling and many were abandoned. Massive restoration work was going on in the midst of tarnished splendour.

One three-story building took up a whole city block and was covered with scaffolding and green netting. The windows were black holes. People swirled around it but it appeared to be crumbling and empty. Not so. Inside it was a gleaming, white department store full of high tech household toys: small electric appliances, decorator items like bonsai trees with jade leaves. Disposable income trophies. All in little alcoves. It was bustling with an air of self-importance. Affluent shoppers carrying fists full of shopping bags.

The building had been erected long ago for seafaring merchants to set up their wares in the alcoves. East met west at Russia's doorstep. Probably defunct during the Communists' rule and just now reviving to serve New Russians.

I stepped into the entrance of another building with a glistening gold dome outside. Inside it was gutted. A once beautiful old church, I could see the onion shape on the inside of the dome but it was empty and dark. Huge pillars and rough walls stripped back to bare bricks. There was chicken wire strung inside to catch falling pieces. It looked bombed. If a war had just ended the state of disrepair and cleanup in St Petersburg would make sense. And maybe a war had just ended. A war of human nature against an enviable ideal of people being fairly and equitably paid and treated. The fair part lost.

Lying on my bed in the hostel I looked out the window at the faded ochre beauty across the street. A building that could have been in New York. I saw the no-longer-full moon above the roofline. Aha, they have the moon here in Russia too.

THE RUSSIAN FACES SPEAK

Sloppy young police hang around on corners smoking cigarettes and looking bored and harmless. They are described as brutal.

People in the street carry unlikely loads — like a car door.

In the cities, young Russian women are tall with long, lean legs. Beautiful women, beautifully dressed, parading high fashion — international high fashion. These women would hold their own on Fifth Avenue, New York.

On the streets beside them, the buses and trolley cars looked truly war-zone, packed with people, some of them hanging out windows. All seemed good natured about it, even body-to-body on a hot afternoon.

I saw on old woman on the street. She was sinewy and darkly tanned as if she lived in the street. She was wearing an old dress, dirty and hanging on her body, but incongruously, she had long, silver-painted fingernails. She had a wooden chair on the sidewalk in front of her that she picked up by the backrest, moved a foot further down the sidewalk and then took a step forward. The Russian walker. She had the inward look of a New York street schizophrenic. People flowed past her.

The weathered faces and gold teeth of the old men and women who have seen so much. And they stood for hours on the sidewalk with something to sell. It might be a single, gorgeous bouquet of gladiolas. They had walked into town with their bouquet that morning from their small, crumbling, rural house. They stood waiting for a buyer. It's all they had. Street vendors sold a handful of garden-grown carrots bound with sewing thread wound round and round dozens of times. One man stood in the row of vendors with only a garlic bud offered in his upturned hand.

I saw a woman on the trolley car in St Petersburg take a banana out of a bag in her lap, peal it deliberately and start eating. I looked out the window. When I glanced back at the woman who had eaten the banana, she was peeling a banana and putting it in her mouth.

That's funny. I thought I just saw that a minute ago. Maybe another woman. A few minutes later I glanced at the banana-woman and she was AGAIN peeling a banana and putting it in her mouth.

This was feeling like one of those movie edits where they can, over and over, show the person going off the diving board. What is happening here? Am I in a movie? Are we all being manipulated in the hands of a giant editor? This time I watched her eat the whole banana. Was this a trick banana? She would open her mouth wide and stick a large section of banana into her mouth and then close her mouth and bite it off.

Elena explained that this is not unusual, to eat three bananas one after another. "Everyone loves bananas. We didn't have them. Bananas are like candy."

And when ice cream bars first came to Moscow, five years ago, even in the middle of winter, people would stand on the street and buy one after another and eat them. Five in a row. "People didn't know what to do with this new thing."

THE CHURCHES SPEAK

Gold leaf was being put back on church domes. I had never seen so much gold. You've no idea how bright pure-gold domes are in the sunlight. Boing! They looked like dazzling mirrors. The contrast between the splendour and gold of the Russian Churches compared to the serf's gruesome life and then, later, to the bleak Soviet times, was disquieting. And now New Russia is whizzing ahead at the speed of light with its western glamour, bustling self-importantly below the newly re-gilt church domes. And among them, moving slowly if at all, the lame, the begging, the old, the broken.

A mosaic-tile encrusted church with a green roof, had been abandoned long ago. It was boarded up and the grass had grown high all around it. There wasn't even a road or path to it any more. The surrounding area had turned industrial. Morning sun was glinting off the ceramic tiles. Each of the tiles had a tiny, raised picture on it: a rooster, a man on a horse, a figure cutting down grain, a woman weaving. Each tile seemed unique. I couldn't find any two the same. The tile patterns were raised to three dimensional and the surface of the building curved and folded organically. The detail of the pattern in each tile gave away to pointillism when looking at them all together. Now the encrusted church is silent and deserted. There is an iron ring to open the giant, bleached, wooden door that doesn't open.

Thoughts of all the doors to beautiful things that don't open. And then of all the beautiful things that disappoint once we gain access.

IS IT EVENING IN CALGARY?

Every day, at some time in the day, I asked myself: "What time is it in Calgary? Is it evening? Are they dancing? Dancing without me?" If I calculated that it was a Friday or Saturday evening I felt agitated and depressed. Monday evenings were a bit of a break. I could relax. No dancing Monday. Sunday was completely safe. No-one dances Sunday now that Sunday Singles has ended. Whew.

TRAGEDY AND A SUMMER CLOUDBURST

If it was classy, clean and expensive, it was New Russian. The clientele had money and the self-aware swagger of schoolyard bullies. They dressed in expensive leather jackets, designer pants and trendy shoes. They had beautiful, slim wives, sporting designer clothes. Their children wore designer clothes too. Nice little people these Russian children. None of that demanding manipulation that North Americans have learned to create in their children.

In one of the restaurant booths a little girl danced on the bench. She was too young to walk yet but she could stand and bob. Her parents sang along with the song, accompanying her dancing. A little, New Russian family at play. The restaurant played schmaltzy music from the West: I am your lady, you are my man. The little girl bobbed. Her parents beamed and held her hands. I ate world-class borscht.

After a mime of putting my hands on my glass of water and pretending it was hot and burned my hands, the waitress taught me how to order vater garyatchi — hot water. Then she brought me a dessert of dried fruit soaked in liquor topped with thick cream and caramelized walnuts. Amazing. And Bryan Adams sang … is all for one, all for love, the one to hold, the one you love. I felt the old yearning to be held, loved, swept away. Music was bringing that up from down inside somewhere and I was no longer thinking of vater garyachi. I was flushed and staring into space. I was looking for something that wasn't there. My tragedy: no soul mate.

Now it was pouring outside. A man ducked inside and I saw him illustrating that the raindrops were the size of the last joint on his baby finger. People wearing summer clothes huddled in doorways. They knew St Petersburg's changeable weather. They knew it wouldn't rain hard for long. A few were holding newspapers over their heads. An international thing that — taking shelter under a newspaper. As they ducked inside, they shake the open paper off to their side and throw it down in the street or fold it and hold it away from their body. My tragedy was swept away by the joy of watching a summer cloudburst — in Russia.

RUSSIAN FAMILIES
Most Russians have only one child. Elena said, "It would be unthinkable to not have a child. No-one ever speaks of not having children." But rarely more than one. Both parents get great pleasure from being with their little person. Couples walk down the street with their child between them, holding hands. All happy. It made me smile. They relished the simple joy of being in each others' company.

THE QUESTIONS
As I wandered and watched, I pondered what I wanted to learn on this trip. Along with turning around my aging image, I wanted to find out if there were business opportunities for a small, specialized, advertising agency in the developing global economy. Or were there brand new ways, waiting to be discovered, for me to earn a living? And could I learn to trust and value myself? My older self? And what was I here for anyway? Surely not to run an advertising agency? Many questions. A tall order. Could I find answers to live by?

FINDING GRANNY
My mind/body/spirit advisor at home had suggested that I would benefit from a spirit-guide as I traveled. Someone to help when I needed it. Someone to give day-to-day counsel. Someone to turn to in emergencies. An advisor.

After questioning me about my family, he suggested that my father's mother, Granny Archibald, would be my best traveling wise-woman. I had been given her middle name, Josephine. She had traveled extensively during a time when that was unusual for a woman. Born into an affluent, banking family in Paris, Granny was a child at the 1900 Paris Exposition when the Eiffel Tower was opened and Paris was the undisputed centre of the world. "There were sidewalks that moved," she told us. "You just stood on them and moved along." Granny had international connections and traveled the world visiting them. When her children were young she would leave them with their nanny and her husband with his hunting dogs and take off for the world.

I have seen grainy, sepia movies, some of the earliest home movies ever made, of Granny on shipboard playing quoit; on giant rugs sitting on the lawns of estates in colonial India, taking tea while uniformed servants watered the gardens from watering cans; tottering in high heels under a frilly parasol along trails to the New Zealand geysers. I saw pictures of her in jodhpurs and high leather boots camping in the virgin BC forest. Granny was a traveler.

My memories of Granny were childhood memories of her "baby-sitting" while Mom and Dad were on holidays. She didn't like children. She hadn't had much to do with her own. And she had no self-doubts. So it was a rough ride when Granny was at the helm. The saving grace was that she served French pastries every day at tea-time.

During one of these visits, the newspaper reported a commercial plane crash. The now-deceased stewardess had told her roommate that she hadn't wanted to go on that flight, that, for the first time, she was apprehensive about flying. Granny said, "Silly girl. What a fool not to heed that."

Granny died in a bizarre and somehow appropriate accident when a huge, thousand-year-old cedar tree in Stanley Park blew over during a freak Vancouver storm, Typhoon Frieda. Theirs was the last car over the Lion's Gate Suspension Bridge, flapping in the wind like the ill-fated Tacoma Narrows Bridge. The Bridge Authority, afraid it would snap, closed it after they drove across. Fallen trees blocked the Stanley Park Causeway ahead. Another tree fell. This one on the car. Granny died instantly. I was sixteen.

After her death we read some of her leather-bound travel diaries. They had onion skin pages and the writing was in fountain pen. She often wrote in French but, surprisingly, she had a few journals in English. She wrote with disgust about Parisians showing unseemly amounts of affection in public parks and wrote sadly of her husband, "poor, dear Howard." As a young bride from Europe, when she traveled by train across Canada, she wrote with awe about the open spaces and the giant trees that she saw for the first time. They kept coming up in her journals, their beauty, how many there were, how tall they were. She loved the Canadian trees. It was ironic to read of her love for those trees when we now knew that one would kill her. In her journals we saw a different Granny, one who observed the world and let it touch her.

For years I have kept a photo of Granny on my mantelpiece. She is wearing a long, white dress, circa 1910, standing on a log in a forest. She is holding a branch with one raised hand. A sunbeam is shining down on her so that her hair and her dress look like the source of light. She is laughing. She looks like an angel in the forest. A beam of light in the dark.

My advisor said that if I learned to connect with Granny, she would be there when I needed her.

As he taught me, twice every day, I sat quietly, and would watch Granny materialize in front of me. In the first few weeks I saw her in various locations, situations and clothes. I experimented with seeing her standing in her black velvet cocktail dress with the white satin collar. Then I placed her as a tiny figure in a forest, surrounded by moss and ferns, sitting on a shelf of fungus growing on a fallen tree. Eventually our visits were in her bedroom in her lovely, Tudor house in the exclusive Uplands District of Victoria. She wore her long pink satin nightie and crocheted bed jacket with fluffy marabou around the neck and wrists. She was always sitting on the edge of her bed with a straight back, relaxed, her hands in her lap.

As we visited I learned more about her humour, her twinkle. I heard the laugh that I had forgotten. I learned things I had never known about her. She became my trusted wise woman. I turned to her with my questions.

BUILDING BRIDGES OVER DINNER

Day five, I left the hostel and moved to an apartment. It was arranged through Elena but the apartment was really her parents'. Elena's Mom was away for the summer, at her mother-in-law's. Her Dad, Mikhail, was back from work and joined us for dinner. Elena is their only child. When she was young, Mikhail devoted every Sunday to taking her to historical places and telling her their stories: the Cathedral of St David, The Monastery of Saints Peter and Paul, Peterhoff. Elena knows St Petersburg and its heroes.

The table was set in the livingroom. Elena had cooked roast chicken that she served chopped in big chunks, boiled potatoes, cabbage, sliced tomatoes, boiled carrots, bread. Mikhail had a delightful sense of humour — "Seeing as I am in charge here I better go into the kitchen and run things." Even in the military he had fun. It showed in a publicity photo taken when he was a "specialist" in Libya. (Remember those specialists we heard about? They aren't soldiers, they are spe-shul-ists. Advisors. Like the American spe-shul-ists in Vietnam.) They kept hamming in front of the camera until the photographer lowered the boom. "Get serious." You can see the resulting smirks twitching around the corners of their mouths as five of them lean over a map, playing specialists.

Mikhail is smart. He had been a "rocket scientist" before being seduced into an army career. He speaks German, French and Arabic. In the military, he belonged to the privileged few who had access to highly desirable foreign goods in special stores. Only people who had served overseas received what they called cheques that they could use to buy clothes, food, TVs, VCRs, sewing machines even cars. Perestroika and glasnost changed all that. Overnight, he and his colleagues were redundant. His forced retirement from the prestige and perks of a colonel in the Red Army left Mikhail bitter about Gorbachov and his reforms. Now he works part-time in the parts department of an auto repair depot and is usually drunk.

With Elena's help translating, we spoke over dinner and on into the evening about Russia - (sad situation); the KGB - (they knew how to control crime); the Mafia - (everywhere), perestroika - (only works for the crooks), New Russians - (have stolen factories, mines and utilities and are getting very rich); the Bay of Pigs and Cuban missile crisis - (all posturing, all politics, they wouldn't do anything); Garry Powers - (we were all doing it, it was what was done); Kruschov - (so unprofessional, so bad when he banged that shoe on the table at the U.N., no class.); health care - (nothing like what it used to be, there were rest places for workers to go and get over stress, now - nothing), free education - (the schools are now hopeless as well as corrupt) and on and on. (Nothing works now.)

We had a grand evening. I felt like all the years of cold war and fear and bomb shelters and distortion were being blown away. Poof - gone. All we had believed - poof - gone.

Elena was cross with her Dad when he left to catch the train and join his wife for several days. He was drunk, weaving and grinning. She feared that he would fall off the train platform and knew her mother would be angry when he arrived that way. But they were obviously close. "He misses her," said Elena.

His mother's house was in a small village. It was a winter house, as opposed to summerhouse, because it was built around a huge, clay, Russian stove. The stove was built first. The house was built around it. The house had electricity but no indoor toilet. "My Dad has made a nice toilet, close to the house, just as nice as inside."

During World War II, when Germans, (Russians say "fascists") occupied their house throughout the siege of St Petersburg, Mikhail's parents lived in an ambulance for two and a half years.

What is the Mother-in-law and daughter-in-law relationship? "They get along. They both like it very clean. They clean every day." Mikhail joins them for two weeks every four weeks.

FAMILY CONNECTIONS

Each evening, as I was dropping off to sleep with my eye still twitching, Elena would go downstairs and visit Olga and Ludmila, another army family, friends of many years. Both sets of parents had been posted overseas. Both daughters had been raised by grandparents. Olga's husband was also forced into retirement and left to alcohol and depression.

Olga asked Elena if I had yet tried Russian mushroom soup. Elena replied that she hadn't had time to make it what with taking me around places all day. (Elena wouldn't let me set foot outside the apartment without being at my side.) Fine, Olga would cook it for dinner and bring it up because I must have some wild mushroom soup before leaving St Petersburg. Up they came, carrying dinner. And she was right. The clear mushroom broth was rich and delicious. She had also made fruit filled pastries for dessert.

We assembled around the table in the livingroom, for dinner. When Elena got up to return to the kitchen, she passed behind her friend Ludmila's chair. She stopped and caressed the top of her head and said, "I love her." Wonderful, easy bond. Sisters. No one showed awkwardness or embarrassment. They knew it was true.

In spite of her husband's reaction to the change happening in Russia, Olga said, "In my heart I believe it is the right thing. You can come here. We will do business with the west. It will get better. But it is hard for some people now."

It came out that I was divorced and had a grown daughter. Olga asked if I regretted getting divorced. I said it was the wisest thing I ever did. She nodded.

They were excited when I told them that my former husband's family had originated in Kobrin, a city in what is called White Russia: between Poland and Russia. I went on to explain that they took their family name, Kobrinsky, from the town. We were even more excited when we found Kobrin on the map.

I was awash with wanting Sonia and her Dad to travel to Russia. There was so much to learn about who we are from what they are, these Russians. Vernon would see that his bitter melancholy has Russian roots. They are all like that.

CENTRALIZED HOT WATER

The phrase vater garyatchi proved helpful when I wanted to know if a hotel had any hot water for showering. You see, the centralist system in Russia includes central hot water generation in each city. Hot water comes to your apartment from a central plant. Russians treat it is an unlimited resource. They wash dishes by leaving the hot water running down the sink. They do not own kitchen sink plugs. When I described to Elena that in the west we fill the sink with soapy water to wash dishes she said, "Yes, I have heard this." In the bathroom the hot water pipes wind back and forth on the wall. Russians hang towels on them so the towels are always warm. In the summer, while the hot water plants are shut down for maintenance, there is no hot water for several weeks. So I used vater garyatchi? to find out if their water was turned off. Usually it was.

RUSSIAN FOOD

Russians eat a great deal of meat. There are butcher shops everywhere. They eat their meat quite fatty so you often get what we would consider greasy meals. Boiled chicken with garlic is rich and delicious. Their beef is old, stringy and cooked for a long time. It has flavor and is filling.

Their passion for wild mushrooms results in some of their most delicate dishes. I saw people heading into forests with baskets over their arms and cars with several baskets strapped on the roof. Children sit beside the highway with three or four huge mushrooms on a blanket for sale.

I pointed at tiny metal cups from which other people in a hotel dining room were eating with small spoons. I wanted some of that. That's how I got to taste mushrooms baked in herbs and a rich cream sauce. Delicious.

They eat bread, cheese and cream cheese with many meals. They pride themselves in their yogurt, which seemed just the same as ours. That popular hazelnut-chocolate spread is often served in people's homes.

Tea is the beverage of choice but coffee is quickly gaining popularity. The coffee interests place articles in the press about the growing popularity of coffee. Russians, eager to be affiliated with the winner, will flock to coffee based on that news. Their beloved samovars will sit unused.

Eggs are served hard-boiled, even for breakfast. Toast is almost unheard of. You get bread with a hard boiled egg at breakfast. They eat kasha, which looks like porridge although they insist that it is not. And in restaurants you order butter separately. In fact you often order each item for your meal separately.

There is a brand of ice cream bar, Maxim, that is available in many places, vanilla ice cream with chocolate coating. It is consistently rich and delicious so probably imported.

The garden restaurant in the expensive, international Hotel Europa in St Petersburg is under a huge skylight. They serve the kind of fancy sandwiches that you could get at any high class restaurant in the world.

THE INFREQUENT HIGH - SPEED TRAIN

I took the high-speed train from St Petersburg to Moscow. It only ran on Tuesday and Thursday. Russians joked that it took the rest of the week to repair the track from the strain of this fast train. My bike was crammed into a tiny room thanks to a bribe to the conductor. The bathrooms had stainless steel squatty toilets that you flushed by sticking a metal pole into them and pushing the bottom flap down. I had a huge picnic that Elena had packed and the train steward brought through odd food packs full of 1950s era sweets like Wagon Wheels. (When did you last see a Wagon Wheel?)

I was met at the Moscow station by a travel agency representative who had arranged an apartment close to the centre of Moscow. But the woman who lived there proved to be unhappy about the arrangement so after three uncomfortable days I moved into Svetlana's apartment. She worked with the Russians I had met when they were in Canada for training.

THE VILLAGE

Walking the city and looking at maps, I could see the peasant-village origin of Moscow. The Kremlin is in the center of the city. There are concentric rings of roads around it, close to the Kremlin and further and further out. The Boulevard Ring. The Garden Ring. Switch to a larger scale map with Moscow on it and there again, rings of highways around Moscow. The centre of the universe. Rings and roads that join the rings. Like a giant spiderweb.

Inside the city, the labyrinthine layout and road disrepair and construction generate regular newspaper articles, illustrated with maps, explaining how to get from one spot to another in the city. The detours are elaborate and lengthy. The frustration of driving a car in Moscow must be off the scale.

GOING NATIVE

Even the Moscow-vites can't find their way around in Moscow. And I must have been blending in because several Russians asked me for directions on the street. This gave me a great sense of pride. Like many travelers, I hated to be perceived as tourista — camcording the quaint and jumping back on the bus. I was thrilled when, one afternoon, I could successfully direct a woman to where she wanted to go. Her speaking Russian, my speaking International mime, worked fine. I walked on air. I'm in. But my eye was still twitching.

CAR REPAIRS

Svetlana didn't drive. However, her boss, who had been a guest of mine in Calgary, wanted me chauffeured. So if I had errands around Moscow I was offered a car and driver. The driver was one of the other men from the office. Svetlana came along to look after me.

The offer of a car and driver sounds quite luxurious doesn't it? But in Moscow that means a small, rusted out, beaten up heap with pieces falling off and dust embedded in the interior.

Sergei, the driver, was married, for the third time. Well it turned out that he and his wife in fact weren't technically married. They had been but they weren't now. She divorced him to keep her job at the KGB. You see Sergei had a sister who had married a man from Chechnya. This was considered traitorous and Sergei's wife was threatened with being fired if she didn't divorce him. So she did. But no-one seemed to follow up on whether they were still actually living together, sleeping together, buying groceries together after they were divorced.

Although Sergei was Svetlana's "best friend," she hadn't known any of this. Their contact, until my arrival, had been at work. Chauffeuring me around, they spent more time alone together than they ever had before. This story came out during one of Svetlana and Sergei's intimate kitchen chats after a day on the road with me. By then I was asleep in the livingroom, they were doing whatever in the kitchen.

Anyway, back to cars. A Moscow gas station only sells gas and each gas pump has a man standing beside it offering to pump your gas for you. These men had no connection to the gas station except that they had arrived and stood beside a gas pump before anyone else that morning. If you let them pump your gas you were expected to pay them something.

Car repairs are done on the side of the road. You see cars along the highways with hoods open, even jacked up with people underneath them. And of course the inevitable happened: Sergei's car broke down on a Sunday excursion. He engaged the clutch and I heard a snap. Oh Oh. That sounds like the clutch cable to me. This'll be good.

We coasted to the side of the road. Sergei advised Svetlana that we had a problem. Svetlana took a blanket brought along for the picnic, spread it on the undergrowth beside the road, sat down and lit a cigarette. "I trust this man. I don't know why, but I do."

Sergei pulled off his T-shirt and lay down under the car. After a while he walked over and discussed the situation with Svetlana. She translated. "We have lost a detail. This detail is important to fix the car. We must find it." They insisted that I stay put while they walked back along the shoulder of the highway. They reported back, "There are many details on the road but not the right one."

Sergei leaned over the hood, he poked around in the trunk and went back under the car. Then the guy working on the car fifteen feet down the highway from Sergei called him over. He had the right detail. "I knew I could trust this man. Others, you know, would blame the woman. Not him. He is a good man." Ah yes, Svetlana, I know the signs, like it or not, you are falling.

After twenty minutes we were back in the car and underway, a bit shaky but underway. I felt fulfilled. I had had a truly Russian motoring experience.

AMONG THE ENEMY, CIRCA 1960

My memories of Russia, the feared giant from the sixties, became ludicrous sharing daily life with contemporary Russians. They had been the enemy. They would annihilate us all before we reached middle age. They would combine forces with the weapons-adoring Americans and knock the planet off its axis and send it reeling, a dead cinder, off into deep space. Nothing left but mutating cockroaches. The history of human life, brief, violent, struggling, finally concluded.

The Cuban missile crisis had been a close call. In spite of my father's usual level-headedness, reading Fail-Safe had left him conscious of what little it would take to start The End. A split second miss-judgement could trigger it all.

We were teenagers. Dad gathered us in the livingroom as the crisis built and told us that the family was leaving Vancouver, a likely strike center. We would move to Victoria on Vancouver Island.

"Once the bombs come it will be too late to get out. The streets will be jammed with people in a panic, desperate to get away. Victoria will not likely get a direct hit. Life will never be the same after the bombs. You'll never go to the store again to shop, there won't be running water or electricity. But you'll be alive and you can start building again."

"But Dad…" we protested. What about piano lessons? Friends? He was adamant.

"Be ready to leave school tomorrow. When the principal comes to get you from your classroom, just gather your things and go out to the car. We'll be waiting for you."

The Soviet boats steamed toward Cuba. Our departure hinged on what Kennedy had to say in an unprecedented, televised announcement. We somberly gathered around the TV. Kennedy told us that high altitude espionage planes had recorded that the Russian tankers, with ICBM missiles on board, had turned back from Cuba. The Russians had blinked. We could stop holding our breath. We didn't have to flee. But we were left with the hangover of a close call.

MEANWHILE IN RUSSIA

While the West looked down the barrel of that gun, new apartment blocks in Moscow were being built far enough apart so that when the bombs came and the buildings fell they wouldn't knock each other down. A Russian businessman told me this apologetically.

MOM'S PEACE MOVEMENT

Through the coldest, darkest days of the cold war Mom wrote letters, went to meetings, baked tarts to raise money, managed displays of the horrific human damage wrought by the bombs at Hiroshima and handed out leaflets on street corners.

And the theme was always the same: we can live peacefully together.

But it wasn't fashionable. What was fashionable was to be a hard liner. We needed to be tougher than them. Smarter, stronger with faster, more accurate, deadly weapons. That's how we were going to avoid war. Peace was oddball. Peace was soft. And anyway, she was our mother. What do mothers know about cold, hard logistics and handling the enemy? We scoffed. We discounted. We rolled our eyes. As today's teens would say, What ev-er.

Through all our sneering and tough talk, Mom kept praying and believing and talking about world peace and disarmament and going to her meetings and writing her letters. And now here I was in Russia. Brushing shoulders with Russians on the sidewalks of Moscow. Walking through the once-dreaded Kremlin. I was here and I was safe. The iron curtain was down. So was the Berlin Wall. Trade doors were open. Travel was increasing. Russians were on our side now, more interested in making money than proving a point

Here I was. A new world dawning and perhaps because my Mother and her friends never stopped praying for and talking about world peace. It should have been my mother here. It should have been her taking credit for never giving up. For dragging the rest of us to détente just by the sheer force of believing it was possible. It should be Mom standing on the Moscow Bridge taking a bow to throngs of cheering Russians.

So I bought a bouquet of daisies and, standing on the bridge, I pulled a petal from one of the daisies and held it up in my hand and said, "This is you, Mom. And you are here in Moscow. You made this possible. You have given me Russia and now I give it to you. You have earned it." And I dropped the white daisy petal into the Moscow River. I watched it float down on the currents of air, light as a prayer floating through the collective conscious as it drifted out of sight. It was gone from view before it hit the water. I cried tears of joy, sadness, pride.

"I love you Mom. I can never make up for the scoffing as you quietly believed. You have given all of us, a gift of great price. You have given us freedom from fear of being annihilated. You have given us nothing less than the world so that I can walk freely in it. Thank you Mom." My tears washed all the fear, for all time, all people — washed away. I felt at one with the quiet believers who have eternally, quietly moved us forward. I was honoring them all. Peace around me. Peace inside me. Mom's peace. My chest was bursting with the power of it all.

WHERE IS LOVE?

Another self-protection technique taught by my advisor back at home had been to fill myself with love. Sounds flaky doesn't it? Particularly when you are sitting at your computer or the steering wheel of your car. But think about this situation. After someone you love phones unexpectedly and you sit in an afterglow that feels like more than a good mood, you have a sense that the love in the world around you has grounded you, filled you and made everything feel right. You feel bathed in...something.

My advisor wanted me to know how to connect with that when I was in places where no-one could call me. He taught me, every day, to visualize a golden ball of light descending from above my head down into my body. He said that the easiest way for him to fill the golden ball with love was to think of his kids. I tried it. And I could certainly fill it with love for my daughter Sonia. That made it rich and golden and glowing. Warm, endless love.

But the love was supposed to be coming from out there into me, so I wanted to fill it with her love for me. And that was, um, just over there somewhere. I caught glimpses of it for brief moments when she seemed to be sending love to me. I could feel it when I recalled something she wrote in a card.

Then why couldn't I connect with that? Why couldn't I consistently conjure it up? I would sit with my eyes closed and think about it and probe and ponder and it didn't come. Now and then it came. But nothing reliable. What came was her resentment, anger, annoyance, impatience. What came was that I was afraid of her.

After a few days of groping for the unreachable I felt defeated. I didn't feel loved by my daughter. I knew that she happened to be particularly impatient with me at that time but I was surprised and dismayed that I couldn't connect with a feeling of love from her.

That left me mourning for several days. Emotional free-fall. Unwanted, unloved, abandoned. I grieved. Alone in Russia, without the daily bustle of running an advertising agency, I finally confronted my reality. Alone.

A week later it hadn't changed. It wasn't going anywhere. It wasn't getting worse.

So was I going to forget about that meditation? Was there any other way I could do it? His kids worked for him. What could work for me? I needed to find love somewhere.

What is love? Where is it? I saw myself smile and sigh, "Ahhh," when I watched a delighted little girl riding on the extra bicycle seat mounted in front of her dad, holding onto the handle bars between Dad's hands, proud and safe.

That felt like love. That looked like love. And again when I saw a kiss on the subway escalator. That wasn't just love between them. That touched love in me too. A beautiful woman, quietly slipping money to a beggar and walking on. A fat little flower blowing over in the wind and bobbing back up. A sunset. A building being tenderly restored. The gentle waves on the shore, over and over, never ending.

I was witnessing a giant pool of love and nurturing that is laced throughout the world, woven into the universe; available to dip into any time I wanted. Without boundaries, without time limit, without question or qualifiers. Just there. Beautiful, infinite, pure love unending, unlimited just — there. I knew I could tap that whenever I needed to fill my golden ball with love.

It was easy to draw that down, like a warm, soft whirlpool distilled out of the pool of life and funneled into the top of my head. It poured love into my skin, bones, muscles, nerves, cells, atoms, soul. No beginning, no end. The weeks of discovering that I felt that no one loved me and the humiliation and shame I felt as one of the unloved led me through to something bigger and unerringly reliable.

Once I started riding my bike it was obvious, that love out there. I was amazed I hadn't noticed it before. I saw it all around me. I rode through it. Some days it crowded out everything else in the world. Just love.

Then I also heard and felt it flowing in from people at home. Did I have to be over-performing to get their love? After nagging myself with that question for a few days I forgot about it and just enjoyed. And have ever since. Everywhere.

That's where the love is.

WE'LL COME BACK FOR YOU.

There was a Russian cruise line with a large fleet of boats going up and down a gigantic, inland water system. It went from the "cityport" two hours outside Moscow, up the Moscow River, through a canal and lock system built by slaves under Stalin's rule and up to the Volga River. This was no little afternoon jaunt. I could cruise a big circle route northwest from Moscow, then east and finally heading south. I could make it almost to the Black Sea. Twenty-nine days of cruising before I would have to turn around. But I wasn't going all the way. Only up to the top, Jaroslavl, where I would begin cycling without Moscow traffic. A two-day cruise.

It was time to go. The boat inched sideways, away from the cityport dock. Before it cleared the boat ahead, there was an announcement on the loud speaker and the boat returned to the dock. Laughter, merriment and gesticulating on the upper deck. A couple had turned up on the dock three minutes late and wanted to get onto the boat. They called out. They were prepared to leap. The public address system said, "Stay there. We will come back and get you." The boat pulled back in. The crew reached over and lifted them and their luggage on board. A round of applause. Everyone loved it.

The symbolism of having someone come back for you — back from anywhere — packs an emotional wallop for all of us. To have two hundred people and a boat of several tons that had departed on schedule, come back for you — now that is huge. That is love.

We pulled away again under the blessing of a vivid rainbow against a black sky in the east. Golden sunlight beamed down on the boat. Did this bode well or what?

SUNRISE IN THE LOCK

I went to sleep in my stateroom as birch trees glided serenely past, silhouetted against the still-light Russian summer sky. A few orange fires dotted the shore where people enjoyed the summer evening on the riverbank.

I woke to a wall of concrete that felt inches from my face but was really inches from the side of the boat. Rust streaked concrete, metal fittings. We were stopped. All was silent. But the sight was like the clang of closing the mother's coffin at the beginning of Dr. Zhivago. Clank. In my face.

I got up and went out on deck. We were enveloped in a fog shroud. The world was silent. Then the halo of the rising sun came through the fog, backlighting the trees along the bank, slanting low through them and turning the fog golden. The ground glistened with countless, tiny, golden mirrors. The sun streamed into the world. Glorious sunshine. Still world.

My brain did a quick scan as I wrote that in my journal. Why am I feeling upset about something? Uneasy? A vague, ghost of something bothering me? And in a nanosecond I landed on — dancing. Maybe people are ballroom dancing in Calgary right now. Without me. I have lost my place there. And the waters have closed over top of me, unnoticed, sinking into oblivion. Good grief.

WATCHING

People on the shore stood and watched the boats, people on the boats watched people on the shore watching people on the boats. There were scores of boats each day and there were hundreds of people along the shore. We never stopped being fascinated by each other.

This boatload of holiday-ers was a happy place. They hooted and whistled and waved to sister ships as they passed. A floating party.

PANIC ATTACK

I'm not learning the language. I missed the chance to photograph an amazing, huge statue of Lenin on the shore because my nose was in my journal. I'm not seeing all I could. I'm not visiting all the museums I should. My waking time could be filled with more things. I'm in the midst of opportunity and I'm not maximizing it.

But, I'm learning when I need to be alone. I'm learning when I need a nap. I'm learning what is happening inside myself while I pass through this wonderland. I can do no better. I can relax. The panic sank back into that janglie place. Why does my eye still twitch?

WOMEN'S WORK

On the back deck, I watched a twenty-something girl annoyed with a young swain for shading her legs. In response, he readjusted his body to shade her more. It was cocky. She had no other sunning spots to move to. People were standing along the railings waiting for someone to vacate their tanning spot so that they could join the sunbathers. And this particular guy had already shown us that he would bully, in the guise of rough-housing, anyone who crossed him. He was strong and ruthless. On invisible provocation, he pushed, shoved, held down and slapped around any of his "friends". The girl knew that.

I reflected on what serious work it is for women to stay beautiful in order to be valued by men. And how interesting it is that this is universally derided by men. They don't grasp the amount of fear and anxiety attached to those issues for women even while they grade a woman on them.

When the young swain decides that tanned skin is disgusting and he wants his hands on a pearly white woman, he will then make fun of her for clutching her parasol, covering her skin, gravitating to shade and insisting they make a detour to buy more sunscreen.

I see myself and my fear. Daily, several times a day, flashes of anxiety about singles at home. Phantom limb. When does it pass?

THE CHURCH IN THE RIVER

It was touch and go. The sun was already below the horizon on the other side of the boat. But everyone wanted to see the bell tower in the river. The whole boat was talking about whether we would get there before it was too dark. Our approach was announced on the loud speaker but it didn't need to be. Passengers and crew were already on deck, on one side, leaning over the railing peering out. If passengers, leaning out, could overturn a boat, we were going to overturn.

The engines were cut as the church steeple drifted into view. All the lights were shut off except one, trained on the white spire. Drift, drift. Quiet murmuring. A reverent hush. There, ghostly white out of the black water in the middle of the river, a silent sentinel. It was tall. It looked like the top layers of a wedding cake. There were forty more feet of it under water. The rest of the town was also down there. Flooded by the waterway expansion.

I asked Olga why such a strong reaction to this and she said: "Their whole town is gone. Down there. They left it all behind. For what? For this water? For electricity? Did we really need it?" I felt like this applied to many things in Russia and wondered how this one captured their hearts.

Then we had drifted past. The engines started, the lights came on, the boat turned a corner and went down another arm of the river.

Passengers oozed over to the other side of the boat and caught that last apricot glow of the already-gone sun. Olga and her husband, Vas, who had dragged me out on deck to see the church steeple, told me that from their apartment, (which is really her father's one bedroom apartment shared with him and her son and his girlfriend), they can see the sunset between two other buildings for a few minutes. And they pause and watch and say goodbye to the day and see the beauty of it fade.

I mentioned that I slept in a room that faces east and I was more inclined to watch the sun come up and greet it and watch it unfold in it's morning glory.

Olga and Vas said that now they will say goodbye to the sun and send it to me. The fact that they say goodbye to the sun when it is midafternoon in Calgary did not diminish the moment. A lovely bridge. Handing off the sun across the world.

RIDING THE WAVE
Back on the shore, after two days on board the riverboat, I enjoyed the slight wonkie feeling I got from time to time as river travel echoed back to me. The ground would shift and wave under my feet. Never at a predictable time. Just there. Tilt. Whee. A free ride. A nice little surprise.

I also liked the road buzz after a day on a rough-surfaced road. I could feel the vibration resonating in my body. It made meditation rich after coming in, washing and changing. Sitting still, tired, relaxed, eyes closed and body buzzing. Like an electrical substation. Hmmm.

Even jet lag and its sense of vague, lazy detachment could feel good when I wasn't rushed. I liked the floating perspective. It was similar to the recreational drugs we took in the sixties.

My body and I were feeling like partners in entertaining me.

REFLECTING ON MUSIC AND TIME
The only privately owned museum in Russia, The Museum of Music and Time, is at the top of the Golden Ring in Jaroslavl, where I got off the cruise boat. Old clocks that chime, lovely gramophones with giant organic trumpets, fabulous music boxes, early hybrids of pianos and organs and a huge collection of bells.

Their wooden music boxes, big and beautiful, played with deep rich tones, quite different from the delicately tinkling music boxes we have on dressing tables. Just once before, years ago, I had heard some antique Dutch music boxes. Like angel music. Rich, mellow, resonating. It was a comforting sound. The tones were so pure that the hair stood up on my neck. Tears came to my eyes to hear that sound again. I wanted it to go on forever.

The Museum's huge record collection included a recording of Stalin giving a speech. I listened. He sounded like any man. Just a man giving a speech. I asked what he was talking about. The guide said "Politicians come to hear it just before the election and they say 'Nothing changes'. He speaks of politicians making promises and not keeping them."

The museum guides played the bells, the music boxes and the record players for me. They also invited guests to play the pianos. They had an early grand piano decorated with gilt and carving. What an honor to be asked to play. I am shy about playing in front of other people. I am self-conscious about making mistakes when other people are listening. And I only know one piece of music by heart.

On the other hand, is this the chance of a lifetime or what? Am I going to let a lifelong habit, that never served me well, interfere with my new, adventuring self? Going where others have feared to go? Not on your life.

There I was in my spandex cycling pants, T-shirt and runners playing Beethoven's Farewell to the Piano on this magnificent antique instrument. Beethoven's tribute to the last sounds of the pianoforte that he could hear. Soon after that, all the beautiful music he wrote was only for us. He would never hear again.

Acquaintances, on shore from the cruise boat, came rushing from other rooms in the museum as I played. They congratulated and encouraged me in

Russian. They gave me thumbs up and snapped pictures and clapped. Shared joy across a language gap. My little recital was a triumph.

THE ANGELS SANG IN JAROSLAVL

Like many Russian cities, Jaroslavl is full of old churches and cathedrals, most of which are being restored. (Where is the money coming from?) This particular one was on the tour circuit so guides were organizing their charges on the sidewalk outside. The English, Americans and Germans, all retired and affluent.

Okay, we have twenty minutes before we need to get back on the bus to go back to the boat. Who wants to go to the market? Who wants to go to the other cathedral? Who wants to walk in the garden? Who wants to buy lunch?

Well what's in the market?

How far is it?

How long will it take to get there and back?

What do you want to do?

Why don't we all just start doing things?

How long are we going to waste time deciding?

Then, back to the first question.

I stood and watched. As long as I kept my mouth shut they didn't know I spoke English. I was just another Russian gawking at them from the sidewalk. I watched them working on their decision. They were in conflict about a tiny window of opportunity. I felt weak with relief to be alone.

Then I drifted inside, staying away from the tight clusters of tours being ushered through and lectured in their own languages. I stood and stared at the vast iconostasis, the wall that separates the common area of a Russian church from the private, clergy area at the back. "No woman is ever allowed back there."

It was made of gold. Gold picture frames, gold accents in pictures, sheets of gold overlaying the paint, gold encrusted with pearls and jewels, a dazzling display of old icons stacked one above the other, rows and rows of them. Byzantine richness. This iconostasis was so high I could see no detail at the top. Just gold.

There was a window along the side wall. It had a deep casement, deep enough to sit in comfortably. An alcove. The morning sun was streaming in there, glinting off the gold. I sat and quietly digested what this was — this grand display of religious fervor paid for by impoverished serfs over hundreds of years and now being refurbished by the newly liberated Russians.

The next tour cluster passed through the room, shot a few snaps, camcorded the wall of gold and filed on through to the next room on my left. Some of them smiled and nodded. No words exchanged. I was keeping my native language low profile.

Then, in the next room, their chatter and clatter stopped and an accapella choir broke into Russian liturgical music. Clear, ringing song with harmonies as rich as the gold icons. The acoustics were perfect. A sound tapestry. As the voices spread and converged the singing took shape and moved and reached out and turned back in on itself. Voices wove around each other. A three-dimensional sound ballet. The sound rang out and clung to the walls. I held my breath, sitting in my sunbeam beside my wall of gold. Time stood still. Present, past and future were hanging in the air. This was before. This was always. This was timeless. I was afraid to move. I didn't need to see them. Their gift was sound.

It touched my soul. Magic.

HOW THE WAR WAS WON

The poor Russian military. They had no idea. Their most high tech, fully loaded equipment was laughably crude and irrelevant in the face of a much finer, more effective weapon. The ultimate weapon. The weapon that left industrial facilities fully intact and operational; the population more or less healthy; the infrastructure operational.

The weapon? American entertainment. It stuck its finger in the barrel of the Russian military machine and said, "Bang, bang."

Instead of body count, retaliation window, landed troops and restoration of basic services there was Gorbachov, Brezchnev, Yeltsin, glasnost, perestroika, New Russia, video stores, Internet, business joint ventures and McDonalds.

The Russians didn't have a chance. No-one was grimly herded into a boxcar. They couldn't get to stores fast enough to buy TVs, VCRs, ghetto blasters, pop music tapes, sticky notes, cellular phones, car alarms, Mars Bars and Coca Cola.

Nike on T-shirts, Reebok on baseball caps, METS emblazoning the back of a jacket. The Russians wear English-language brand names and slogans with pride. Bear in mind that not only is their language different, their alphabet is different. No problem - which is the first English they learn. If they can't buy it they scam it or steal it.

So now that the war is over and the west has won, it's time to see what the enemy looks like. Time to look at Russia from a bicycle.

BUILDING ALLIES

I tried to ride softly into the lives of Russian strangers. Russians were suspicious of strangers at first glance. They frowned. Their faces closed down. Harsh, angry looks. It was easy to fall into mirroring that look back to them. But I discovered that I could shift the tone to friendly contact by smiling at strangers and nodding, like a little bow. Head a bit to the side. Eye contact. A formal, old-fashioned, slow nod. Their instinctive distrust and resentment dissolved.

I had to work at this. I had to remind myself to do it. It was so easy to mirror their frown. But I wanted these people to be my friends. Who knows, I might have needed one of them further down the road or later in the day.

Maps were new to Russians. In fact, until recently, they were illegal. So Russians had trouble orienting themselves to these two-dimensional landscapes. A person would hold the map, stare at one spot, follow a road with his or her finger. I would point to the name of the place we were standing and say it. Next thing they'd have the map upside down or be staring thoughtfully and muttering at a distant corner of the map. I'd stand there and think, "Clue-less." Then the problem was getting the map back.

I was better off to switch to verbal directions and explore getting to the next town rather than to my destination for the day.

I would say the name of the next town with a questioning inflection in my voice. At the same time I pointed down the road which I thought would get me there.

The answers would usually be long and complicated and, of course in Russian. I always listened with interest to all of it, said, "Da, da," thoughtfully and after they finished I repeated the name of the town with a question in my voice and pointed down the road again or down the other road they seemed to be indicating.

If I could, I would ask several people until I got a trend in the answers. Three answers the same was solid.

I don't know the Russian words that they used but I could tell when they were asking where I was from. I would say, "Can-a-da", emphasis on the second syllable. "Canada? Canada?" The babushkas (old grandmothers) would shake their heads and laugh. They exclaimed in Russian. Sometimes I could tell that they wanted to know where I've been on my velocipede. I pointed into the distance and said "Jaroslavl, Rostov, Pereslavl Zullisky, Yriev Pilskij, Suzdal." Their mouths dropped open. "Velocipede?!?" They shook their heads. Then they threw themselves into giving me detailed instructions in Russian on how to get to the next town. I said, "Da, da." thoughtfully.

And I could tell when they wished me a safe journey and I said "Spaseeba" and they said "Pashaltzta" which is something like, "No trouble." And then we said "Dasvadanya" to each other and waved and I rode away. Anyone who harmed me would answer to the babushkas.

Even between spread out towns and villages, there were people on the road to ask directions because they walk for miles. I saw a woman wearing a dress without a purse or anything else in her hands, walking along a road that didn't have a house, building or town in sight in any direction.

I also saw people carrying huge sacks of potatoes or a big bundle of hay wrapped in canvas, pieces of sheet metal tied with an old rope or bundles of flowers to sell. These loads may be pushed or pulled along the road on every manner of conveyance with wheels on it: bicycle frames, dollies, baby buggy frames, wheelbarrows, little wooden carts.

The days I spent on the back roads taught me to feel safe with these people. I felt their genuine concern for me. I saw their humour.

THE GUARD AND THE PANTILINER

Like every large, old town, Rostov has a kremlin. The kremlin was the original, walled fort, the seed of the town. There were always several churches inside the kremlin. My Lonely Planet Guidebook said I could get into the kremlin in Rostov through a back gate and stay at a hotel that used to be a monastery. The handsome young Russian soldier guarding the gate waved me away and around to the main entry gate on the opposite side of the kremlin. But when I got around there I found a sign with a line drawn through a bicycle so I went back to my guard.

In an attempt to explain I drew the sign and pointed at the other gate and pointed at my bike and said "Niet, niet," and shook my head.

Unlike most Russian guards, the nice young man, as my mother would say, was trying to help. He actually took off his hat and scratched his head. He said many things to me in Russian and I could see that I needed to explain that I was trying to get into the hotel, inside the gate, with my bike. So I hauled out my Lonely Planet to show him the diagram of the kremlin layout and pointed at the hotel where I wanted to stay.

The gate was a huge metal crossbar affair with square openings. I stuck the Lonely Planet through one of the squares to him and pointed at the hotel diagram. As he looked down at it a pantiliner that I had stuck into another page, plopped out and landed on his boot. He looked down at it, bent down, picked it up, looked at it and handed it through to me. Did he know what it was? Should the ground open and swallow me up? I smiled and said "Spaseeba," (thank you) and carried on. Bluffing through seemed the only way. I didn't even blush.

Shortly after, an official looking car drove up from inside. They opened the gate to let the car out and they let me in at the same time.

COMMUNIST SYMBOLS

The idea was wonderful. Reward for pulling your weight, regardless of how menial your role. Janitors and doctors fairly and evenly rewarded. I saw it in the architecture, the statues — heroic and huge, the paintings. Communism and the worker put at the centre of the stage.

But it didn't work in the real world. It was twisted by paranoid leaders who needed control, who trusted no one, who created a police state. And true to human nature, greedy people gathered wealth and power.

Statues and symbols are all that is left. Beside a country road, surrounded by open fields, I cycled past a concrete pillar fifteen feet high with the hammer and sickle on top, a sheaf of wheat and a blowing banner. Faded red and gold on grey. Workers in the fields you are the heroes. You are Mother Russia. You are part of a brave new way to be, a fair world.

Now young Russians scoff at that. They sneer about the rallies at which they stood as children, masses of them, each waving a tiny red flag on a wooden stick.

Riverboat passengers were irreverent when we passed the gigantic two-and-a-half times life-sized statue of Lenin at the edge of the lock system, one arm up in the air, striding forward in his top coat, gazing fearlessly into the future, heroically pointing ahead at the locks. The passengers smirked and got their pictures taken wearing their bathing suits and leaning on the railing with Lenin in the background. The Russians said, "The canal was built on the bones of people who died building it. Thousands of them."

UNDERGROUND ART GALLERIES

However much young Russians sneer at Communist history and Soviet images, they do not deface. There is no vandalizing in the metro stations where you find perfect examples of the 1930s and 40s heroic-worker art genre as well as first class neo-classical design. I saw subway stations with arched, carved ceilings like something you would expect to see in Rome. They were stunning. Taking art to the people in their daily lives.

When I came out of the grubby, chaotic St Petersburg streetscape into the metro, I descended the longest escalator I had ever been on in my life. Tall, elegant art nouveau lamps marched in a row down the middle of the polished, rich, dark wooden divide between the up and down escalators. Women with soft cloths rode up and down wiping off the dust. The polished wood reflected the row of lamps.

People serenely glide down and down and down. Each step has a person on it. Two people together will stand one in front of the other. As soon as they step onto the descending stairs, the front person turns around so they are facing each other. You can see they have done this before. The tallest in front so they are closer to being level to talk. That means if it is a man and a woman, the man is usually in front, turned facing the woman. Many lovers kiss and snuggle as they ride down. I saw a woman standing on the escalator crying as she silently descended. Tears were streaming down her face. I concluded: man trouble. But maybe it was a dying child or the humiliation of a tyrannical boss.

In the Moscow metro there were murals and statues to the heroic worker. And as everywhere in the world, public art was ignored by the locals. Russians hurried by without noticing statues of the brave young men and women beside each pillar, looking clear-eyed into the distance, their eye on a dream. I saw a beautiful statue in something like polished pewter of a larger-than-life young woman wearing a gun slung over her shoulder and looking off to her left. She had the air of an Israeli soldier. A figure of calm and dignity and purpose. Andrei, my guide to the legendary Ismailovsky Market that day, was embarrassed to be photographed beside it.

RUSSIAN MENTALITY

They watch their government spirit away money in huge chunks. Now that they were allowed to regionalize their learning materials, the school districts were allocated one hundred and seventy billion rubles to produce new textbooks. Only seventy billion ever turned up in the districts. "How can you run a country that way?" the Russians ask. And they shrug with their palms up. "Russian mentality," they say.

The miners in the east haven't been paid for nine months, the headlines blare.

"Why not?"

"The mining company doesn't have the money to pay them."

"Why not?"

"Because the mines do not get paid by the utilities that they sell to."

"Why not?"

"The utilities have no money. Officials have been stealing it".

They shrug. They say, "Russian mentality."

They have little scams that work against their fellow citizens and everyone goes along. On a weekend afternoon, Svetlana and Sergei took me to a lake — sort of a water-filled depression in a field. As we pulled off the highway, we pulled up to a barrier across the access road. There was a woman standing beside it.

"Is this her lake?" I asked, interested in private enterprise.

"No," laughed Svetlana.

"Does she own the park?"

"No," again laughing.

"Does she own the road?"

"She owns the barricade. That is all. She put up a barricade. She lets you in to go to the lake if you give her cash. That is all." We gave her cash. Russian mentality.

WHO ARE THE AUTHORITIES?

Russians don't pay their taxes. Why pay taxes? Who knows if the government will still be in power next week? The International Monetary Fund refused to give Russia more money until they improved this tax compliance problem.

They don't pay their bills either. After all, no-one is paying them. They may not even be getting a salary.

Law enforcement is variable and based on each-man-for-himself. The police used to have empty holsters. Now they have machine guns. And they have a crack force of police who wear masks so that they can go after the Mafia without fear of reprisals against their families. But the police are full of Mafia too.

Mikhail, a Russian management consultant said, "The Mafia will probably end up controlling it all. They are the only ones who can make things work." And already they successfully collect taxes in the form of the protection money that, unlike government taxes, every business pays.

TRAFFIC BULLIES

Russians are afraid of bullies and yet quite happy to bully others. I saw this in the streets: cars bully pedestrians and pedestrians are bullied until they find a car they can bully. Then they take charge. They never wave a thank-you or smile at a driver. The driver never gestures permission to a pedestrian to cross. A weak driver that doesn't bully pedestrians can end up wrapped in a sea of pedestrians flooding, non-stop, around their vehicle. And them stuck in the middle, in their impotent metal cage.

I trailed a group of pedestrians across Nevsky Prospect, the big, wide boulevard down the middle of St Petersburg, only to have a police car rip around a bend in the road and come bearing down on us. He railed at us on his loud hailer as he sped by.

Before switching to green, a red light changes from solid to flashing. It is sort of an on your marks signal. On that signal, pedestrians better run because cars are going to floor it and come at them before their light turns green.

According to the Moscow Chief of Police there are 300,000 new cars on Moscow streets every year. Due to the fact that five years ago in Moscow there were no cars to speak of, that means 300,000 new drivers each year. It isn't surprising that they drive like they are teens in bumper cars, honking their horns as they bear down on pedestrians at full speed. They aim for pedestrians. They never deviate from their course to avoid one. They deviate from their course to get them. Men in snazzy suits, little old ladies, priests — they are all targets of guerilla motorists. Time on your hands in Moscow? It's fun to just stand watching the traffic. In the midst of that traffic-combat, diplomatic limousines with black windows, flags whipping and siren-blazing police escorts routinely tear around the city. No-one even turns their head.

Highway speeds don't dampen this game of dare. On a section of two-lane highway I saw a police car - lights flashing, sirens blazing - charging down the middle of the road followed by three tour busses. The police car forced the on-coming traffic to hit the gravel shoulder. When I asked who would be on those buses I was told "important people." An interesting display of power. Important people being rushed down the middle of a highway in buses.

ANIMAL BULLIES

Gigantic guard dogs, bred and trained to be aggressive, are currently popular in Russian cities: German Shepherds, Rottweilers and Dobermans. These huge animals are all the more inappropriate in view of the fact that they are housed in their owners' tiny apartments. Portable intimidation. They are led through the streets on short, thick leather leashes or chains, wearing muzzles.

OFFICIAL BULLYING

Entering the Canadian embassy in Moscow I encountered bulletproof glass and an unfriendly guard. The ugly, retrofitted reinforcement looked like a security bulkhead and made no pretense of fitting into the pre-Revolutionary décor of the lovely old building. They had an elaborate entry system involving speaking into boxes and being ignored for a long time. I loved to pretend I was the spy who came in from the cold, the perpetrator of some foreign intrigue, the key player in a huge dangerous drama. The lobby told me someone else loved playing foreign intrigue too.

SERVICE WINDOWS

In Russia many transactions need to be performed at service windows. Cashing travelers' cheques gave me exposure to the most amazing example of Russian service.

These service windows are set up behind one-way mirrors. I was on the outside. I only saw mirror. The opening in the mirror, through which I performed my transaction, was usually six-to-eight inches high and a foot long. I stood with the window at about the height of my waist. So my whole transaction was conducted bent over.

Inside I could see a fragment of the room behind the mirror. I could see women sitting down at a desk or long table. I never saw it all so I didn't know. There were men walking up and down behind them, observing. All I could see of the men was their hands, clasped in front of them. Hands were all I really saw of the women as well. And maybe a bit of chest and sometimes a chin. I would lean over and try to ask into the window if they spoke English. Sometimes I was waved to another window, sometimes someone inside was consulted although they never came over to assist with the transaction.

I bumbled through pushing my travelers' cheques and passport through the window. They had me sign several different forms. I didn't know what any of them were. I would see their hands put a stack of rubles into a counting machine beside them and I would hear the machine swish through the stack. Always a big wad because purchases in Russia are in the hundreds of thousands and millions of rubles. Eventually they would push the money through the hole to me and I would go away.

All the way through this transaction the other people in the line were clustered around me, looking over my shoulder. Sometimes their knees were in the back of my knees. Usually some part of something they were carrying was sticking into me somewhere. They were line hopping aggressively and the minute I started to move away from the window the next three people pushed their way to the front.

Often a line-person, from further back, claimed an important question needed to be asked and barged to the front and then virtually dealt with their whole transaction.

It was all power. Claim power or grovel.

LIFE AS THEATRE

To get around other bullies, Russians stage dramas, even when not necessary. Svetlana and I were waiting in a long line-up outside McDonald's Restaurant in Moscow. The line went all the way through the parking lot. The young woman managing the door would let a few people in and then close the door for a while. When we got close and she was about to close the door, Svetlana barged through saying "foreign visitor." I was dumbstruck. No questions asked. We're in.

Again, Svetlana wasn't satisfied to just bribe my bike onto the train, she created a cock-and-bull story about the fact that I was her American sister and I was leaving and we wouldn't see each other again for years and that I was going off on a bike tour and meeting up with a group at a particular time in Paris and HAD to be on that train, WITH my bike. Never mind the fact that my passport was Canadian, that she had jet black hair and I am blond nor that she spoke perfect Russian and I didn't speak a word of it — never mind all that — that's her story and she's sticking to it. And having fun.

I was horrified that I was supposed to carry out this ruse for two days on the train. She made a big show of grief and even cried as she hugged me while whispering in my ear — "Remember, you are my sister."

I noticed that as soon as we pulled out of the station my compartment mate, Irenie, (who spoke English) and the conductor in our car, (who had taken the bike bribe), dropped the whole sham and dealt with me as me. Thank heavens.

YOUR FORCE FIELD

Before leaving home my advisor had taught me to create an atmosphere of peace around myself as I moved into unknown situations. Peace be with you. When you are tired and annoyed and the bureaucrats are getting to you and the people in the train station won't put your bike on the same train as you and you can't go to the washroom with your bike because it doesn't fit in the door and you are tired and it is raining, remember that little trick that turns things around.

From your heart, from inside your heart, send out Peace be with you. From the top of your chest where your heart is, from there you beam Peace be with you out to their forehead. Feel love travel along that. Pause. Feel it. Things shift a little. You present a different person to them. Do doors open? Fares get cheaper? Bikes get put on trains? Maybe not. But something shifts. And sending out that wish for peace changes what happens between you and other people.

As I traveled alone through countries where everyone said I would be in enormous danger, I particularly used it when I was uneasy. And I gradually came to think that my safety was built on people perceiving me as protected. In some kind of power field. Was it that any woman alone had to be crazy and crazy people are dangerous? Was it that they expected me to be afraid and when I wasn't they assumed I had a gun? Was it that they were impressed that I made this choice and therefore saw me as a magic woman? Did they feel safe around me because I was grounded and open? Did they get sucked into my belief that they would be nice to me? I don't know the answer. All of them and more.

WHO'S RUNNING THINGS HERE?

I tried catching a glimpse of my decisions being made. Where did the decision come from? By what process? Walking down the street, I wondered which road ahead I should take. This road or that one? This or that? Which one? One went toward that amazing church with the sun on it, the other a winding lane that's supposed to lead to a worthwhile museum. Which? (Still walking toward the Y.) I'm getting hungry and neither offers food. Which? (Still walking.) I could ask someone. (Someone passes. I don't try and stop them to ask.) That one's a bit more downhill and I am tired. (Still walking, now at the intersection.) I'm grinning now. What will happen? Which will I choose? Will I stop? The options seem balanced. Nothing to give one street the edge over the other. In the middle of the intersection now. What will happen?

The body chose. The body didn't break stride. I kept walking. I haven't slowed down. Which did it choose? Ah. This one. This is nice. But the other was nice too. Am I disappointed? No, this is fine. Why did it choose this one? I don't know. Am I happy? Yes. Have I just seen the footprint of the Other Traveler?

THE TEAM

I quite liked being alone, except when eating in a dining room, such as on the cruise boat. It was funny how at those times the idea of being alone could seem sad and abandoned. I felt awkward and embarrassed because all those people could see that no one wanted to be with me. I was an outcast. I was unloved.

However, once settled, I shamelessly watched the other diners and got caught up in their dramas. Family groups, couples, business people, all acting out their strange relationships and leaving me relieved that I had no-one there to treat me with disdain.

But, in fact, I wasn't alone.

I had a whole team with me and they loved me and cared about me and were proud of me. Not for a moment was I lonely. I certainly craved conversation sometimes, but I wasn't lonely.

During travel hardship, I could hear the reaction of my people as they walked into the room with me. I could hear their shock, amazement and amusement. They were dazzled by me and what I was doing. They encouraged me, counseled me and applauded. It was a team effort and I never lost touch with my team.

I wore their love like a blanket and snuggled inside it.

COME BACK AND SEE ME.

I needed a place to stay in Jurjev Pol'skij. I had traveled an extra 18 K that day to go back and find the pannier that fell off behind some trees after a bathroom break. And I had changed a flat tire as well. It was mid afternoon and I was ready to stop riding. It would be a long way to the next town and I wanted to explore this one. It had a huge kremlin with several stunning churches. This was the hometown of the first Russian astronaut: Yuri Gagarin. It was re-named Jurjev Pol'skij Town in his honour. (Yuri being the diminutive for Jurjev.) It was in the middle of the Golden Ring.

While gazing around I noticed a bank. Seeing as I am right here why not find out if they cash travelers' cheques? It's a long shot but, why not.

I got handed down the line to Marina in a little office at the end of the tellers' line. She explained that she was very sorry but her English was bad and they did not have the means to cash this. So I asked about a place to stay.

"I am very sorry. We do not have this here."

"A hotel? Hostel? Any place to sleep?"

"I am very sorry. Small place here. Not such place."

"I am too tired (acting out tired) to make it (acting out riding bicycle) to the next town (pointing down the road) today. I will pay (point at wallet) a family to sleep with them. (International gesture of sleeping: palms together, held at ear, head on side). Can you (pointing) find a family for me to sleep with?"

Marina made several phone calls. Between each one she said, "I am sorry, take a while." She talked in Russian with other people in the bank and with people on the phone. Then, during one call she asked me several questions:

"Are you one?"

"Have you rubles?"

"How much?"

Then, "There is a place. I am sorry. Not special. You can sleep there. She will take you there."

This was some kind of women's flophouse. Most of the women there were pregnant, many had children. They chatted and laughed with each other cheerily and seemed to be having a good time. I was given a room alone with two cots in it. The bathroom was something out of Gulag Archipelago. When I walked in I could hear the chorus of reactions from my Team.

This will never do.

Oh dear, oh my dear.

Fuck this shit.

Oh Marg you poor thing.

This is unworkable.

Once settled in, I passed the bank on my way to the market for food. Marina was standing on the stairs in front of the bank talking to a man. I walked over to thank her and the man drifted away.

We chatted about her and her husband, about living with her parents and building their own house with the help of her father and brothers. Her father drinks. She has a degree in textiles but cannot get work in that field so works in the bank. She learned English in the technical college but regrets not getting much chance to practice it.

I asked about her husband. "I like him. (Pause.) I like him. (Longer pause.) I love him," she added laughing. Her husband is a soccer coach and does not get full time work.

As she went back up the steps into the bank, she turned and said, "Come back and see me," over her shoulder. A gentle connection offered. Of course I will come back to see you Marina. You have asked me to.

I was looking forward to Suzdal. Lonely Planet reported that there was a small hotel there — formerly a museum and, before that, a tiny monastery. It sounded like a special place to stay. But I had no idea what time I should expect to be pedaling into Suzdal. The map I was working with was old so I knew it had been purposefully distorted. A security risk you understand. But I did know that Suzdal really existed, in that general area, and that I was heading toward it.

After a morning of riding through fields I was now among some houses. I also noticed that when I asked a man, playing with a delightful fat puppy outside his gate, if the road ahead was the road to Suzdal, he seemed to hesitate before saying, "Da, da," and waving me on. Oh dear. I'd better ask someone else soon.

Around a corner and down a hill. A few more houses but the road petered out and turned to sand. Ahead of me was a creek and then a steep hill with only a rough footpath up the other side. A giant fort or castle or monastery or something was all I could see at the top. A big wall around something. What the heck was this place?

A mother and daughter were walking beside the road. My "Suzdal?" question put them in confusion but they were clear that I should go up the path and around the wall.

So I crossed on the footbridge and started grinding my way up the steep path. It was deeply rutted and quite a struggle pushing a fully loaded bike but I was buoyed by the accordion music coming from the top. I could hear the cheery Russian folksong, Kalinka. And there were voices singing. Seemed a bit strange, outside at midday, but I was intrigued. As I labored up I recalled hearing Kalinka as a teenager in the huge forum in Vancouver. At the height of the Cold War, Mom dragged us down to hear the Soviet Army Chorus. We were full of doubt about the dreary afternoon we faced and ended up amazed and dazzled by their singing and their Cossack dancing, leaping and whistling. Kalinka got us clapping, stamping and roaring our approval. Along with everyone else, we cried during the standing ovation. Later, in the parking lot, we flocked the bus, shoved our programs in the door to get them autographed by the chorusing soldiers looking awkward sitting straight up in their seats.

Now I was in Russia. I was among the people raised singing Kalinka. Cresting the hill I found the musician playing an antique accordion. There was a couple with him. They looked downtown-Moscow-sophisticated in fashionable black. He was 35 or 40, she was younger, maybe mid-twenties and pretty and not as boisterous. Also, not as drunk. It turned out to be his birthday. He was continually drinking from a tumbler of vodka. She was sober and shy. He asked if I wanted some too. No thanks.

I wanted to say; "I know this song. I love this song. You make me happy." We hugged and kissed and sang and I eventually asked my usual question: "Is that the road to Suzdal?" He pointed, we consulted the map, we talked around it, he seemed to say yes. Yes definitely. Yes take that road to get to Suzdal. Out past the fort and go right. Pause.

Then quietly, from off to the side where she had relegated herself, the girlfriend said, "This is Suzdal."

TALKING TO THEIR ANIMALS

It was early morning quiet in the Russian village. The sun was shooting golden rays flat across the landscape and down the streets and into the fenced back yards. High wooden gates were opening and the family cows were coming out. Usually just one. Ambling out to the road. They paused and ate a little grass, ambled some more. They looked down the road at the other cows. Some were plodding down the road starting out to the fields on the edge of town where they would spend the day. No one was rushing them.

Beside the road, waiting, was a tiny, old and wrinkled woman. Gumboots, head scarf, heavy skirts, layers of sweaters and an apron on top. She had deep lines around her black eyes. She and her cow were standing side by side, facing the road. The cow was munching on the grass. The woman had her hand on the cow's forehead and was absent-mindedly scratching it with her fingers. Neither of them was doing much else except scratching and being scratched.

I could see them crossing the road ahead of me at a break in the traffic. A woman and an animal. When they reached the far side the animal jumped straight up and soared through the air. It bounded like a gazelle. Could it be a gazelle? A gazelle in Russia? It leapt through the air with such ease. Back legs out behind and front legs tucked up. Up and over something. Then after landing on the other side it turned its head back to the woman and stood watching. She paused at the side of the road. I was getting closer. She seemed to be at the edge of a ditch. Then she found her footing and jumped across, landing on one, outstretched leg. All this time, the animal stood with its head turned back, watching her. Once she was across, the two of them continued walking forward. What the heck was it?

Aha. Now I could see. It was a goat. And as she and her goat walked away across the field, she leaned down and picked a handful of long grass and held it in her hand at her side, without looking back. The goat walked behind her and occasionally pulled some grass from her hand and chewed as it walked. I couldn't have been more delighted if I had watched a unicorn.

In a small field inside Suzdal, a weathered old man with four goats had gathered them together to head down the street. They trotted off. Half a block down, he turned back and saw that one was far behind. The other goats also stopped and looked back. A couple of them took the opportunity to snack on grass beside the road. He scolded the straggler. His tone wasn't harsh. It was more; "You should be ashamed of yourself. Can't you see that we need to stay together?" The straggling goat broke into a trot, came up beside him and then resumed walking. Now together, they all continued on.

Everyone lives in apartments in the city. There are no houses. In villages there are only houses, no apartments. These village houses have sitting places outside the door and again outside the gate: chairs, stools and logs.

The older men and women sat there in the sun or shade outside the door or outside the gate. Often there was a cat on their lap. The cats were sometimes asleep, sometimes standing in their lap pushing their foreheads up on the person's chin, demanding attention. They got stroked and talked to. I rode by and heard people talking but when I looked it was only one person and a cat talking to each other. I smiled. A gentle bit of love was leaking into the world.

A young cat trotted into the lobby of the somewhat seedy Belgrade Hotel in Moscow, past the security guard, who grinned as he saw me watching it. It jumped up beside a young boy in a lobby chair and curled up behind him, settling into the chair.

Across Moscow at the classy, expensive, western, Radisson Stanislayovskia Hotel, thick-chested, no-necks with buzz cuts, lumbered around outside the front door. The doormen. The bodyguards. (Postscript: The manager of that hotel was gunned down in a what the media labeled a mafia-style-slaying since I left Russia. I guess the body-guards were for more than show.) I saw a kitten curl its legs underneath itself and then drop onto the carpet beside the front door. It was ignored. I picked it up, stroked it and when it cried, still that baby-ish kitten cry - I put it down again. It curled its legs underneath it and again settled in. These cats are not skinny and dirty. They are just young cats out there in the world on their own. What will their stories be?

Stray dogs live a life of freedom and fun in Russia. They hang out. They join their friends for some trotting around and then swing out on their own. They lie in hollows in the ground, sometimes beside busy roads, and sleep soundly. They sit outside stores and get thrown scraps. They sniff around in garbage. Rarely are they kicked at or shooed away. People in Russia live trickle down economics. They give to beggars in the streets, they buy from tiny street vendors, they hand money over to churches and religious people, they feed stray dogs.

I saw a street vendor, a woman, feeding two young cats — one really just a kitten the other maybe its young mother. Both wearing permanent dirt. The woman had a bag with broken up wieners and some stuff that looked like Meow Mix. The cats crouched on the edge of a granite planter hidden in the plants. They gobbled it up. How do they survive a winter?

Dogs, cats, chickens, geese, goats live together peacefully. I saw them mingle and never saw one being chased.

SCRAM

I developed the skill to identify Russian no-goods that tried to attach themselves to me. The men who were drunk and fancied themselves glamorous. I even learned how to get rid of them when they caught me by surprise. In fact I ended up staging a scene to shake one loose. It happened in Suzdal. I was strolling and browsing along a row of shops on a warm afternoon. A drunk, blind man who spoke a few words of English decided he was going to take me to a place to get my pictures developed — while everyone else I asked said that you could not get pictures developed in Suzdal.

It soon became clear that he was just hanging on. I wanted to get rid of him. I tried nicely to thank him and say I would manage myself. Next thing he would be after me again. I got firmer and firmer. "Niet spaseeba. Dastvadanya." (No, thank you. Goodbye.)

When he sidled up to me once again in a small store with five other people in it and said, "Don't you like Russian men?" the absurdity of the question and the arrogance of assuming that that would be the reason I rejected his annoying intrusion pushed me to fury. I yelled, "Dastvadanya!" Everyone froze. Silence. No one moved. All eyes on him and me. (One thousand and one. One thousand and two. One thousand and three.) He turned and scurried out. (He managed well for a blind drunk.) The tableau in the store came to life again. I think he left because he was afraid of pressure from them, not of anything I could do.

The problem with a drunk is that they have lost touch with anyone else's preferences. They are only aware of themselves.

LOST IN THE FOREST

I had been uneasy about my source of directions. He had latched onto me in the market in Tzeecova, went back to his apartment and got his velocipede and led me out of town. Further and further we went. I got more uneasy. He in front, just in view.

I saw him pull off his t-shirt to reveal a lean, muscled, tanned back. Oh dear.

He was clearly sending me off on an unusual route to the next town. When a bystander challenged his map drawn in the dirt beside the road they had an animated conversation in Russian and then the other person seemed to back down. Was the main road under construction? Broken down? Unsafe? More than usual?

None of us could say enough in the other's language to find that out and it didn't lend itself to international mime. He wanted to accompany me further. "Niet, spazeeba," I said and pointed at him and pointed back at town and said "Dastvadanya". Thank goodness he left.

So off I went, on a granite military road. The granite treads were two feet wide and about ten feet long. Every ten feet there was a crack before the next granite tread. The crack could be half an inch to three inches wide. So it was like an old train track, before continuous tracking. Lub-dub. Lub-dub. Sometimes the crack was so big I had to stop and walk the bike across for fear I'd end up on my nose.

After three minutes I got off my bike. This was a prank. But then it was probably worth seeing if there really was a turnoff at the three-kilometer point as my guide had indicated. (Thank goodness Canada had switched to kilometers. At least I didn't have to deal with that disparity.) It wasn't until three and a half kilometers that I reached the turn. Well close enough for a guess. But I was unnerved by the fact that the rare people I saw on this road walking or on giant machinery, shook their heads. No, I could not get to

Komsomol'sk this way. One nodded "Da." Hmm.

Well I was far enough along now to keep going. But I felt more worried than usual and stopped several times to ponder bailing out, going back to Tzeecova and trying to find someone else to direct me. I kept trying to draw on some cosmic wisdom to guide me. Granny said, "We don't have enough information yet. Stay alert, be ready to go back, find out more." Okie-dokie.

Meanwhile this granite highway from hell was wandering aimlessly. I was now in a forest and the cracks were getting bigger. There were fewer and fewer other people. Then, no-one. The road had wound around. It felt like I was heading back to where I had come from. Was it a loop? Would I come around a corner and find my source of directions and his friends sitting in a truck waiting for me? And laughing? That was unnerving.

Another turn, this one seemed to be going in the right direction. But the wind was increasing and the sky was darkening. Leaves were falling. It was late August and I was in Russia so it made sense that fall was starting to happen.

More wind. Darker. Was that thunder in the distance?

Then I discovered — two days after the end of my period — that my snazzy fluorescent green cycling shorts had a large, almost-perfect circle of bright red blood on the front of them. The size of the bottom of a Coke can. Right in front of my crotch. Oh yeah, how long have I been sporting this trophy?

With the wind whipping around I struggled out of my latest pair of bloodied shorts beside the road.I tried to find something else to put on, and pantiliners — which of course I've moved to the bottom of the pannier because my period was over. This would be a fine time for buddy and his friends to happen along.

Was that thunder getting closer?

Rain drops. A few. Scattered. A few more. Bigger. Heavier. Wetter. Hmm.

Time to suit up. All-weather jacket, long spandex pants, gloves at hand. Camera into its plastic baggie, map into a baggie, everything else checks out ready for a downpour.

First thoughts were, "Oh shit. What am I supposed to do in a forest in a thunderstorm? Okay I know the don't-stand-under-a-tree rule. What about in a forest? Under one of the shorter trees? Surely a metal bike in the one clearing in a forest in a lightning storm, surely that would be a target? So should I separate myself from the bike?"

I hadn't seen anyone on the road for a long time. Now there was lightning and rain. Wind, lightning and rain in a dark, deserted Russian forest.

I panicked. I am in a thunderstorm in a forest in Russia. And I'm lost. I felt the urge to run, to pedal faster, to escape the danger. The forest had turned into the evil black forest that reached out tripping and grabbing at Snow White. Forest as enemy.

I stopped. I have been here before. I had explored deep, dark, mythical forests before. They had taught me to stop. Just stop it all. I stood and listened and watched. The magnificent, huge trees were bending in the wind, throwing leaves, bending back, swishing, whipping around like saplings. The wind was blowing out the summer season. The air was full of leaves making a soft chattering sound. They swirl everywhere, in all directions, like the snow in a child's glass ball. Sky boiling. Thunder and lightening almost continuous now. No one around. Just me.

My smallness in the midst of these huge forces now seemed reassuring. This was fine. These forces are out there all the time and now they are showing themselves. A private performance.

How could I be lost? I was on the planet earth. I was in no danger of floating off. I was even on a road and roads always go somewhere, eventually, in one direction or the other.

I smiled. The rain fell. The wind blew.

I was lost in a thunderstorm in a forest in Russia. I was happy. I came out into the world to touch life. I have arrived at my destination and I would keep arriving at it over and over. Today, life in a Russian forest. Life in a Russian thunderstorm. Thank you.

THE OTHER FOREST

It was an imaginary forest that had come to mind in the Russian one.

Its powerful lesson came months after my father had died while I was still consumed by grief. I wanted to learn what was going on inside myself. What was that knot in my chest? I tried visualization. I visualized going into a dark forest as a metaphor for exploring hidden stuff within. I found myself running and afraid. It was dark in there. It was damp. A forbidding wind was howling, big dark trees were bending menacingly. My face was being whipped by branches and cobwebs. My arms and legs were being scratched. I was tripping. I was out of breath and crying. My heart was pounding. I kept running as fast as I could. The forest scene from Snow White. You've seen this.

Then I remembered that I had come into the forest to see what I could find. I had seen plenty of scary, dark shadows, what else was there to see? I stopped. Silence but for my heart pounding, breathe panting and ringing in my ears.

Silent. Still. A shaft of light. The only noise was my still heavy breathing. More light. Moss. Carpets of tiny wildflowers. A small brook. A decaying log with a fairyland of mushrooms, fungus, minute flowers. A still soft place. It was beautiful. A sanctuary. It was the opposite of what I had turned it into by running. There was no storm here.

Now I go there when I meditate. Sometimes I meet Granny in the tiny fairyland and sit on a piece of fungus or lounge on a carpet of moss.

In the Russian forest I felt as if I had been given a chance to live that visualization and the pleasure I felt becoming grounded and safe in that storm was coloured by the layers of feeling and memories of Dad, death, loss, insight and huge respect for what we can learn when we travel inside ourselves.

LESSONS THE TREES TEACH

They just stand there. Short ones, tall ones, bent ones, bushy ones. They don't have self-doubts. They don't wonder if they should be another kind of tree. They don't ask, Why me? They root. They reach. They grow. Some of them struggle. Some thrive. They drink the rain that comes their way, soak up the sun and bend in the wind.

That's a tree's job description and they do it beautifully. Can I learn to model their world view? I find myself standing and watching trees. Watching, listening, touching, smelling. The smell of warm, dry needles and leaves in forests. The smell of rich, damp forest returning to earth. What do you have to tell me? How can I read your secrets?

STILL LOST — BUT ONLY TECHNICALLY

So I had ridden to the planet Earth. I had ridden to the knowledge that plant Earth was just fine for a location. Enough of a location. But for, uh, practical purposes, where exactly, on planet Earth, was I? The beloved granite road took a pronounced curve to the left. A giant U-turn off into more forest. On my right, a mud road, a gumbo road, and along it was coming a little rattletrap car. The driver, apologized over and over that he had no English. He drew me a map to Komsomol'sk. And three hours later it blessedly got me there when I had long been thinking that I would spend the night under a farmer's haystack. I may never find that road again, but I know it was on Earth. And I know that finding that was the real find.

SHE WAS IN CHARGE

Komsomol'sk is not a pretty little village. It is a grey, Soviet town with a huge hydroelectric dam. (Isn't everything Soviet huge?) High tension powerlines march off to the horizon. The only reason there was a gostaneesta (hotel) was because of the dam. People come from out of town to work on it from time to time - that was my theory anyway.

I locked my bike to the pole in front of the gostaneetsa and turned to go in. There she was. Short. Shorter than me. Maybe five feet. Fire hydrant shaped. She was watching me with her arms folded over her chest

"Tourista?"

"Da."

She laughed. She motioned for me to bring my bike inside as she told me so in Russian. So I unlocked it and took it through the double doors that swung open like in a saloon. The lobby had concrete walls painted two shades of brown: chocolate brown on the bottom, café au lait brown on the top. Brown high gloss. A couple of 1950s style vinyl covered chairs. Linoleum floor.

She talked in Russian. I didn't understand a word, but my international mime told her that I wanted to sleep there for one night and that I was one person, alone. I didn't care what it looked like, what the bathrooms were like or how much it cost. I just wanted a bed. I was beat.

She went into her little office on the other side of a small window and handed through a registration form. Like so many forms in Russia, it was printed on newsprint. It was also in Cyrillic. Fine. I could handle that. What could they ask for on a registration form? Name? Address? Maybe visa number?

I put in basic stuff where there were lines and handed it back.

She wasn't happy. She scolded me in Russian and returned it to me, pointing at what I had written. I kept adding other things and handing it back. She kept pointing at what I had written and scolding. So I added my home phone number and cat's name.

Back in her hands it made her even more cross. She pulled out some of her completed registration forms and pointed at what others had written. Of course they were in Cyrillic too so I have no idea what was there.

She was angry. Like most people, she seemed to believe that if she talked insistently enough to me I would suddenly understand the language. She tore up my registration form and handed me another one. She had the power to bounce me out on my ear. I couldn't possibly make it to the next town in daylight — it was already dusk — and chances are that the next town didn't have a hotel. I was dog-tired. I had been riding for twelve hours. I had come through a storm, being lost and coping with the possibility of not finding accommodation. I needed to work with this lady and keep her happy.

I walked around into her office and knelt on the floor beside her desk. I tried to get her to explain to me what she wanted in each blank. Then I realized she wanted Cyrillic. Right, Cyrillic, of course. My only hope was my Russian visa which was typed in Cyrillic and I assume had things like my name on it.

I hauled it out and painstakingly copied some of the Cyrillic script items from it onto the registration form. I would copy an item, show her and listen to her explain at length in Russian what else I had to do. I would pull one more thing off my visa, slowly print it in and show her again. At one point we were both laughing, neither of us having a clue what the other one was laughing about. She talked away in Russian. After an hour she was happy enough to take some money. I gave her thumbs up. She liked that.

Now I was concerned about leaving my bike in the lobby while we went up to the room. Even though not a soul had shown themselves since I arrived I had picked up her protectiveness. She marched over to her office, picked up the broom, walked to the pair of double swinging doors and stuck the broom handle through the two door handles with a flourish. She turned back to me and dusted her palms together like in an old silent movie. I cheered and off we went. She was pleased. So was I.

Her upstairs corner room had the luxury of windows on two sides and was painted a lovely robin's egg blue. The matching blue plastic curtains were held on the shower curtain rods with shower curtain hooks. I guess they were shower curtains. There was a broken down brown table and chair as well as a small bed. It is easy to see where Russian hotels fall short but there are nice things about them. Russian beds are all firm and comfortable and the blankets are inside two sheets sewn together with a round hole in the middle of the top sheet for fitting the blankets in. The bed was turned down and the pillow was plumped up and sort of stood up on its side. This was going to be much better than wriggling under a haystack.

The bathroom was at the far end of the hall. Toilet in one room, sink in another. No hot water.

She stood guard beside my bike in the lobby while I carried my panniers upstairs.

I went down after washing my hair and sponge bathing in cold water to get some hot water to drink. I also wanted to take her picture. She gave me an electric teakettle for 500 rubles — at that time a fraction of one cent Canadian. It was the shape and size of a teapot but made of metal and had a frayed cord and plug. She said "Niet," laughingly, to the idea of having her picture taken but even as she was saying it, she pulled out her comb and smoothed her hair back into its tight bun. Then she patted it with her hands.

I set my camera on her counter and stood beside her while I triggered the picture with my remote. We had done something together. We had succeeded. She had a bed for me. I loved her.

THE GIRL AND THE MAN

I fell asleep as soon as it was dark and hardly turned over in the night. Wonderful, zonked sleep. I woke at 5:40 AM. It was still dark but I knew it would be light soon. I felt well rested and wanted to get a good start on whatever this day was going to bring. (Little did I know.) So I dressed and went down to the other end of the hall to the bathroom.

The only other person in the hotel appeared to be a man I had seen with "my" hotel lady just after I checked in. He was 40-ish but looked beaten up and weathered — hard living and hard drinking. The average life expectancy of a Russian male is fifty-two years. He wasn't going to beat the numbers.

I could hear movement as I approached the bathroom. When I reached for the door handle it opened in front of me and out of it emerged a beautiful young woman. Maybe sixteen years old, maybe eighteen. She was wearing a brightly coloured cotton summer dress, had lovely olive skin and shoulder length dark brown hair that was tangled and unkempt. Her eyes were bloodshot and she looked at me in confusion. She almost went back into the bathroom when she saw me.

Then, from behind me, I heard the man's voice. His door across the hall was open and he reached past me and out to her. He picked her up like a small, confused child and carried her back through his door and closed it, talking quietly to her.

I heard nothing more. I saw nothing. I left.

What was their relationship? I decided that he drifted and floated to where there was work. He came to town working on the dam. She was not much more than a child, bored in this isolated town and he offered glamour and sexual liberation. But there was nothing to do there. So they stayed in a hotel room (how glamorous!) and drank (wow!). Her bid for freedom. His perk.

Okay — what scenario can you come up with?

BACK TO ME.

Often my questions to Granny were complex. Should I move to a new location in Moscow — seeing as the woman in the current apartment is escalating warfare about what the agency was paying her? Should I stay in Moscow long enough to try and get some business opportunities going? Should I cycle out of Moscow? Or find some other way to get myself and my bike out of Moscow? Or should I heed the warnings and forget about riding in Russia and just get to another country? And if so, where? Try and answer that one, Granny.

For weeks Granny discussed, advised, helped out. Then I noticed that she smiled enigmatically and said; "You know the answer." And she was right. As soon as she said that, I did know. I had just wanted her to say it. Then I would feel advised. Right Granny. I know. We know. I would tell her what I knew. She would smile. Sometimes she said she was proud of me.

Then, a new development: Granny would say, "Well we don't know enough yet, dearie, to make this decision. We have to pedal a little further". Sometimes she would add, "You will know when you know."

At first that frustrated me. I thought she was copping out. Come on Granny. You are the oracle. What's the decision here? Then I took her responses more seriously. I started exploring that. Could I be at peace with the fact that I didn't have enough information to decide? I tried it on and it fit. Right away I felt settled in not knowing. It was just fine not to know yet.

Just fine not to know? Where was the grim drive to closure? The commitment to decisiveness? They were somewhere else.

I didn't know. Okay? I just didn't know and that was fine. I would know when I knew. Now I knew I didn't know. And I knew that was a place to be, not a state of transition to speedy resolution. I could live there, eat there, sleep there. And get up the next day and still be there. And that was fine. Things would happen and then I would know. Until then, I was fine not knowing.

Sometimes I wouldn't even know when the additional pieces fell into place. I wouldn't even make a decision. I would look and notice that the decision had been made. For a while I didn't know and then I just knew. From where? What was the process?

Who knows, but I loved it.

I began to understand that Granny was connecting me with my own internal wisdom and that I was gaining confidence in processes that happened separately from cognitive thought. Control had shifted from me to Granny and now was shifting back to my internal wise self. And my wise self was connected to the cosmos. It felt comfortable and safe and right.

MUSIC FOR THE HOME STRETCH

Downstairs, next morning, "my lady" was replaced by another short, middle-aged Russian lady. I had the feeling that she had been briefed about me. She treated me kindly in spite of the fact that I woke her up in her little lobby-side office/sleeping room. She wanted to carry my bike downstairs for heavens sake. I wouldn't wish that on an enemy.

She hovered patiently and supportively as I saddled up and she pointed me in the right direction. She also seemed to be telling me there wasn't asphalt all the way to Kostromi. The road was bad. She was worried. (How right she was.) Before I rode off I put my hand on her arm, leaned over and said very quietly, "Spazeeba." She took my hand and wished me well in such a heartfelt way I couldn't have felt more blessed if angels had come down and sprinkled fairy dust on me.

This was to be my last day riding the roads inside the Golden Ring. Once I reached Kostromi, at the top of the Golden Ring, I would arrange transportation back to Moscow to stay out of the heavy traffic. The thunderstorm truly had ushered in different weather. It was heavily overcast and a relentless headwind was blowing. But I had a dumpy little Russian lady who wanted me to make it through and, by gum, I would.

What she knew and I found out was that the road just stopped in the middle of nowhere. At least the pavement stopped. The only way to proceed was to traverse (portage?) a stretch of loose, jagged rock that went for heaven-only-knew how far. This wasn't gravel. This was bigger stones. Like a man's fist. And jagged. And loose. Just kind of dumped in there. In some places it was difficult to walk. I was appalled. In parts I had one foot on a pedal and pushed myself along the ground with the other foot, keeping it close to the ground. In some stretches, any sort of riding was out of the question. As I struggled along I thought: Cycling in Russia isn't without risks. But then so is getting out of bed in the morning.

Within minutes, my team was on duty assessing the situation and advising and commending:

Holy shit, I don't believe this. - scolded Sonia.

Right on Marg, you are doing great. - beamed my friend Noah.

Oh Honey, how will you ever manage? - worried Mom.

Good for you Marg. - chuckled Andrew.

The rock pile probably lasted five kilometers but I really have no idea. It gradually improved to rocks in sand and became rideable. Further along I came to some kind of outpost town. It had Soviet-times houses and deeply rutted streets of mud gumbo. The ruts were huge. It looked like tractors were the main transportation, even inside town.

Once across the boulders, sand and mud, I discovered that I still faced 40 K more than I expected to get to Kostromi. And still a spirit-breaking headwind. I needed something. I made it by treating myself to music. My nephew, Andrew, had taped Neil Diamond. I forgot how much I love Beautiful Noise, and Forever in Bluejeans and Longfellow Serenade.

I felt tired and alone and as music often does, it unleashed something. I cried all the way to Kostromi. I cried for all the love I had looked for and never found. I cried for the fact that this trip will make most men all the more unsuitable for me. I cried for Brenda, my cat, that I so desperately wanted to protect and didn't seem able to. And I cried because it felt great.

Late afternoon in the Kostromi Motel, I couldn't get warm. The lukewarm shower didn't help. I wrapped my hair in one towel, and my body in another.

What a luxury to have two towels. I put apres sun cream on my burning face —
not from sun but from the wind. I climbed into bed under three heavy
blankets with my head propped up on the pillows from both beds. I plugged in
the Walkman and closed my eyes. I felt the roadbuzz, the warmth coming
back, the fatigue, the triumph. I had finished cycling the Golden Ring of
Russia. This was my reward. Lying listening to Neil Diamond, drifting in and
out of consciousness, limp, safe and, finally, warm. A flood of feelings and no
effort required of me. Just feel them. And listen to my team.

Oh Honey, how do you do it?
I can't believe you did that.
I never doubted for a moment Marg.
Sweetie you are amazing.
I'm sooooo proud of you
Yeah Mom.
Cool Marg. The intrepid travelling aunt.
Right on Marg. Good for you. You should be proud of yourself.
Well there. You've done it.
Good on ya.
Well now we can all continue as if we're normal.
I knew we would darling.
Yes, we are good aren't we?

MY TWITCHING EYE MEANS...SOMETHING

It was still with me. Many times a day. Sometimes I barely noticed it, working
away, in background overdrive. Flutter, flutter. Was my body frightened by the
lack of structure? All my schedules and habits, many of my assumptions and
priorities were gone. No more structure to anchor the whole operation. My
body was grappling to find something to hook onto. Bedrock. The bottom of
the pool. A constant horizon against which all else can be reckoned.

I don't know why that felt like the source of the twitch and intellectually it
didn't look like a tight fit. But it kept coming to mind. Phantom limb. Vestigial
perception. Let me see now, we are... eyes narrow in thought, straining to see
the obscure. Squinting through the fog. Nothing there. Nothing to hook onto.

I wondered if it would last the rest of my life. Is this part of me now? It felt
like a tattle tale of my not really having this travelling thing aced. It
embarrassed me. Thank goodness Russians won't know the language of
dysfunction, I caught myself thinking.

Yeah? Says who Marg?

I'M ALIVE

In some way, cycling in Russia is like cycling anywhere. New views and
adventures unfolding over each hill and around each bend. Lots of boring
slogging; moments of great joy and wonder; navigational confusion; asking
strangers questions; loading up and grazing through snacks; layers of clothes on
and off as conditions changed — pedal, pedal, pedal.

First of all, find the road. Constant work at that. Keep checking, keep asking, keep looking for confirmation and info on the next leg as I rolled ahead. Then find the town. Toilets. Food. Water. Then find a place to sleep. Once I was outside the sphere of Lonely Planet it seemed insurmountable. I had a panic attack. Then I acknowledged that I was already getting to know the scene in Russia. I knew how things worked. No sweat.

First let me say that the cycling inside The Golden Ring was awesome. Very little traffic once off the busy Golden Ring highway. Great roads — with that one exception. Thank goodness I didn't let people talk me out of that. To have missed that! And the rare cars stop for horse drawn carts, tractors and geese crossing — because geese don't change their plans for anybody.

Wonderful scenery. Forests, meadows, a few valleys and rivers — rare enough to feel like an event. Sometimes in the morning the dips were full of mist that clung to the ground and pulled away reluctantly leaving wisps behind. The villages were small and have chickens and geese and shy residents who wore gumboots and had hard work bent into their bodies. Each village had several wells with a pump or just a bucket on a chain. I loved every minute. This was the best-kept secret in Russia.

When I got a flat tire, well, you all would have been proud of me. I didn't break stride, (cadence?) Off the bike, off with the panniers, flipped it over, tools out, wheel off, tire off, new tube in, pumped up, checked, old tube patched, bike back up, brakes re-attached, luggage back on, hands washed in no-water grease cleaner, back on the bike and on my way in a FLASH! The wink of an eye, as we say. Very proud of myself. The crowd roared. I was pleased to have that hand cleaner with me. I was elated to have completed the task without bandits stopping and — bandit-ting me. I remember thinking that if the banditos, or Mafia, or whomever they all imagine, comes now, I ain't going anywhere. I have no means of escape. But they will have to deal with someone who is too busy to put up with them and their demands.

My adventures were not life threatening. I wasn't robbed or beaten. I was just called on to be tenacious and creative and it gave me enormous satisfaction to come through these challenges — and I had convinced myself that everyone at home was proud of me.

But these are the same adventures that you and I face at our desks and on the phone and in our kitchens and cars every day. Little tests that demand courage and wisdom and creativity. No-one admires us for them because they are diminished by being usual. I was amazed and thrilled that simply by putting the show on the road I was a hero.

I gathered crowds in Russia. They were kind to me. Where were they while I was slogging it out at my desk looking down the barrel of a bankruptcy gun? Dealing with men I couldn't get rid of and men I couldn't keep? Huh? Where was the cheering section then? Riding a bike in Russia is chickenshit compared to keeping a tiny advertising agency afloat for eighteen years, raising a child, maintaining a house. We're all heroes.

BACK TO MAXIM

I had ridden the Golden Ring plus the roads inside it. I was alive and well. Back in Moscow, Maxim, who had done everything he could to dissuade me from going out there on my bike, asked me how I managed to do it. I told him that I learned to say, "Ya goste vashyay stranya." (I am a guest in your country.)

Maxim blinked, translated my terrible Russian accent in his head, smirked, then broke into a laugh and shook his head. "So simple. So simple. That's what we needed to give you. Something that simple. Why didn't we think of that?"

I didn't add that I hadn't left room in my world view for anyone to harm me. They didn't have a choice. I was directing the movie and I had decided it would be a happy movie. I didn't try and tell him that.

BRIBING LESSONS

First of all: the bribe should be in American cash. Keep it handy. Twenty-dollar bills are the industry standard but a five here and there gives you flexibility. Don't start offering bribes until you get to the right person. This isn't always easy to figure out. If an individual shrugs, walks away or points you to someone else, they don't have the decision-making power in this situation. On the other hand, if the person gives you many reasons why you can't do such-and-such, chances are he or she is a candidate for a bribe.

Then you ask how much it costs to do - whatever you are trying to do: put your bike on the train, get a visa, get inside - whatever. You ask him this after he has told you all the reasons why you can't. (It was always a he when I was bribing. Shes didn't seem as aggressive in this regard. Shes tended to sneer and blockade but not to have bribe-able solutions.) He may say an amount. Ten dollars. Or he may shake his head. Now it is time for you to make an offer. "Twenty dollars?" Even if he knows no other English, if he is receptive to a $20 bribe he'll know what "twenty dollars US?" means. Holding a folded twenty in your hand and showing it to him as you ask is good for impact. You don't have to do this surreptitiously. It can be in full view of other people crowded around making all their demands as well. If he accepts it, he usually puts it in his shirt pocket. He may then ignore you for a while, after which he gives you instructions on how you proceed. This person is now your protector and will stop anyone else from interfering with you.

On the train out of Russia the Hungarian border guard frantically flipped through his manual trying to find where it was written that he could charge me for having my bicycle on the train as it traveled through Hungary. It was "my" conductor, the one who accepted twenty dollars US to get my bike on the train, who took him aside and told him I had already paid. He claimed to me after, that he paid the Hungarian official some of the money I had paid him. Who knows.

I got into an interesting situation once with my hostess, Elena, negotiating with two different train conductors to get my bike on the train. She got tired of the first one stalling and seeming to be uncooperative so she switched and paid off the other only to have the first back complaining that we were supposed to be dealing with him. Go figger. The bike was on and the payee was then protecting my interests.

THE TRAIN TICKET TRANSACTION

It took Svetlana, a Moscow native, half the afternoon to find the place in Moscow where I was to buy my train ticket from Moscow to Prague. When we arrived and told the woman at the counter I wanted to buy a ticket to Prague, she said it would take fifteen minutes. We sat in a courtyard for twenty-five. We could see her through the door and in that time she didn't seem to be involved in preparing a ticket for me in any way. She walked around, chatted with her colleagues, moved pieces of paper. There were no other customers.

Svetlana went back in. The woman spent five minutes talking to another woman behind the counter, then nodded to me outside. I went in. The woman then spent fifteen more minutes flipping papers, calculating, filling forms, numbering forms, creating triplicates by putting carbon paper between identical newsprint forms, opening drawers, taking things out, telling us numbers, discussing with other people (this was more or less on-going) consulting lists and charts and taking numbers from them.

She repeated all these steps several times. As the process elongated I became increasingly fascinated and wanted her to keep going forever. Then she told us the price. Then she told us it would be a new price because I was travelling after September first when fares went up. Then she told us there would be additional cost for insurance. After that was settled she consulted with someone else and then she said there would be a surcharge because I was a foreigner.

It was a dazzling display of bureaucrat-eeze at its finest. And much to my disappointment, she finally counted my money twice, gave me change, explained everything on the ticket and sent us to another counter to find out if I needed transit visas for the countries I would pass through while on the train.

There were people at the other counter but it was past closing time so they wouldn't answer the question. They did, however, give Svetlana a phone number to call the next day.

ENDING THE COLD WAR TOGETHER

It was my last dinner in Moscow. I was catching the train out of Russia to Prague later that evening. Svetlana bought ingredients from venders on the side of the road to make a "special" goodbye dinner for me. Sergei was a guest as well. Over dinner I told them about the Cuban Missile Crisis and my Dad's plan to evacuate us. Svetlana and Sergei were in their late thirties. They had heard about it from older Russians. Their eyes filled with tears. They shook their heads sadly and reached across the table and took my hands. I said, "And now I am here, with you. We are together. We are safe." They raised their glasses of wine and said, "To you, being here."

Before walking out the door with all my things, we sat down in the livingroom to reflect on the time we had spent together, review if I had everything, think about what was ahead. This is a Russian custom that they perform religiously.

CHASING THE SUN SOUTH

SKIPPING THE BALTIC STATES

By late August it was getting cooler in Russia. I felt the pull to follow the sun south. My original idea had been to leave Russian via St Petersburg, sailing southwest through the Gulf of Finland to Tallinn in Estonia. From there, in spite of dire warnings, I would cycle down through Estonia and Lithuania. The plan depended on fall coming late to northeastern Europe. I would just ride the conditions.

The bloom went off that plan when the weather cooled but its death knell came from another direction altogether. With the help of my St Petersburg hostess, Elena, I tried to contact someone about passage on the boat. It took half a day of frustrating phonecalls to find out that the boat was no longer running. The Board of Directors had all been arrested for not paying their fuel bill. So it seemed time to just skip ahead to Prague the easy way, by taking the train from Moscow.

CROSSING THE FRONTIER

I met Irenie when we moved into a our train compartment together. She and I plus my bike and her desktop computer. It was all packed in there but she was cheerful and we worked around these bulky compartment-mates. Her work often took her out of Russia to formerly satellite countries training hotel employees on her company's computer system. She spoke good English and was willing to chat and also to sit quietly reading or looking out the window.

The border guards at Belarus decided that she was carrying more cash out of Russian than permitted. (Why should they care? The ruble is as valuable as toilet paper outside Russia.) Like all Russians, she had no cheques or credit cards. Even traveling on behalf of her company for three full weeks in Hungary she was going to pay for everything with a wad of cash she carried with her. She knew that there was a limit to the amount of cash she could take but she understood that the limit was higher. The guards got angry and took her off the train.

When she finally returned she muttered, "They change the rules all the time and don't tell anyone."

"So what did they do?"

"They kept the extra."

"A fine?"

"No. They just put it in their pockets."

Later that afternoon Irenie and I were chatting when the train slowed and pulled into a huge shed. Looking past Irenie at the window I could only see that there were other trains in there.

I asked her what was happening. "They're probably changing the wheels."

"Of the train?"

"Yeah."

Yeah, sure Irenie. Why would they change the wheels while we were on the train? Even in a crazy country they would change the wheels when the train was out of service. These Russian people do have odd gaps in their world knowledge. Where-ever would Irenie get that absurd notion?

We continued chatting. Fifteen minutes later we still weren't going anywhere. What the heck was going on? I went into the corridor and looked out the window. The train beside us was ten feet in the air and, sure enough, the slouching workmen, smoking cigarettes and joking amiably, were rolling new banks of wheels under it. And we were up in the air just like they were.

"My God, Irenie, you're right. They are changing the wheels."

"Yeah, I know."

"Why are they changing the wheels? Why would they do that with us in it? In the middle of a train trip?"

"Stalin wanted to protect the country from invasion so the railway tracks in Russia are a different size than in Poland. When you cross the frontier they have to change the wheels."

"You mean every single train that goes in or out of Russia gets jacked up in the air and different sized wheels put under it?"

"Yes."

There's the planning of a madman. And in fact Russians now say, "Stalin had a disease, in the head. It was from too much work. It made him ill."

The guard at the Polish border looked like he was with the French Foreign Legion: slight build, moustached, with a visor on the front of his pillbox hat and a leather belt over one shoulder that came down and attached to the belt around his waist. He was annoyed. Irenie explained that I had been told by the Polish embassy in Moscow that as long as I stayed on the train I did not need a transit visa to go through Poland. He got more annoyed.

He looked at my passport and Russian visa again. He spat out Polish. It didn't need translating. He was having none of it. Irenie tried again. He closed my passport and slapped it against his hand impatiently and turned away. Irenie said I had to go with him.

"Go with him? Where?"

"To the bureau."

The conductor intercepted in the hallway. He held his hands up at his shoulders trying to defuse the situation. Irenie stuck her head into the aisle. They all talked in Russian. The Polish border guard stomped away. Every so often he turned back and motioned angrily for me to go with him.

"You'll have to go", said Irenie.

"What will happen?" I asked alarmed.

"Who knows?" she shrugged. She didn't look happy.

Rushing along the platform to keep up with my guard I looked plaintively at the conductor who was leaning out from the top step, holding the handrail and watching. He waved me on.

Well here we are. Bike and luggage on the train. I'm in some nothing place at the border between Belarus and Poland being ushered into a cold, concrete building and up stairs. The brown walls were nicked and banged — from bullets? Struggles? People trying to escape?

Aha. Yes. A border. An iron curtain within the iron curtain. He ushered me into a little room. There was a wooden table in there and a couple of chairs, graffiti on the walls. The windows behind the bars were open. A prison cell. How many terrified people have been held in this room before me? Tortured? Interrogated for days? What kind of trumped up charges did we get laid against us in this room?

Maybe they have mistaken me for someone else. A spy. A Mata Hari. They would interrogate me for days and then leave me in a dark cell. My family would notice they haven't heard from me for weeks. The Canadian embassy would bumble around, unable to help. The story got more vivid. I was scaring myself. Soldiers with machine guns came and went on the stairs outside my door. They chatted and laughed. Cruel brutes. Trained to shoot first, ask questions later. The train could leave with all my stuff and I would have trouble convincing these humorless guys that I needed to be re-united with my bicycle. I had butterflies in my stomach. Maybe I'd better de-escalate this adventure story. I could make it come true. Peace be with you.

I looked out the window. There was a rug spread on the rooftop of another wing. Was it drying? Why was it there? It seemed impossible that torturers would shake out a wet rug and carefully place it on a roof to dry. Anyway the guy probably just wanted $10 American.

He marched back in with papers. New papers as well as all my papers. He put the papers on the table, leaned over and wrote on them. He said "Ten dollars." I said, "Okay" and got it out. He handed me the pen and showed me where he wanted me to sign. I signed. He gave me back my papers and visibly relaxed. He walked me back to the train. We tried a fumbled conversation. He spoke some English. He shook his head in disbelief at those idiots in Moscow who don't know anything. He showed me which train to get back on. I wanted to say "Come on, level with me, you're really from the French Foreign Legion, right?"

The conductor nodded and slapped my shoulder as I went by his compartment. Irenie looked relieved. Veterans of the border wars.

CZECH REPUBLIC
Prague at its un-finest

Andrew, my traveling nephew, said, "You'll love Prague." Everyone said, "You'll love Prague." I had some contacts there, again through my International Marketing Course and was ready to enjoy the architecture and culture of the oldest city in Europe. I looked forward to seeing the buildings that Europeans had been living, working and worshipping in for a thousand years.

The train pulled into Prague two days after leaving Moscow. Accommodation was tight. I had unwittingly timed my arrival to coincide with Michael Jackson's who drew thousands of East German teenagers. The only economical accommodation I could find in this tourist-packed city was a room in a hostel behind one of the train stations. Panhandlers, drunks, vagrants and street people lay on the benches and sidewalks and approached as you passed. It smelled sour. Garbage was piled up. Coming and going was like running a gauntlet.

I was apprehensive about the three German guys in the next room who drank and partied most of the night. The walls were paper-thin. When they played cards I could hear the cards snap onto the table. You can imagine how loud their voices were. It was as if we were in one room together. I tried hitting the wall and calling please be quiet. But the next night I was wakened when they returned late from drinking. One of them was giving a drunken, tour in English: "Here is the bright light to be sure you don't get lost. Here is the woman. Here is the elegant room we share."

"Here is the woman". Oh dear. Three drunks next door, no one else around. I didn't pound on the wall. I didn't call out. They knew I was there. I kept as low a profile as I could and spent the rest of the night reading and planning my escape from Prague while they talked loudly, guffawed, drank beer (crack, fizz through the wall). I had had it with wandering the streets, being charged absurd amounts for food and discovering that every lovely building I was looking at was being photographed and camcorded by dozens of other people. I was part of a pack and part of a pack wasn't what I wanted to be.

EINE KLEINE NACTMUSIK DOESN'T CUT IT WHEN YOU WANT MICHAEL JACKSON

I stayed an extra day to meet a contact and get some instructions on a cycling route out of the city. I was determined to fit in a cultural event while I waited. Mozart's Eine Kleine Nactmusik, a long-time favorite, was being performed by a string orchestra in a tiny downtown church. Very old. I imagined that Mozart wrote for this setting. Maybe Eine Kleine had been performed in this church while he was still alive.

I noticed that the five front rows where reserved. This was just the kind of event that a high school teacher would try to inject into a Michael Jackson school tour. I felt uneasy.

Right you are. Just before the performance began a group of German high school students arrived and that was that. They giggled, whispered, poked each other, passed notes, tugged sleeves and hair and conducted rivalries and flirtations throughout the concert. They were like a wall between the rest of us and the music. Several people tried shushing them, to no effect. I felt sabotaged.

WALK ON THE WILD SIDE

Walking back to my frightful hostel I passed two American couples strolling up and down under the generous canopy at their expensive hotel. They were wearing evening clothes. One of the men was saying, "I just love getting out and seeing what it is like in other places. I always want to see over the next hill."

I felt like saying, "You want to see over the next hill Bub? Come with me, I'll take you over the next hill. So far you haven't left the US of A."

YOU ARE MY HERO

We've wanted to be heroes. Our heroic chances are so rare. The rescuer. The leader. The see-er of opportunities that are fearlessly faced. When do we get a chance to be those? Arnie, Thelma and Louise and the body-built mother in Terminator. There is a wonderful movie with George C. Scott and Joanne Woodward called, Once were Heroes. Strange little movie about little people, kind of crazy little people, who were brave in the face of mythical evil.

In the grubby hostel in Prague, populated with people I would cross the street to avoid, a lovely, tall, young woman chatted with me in the hallway. When she heard that I was traveling by bike, alone and out to see the world, she said gently, "You are my hero." She touched me with a magic wand. She reached out and turned me into a hero. Taller, stronger, faster, braver. She made more possible because she saw me as brave. She gave me a gift. Thank you girl in the hostel in Prague.

TRAVELING ALONE

I felt like an outsider in the network of travelers. Apart from the pair of the middle-aged sisters in St Petersburg, all the hostlers were in their twenties. I have close friends in their 20s, but hostlers in their 20s categorized me as a parent. A weird parent but definitely a parent. After an evening of chatting they pronounced me cool, which was gratifying, but not the same as a kindred spirit. People my age were traveling in a more protected stream. Rental cars, high-end hotels and fine dining. They were the elegant couple taking the air under the canopy of their luxury hotel.

But a bigger question wove through my interest in kindred spirits. Somewhere inside I knew that we live alone and die alone, appearances to the contrary. Could I come to grips with our aloneness? Transcend our illusion that we are not alone? Settle peacefully into being alone?

There it is: our aloneness. Like the astounding space between subatomic particles. Atoms are mostly space. You are mostly space. So is the chair you are sitting on. The only bond between the particles is energy. That energy, like gravity, holds them together. But there is no contact. Mostly space.

The same with people. There are huge gulfs of space sitting quietly between our connections. The void separating us from all else. From each other. When it surfaces we are shocked, dismayed, frightened. But it has been there all the time. The void. With an undercurrent of yearning to bridge it. That's the energy that holds us together. Now I could learn to be at peace with that aloneness.

Granny and I were alone. Thank goodness I had her. And the team of supporters that I carried in my heart.

ENOUGH

Before leaving Prague I met with a local lawyer, a connection through my Canadian Czech friend. We met at the downtown KFC location which was easy for both of us to get to, she in a business suit rushing to another meeting, me in cycling clothes. My backpack, holding my everything-importants, was in my lap while we poured over maps. She pointed out the quiet roads for cycling out of the city. After half an hour she reached back to pick up her purse from where she had looped it over the back of her chair. It was gone. Not under her chair, not on one of the other chairs, not on the floor. We asked people around us. No one had seen anything. Shaken, she went off to the police. And I determined I had now seen enough of Prague.

THE BENESOV MUSIC FESTIVAL

I fled Prague at first light, hoping to beat the morning rush hour. I headed south to get warm weather as fall closed in on northern Europe. That took me to Benesov, the Czech Republic at its finest. Benesov has an old town square surrounded by stores: bookstore, stationary store, tiny grocery stores and pastry shops – amazing pastry shops. These stores worked on the Russian model of clerks behind glass cases with shelves of merchandise behind them. You asked the clerks for what you wanted. It was slow.

My hotel was on the edge of the town square too. Their fax machine had broken down so I asked at the post office about other faxing options. Fortunately a medical doctor behind me in the lineup spoke English. After lengthy discussion with the postal clerk, the doctor decided it would be easiest to take me to an office a few blocks away where she knew there was a fax machine and weekend staff. She expressed appreciation for the chance to practice her English as we walked over.

It was Friday afternoon and the office was already closed but the woman there was willing to let me fax. She spoke zero English so, again, my doctor was invaluable arranging for my return, with faxes.

By the time I had them written the next day, it was raining and the hotel fax was fixed. I could easily have faxed from there. But I knew the lady in the office was expecting me and I had a vague feeling that some opportunity would open for me if I went the six blocks back to her. I didn't know where that feeling came from but with my newfound respect for the inner voice, I trotted off.

The lady and I quickly got bogged down in the language gap. She was trying to explain the costing structure for each fax. It was complicated. She called in a young woman practicing the flute in her mother's empty office upstairs. A music student. She knew a teeny amount of English, enough to get our faxing sorted out. Then, I asked if there was any music in town — really just to be conversational. I doubted such a small centre would have live music.

In fact, yes, there would be music in town that night. And the next and next nights. Which happened to coincide beautifully with my plans to wait out the rainy, cool, weekend lying on my bed reading a long, multi-generational Russian novel, grieving the loss of Russia and spoiling myself.

The Benesov Music Festival. She drew a map showing how to get from my hotel front door to each of the venues and was able to say that these were all free, although I wasn't sure that we understood each other correctly on this. I couldn't believe my good fortune to have stumbled upon a music festival and spent the rest of the day grinning like a fool.

After dinner I walked out across the square and up the hill, as she had directed. I was wearing layers of my warmest cycling clothes which meant spandex pants, running shoes, turtle neck sweaters and a hooded rain jacket. At 7:45 it appeared that no one else was going to be attending this event, due to start at eight. The church was empty. I went back outside to see if I could find someone to confirm that this was the right place and, indeed, there was a concert there this evening.

I saw a fashionable and lovely young woman — who turned out to be a recitalist — and her handsome man, standing on the grass behind the refectory embracing each other and talking quietly and gazing into each other's eyes. They looked like they were out of a movie. A whole world inside the circle of their arms. Lovely. Ah. Pang. But also relief that I was doing what I wanted without conflict, without accommodating what someone else wanted, without monitoring someone else's wishes more closely than I was listening to my own. Am I gradually settling into my alone-ness?

Calmly, alone, I went back into the church and sat near the front in the remarkably uncomfortable pews. People then arrived quickly and filled the church. During this, white-haired members of the orchestra had assembled in the space in front of the alter. The man in his early twenties, wearing torn jeans and Moroccan jacket, stuck out among them. He had dark brown, shoulder-lengthed hair that fell easily from a natural part in the middle. He had perfect features. A slender, patrician nose, even eyes and a chiseled mouth. He was a Chopin.

He sat on one of the metal chairs and chatted with a senior cello player. He appeared to be a friend from the audience. Then he went in behind and emerged in his own tuxedo with his own cello and settled beside his older friend. Others drifted in, tuned, chatted. A small black and white dog trotted up the aisle and walked in among the orchestra. The beautiful young cellist noticed, pointed and laughed. No one was concerned. Several stroked the little dog.

The conductor came from behind the orchestra. Applause. Bow. Then from the back of the church, up the aisle, came four soloists, two men and two women. The women dressed beautifully in sedate evening clothes, men in tux, poised and elegant.

Full orchestra, full pipe organ, full choir and four soloists — all professional caliber. The soloists' voices, particularly the soprano's, were so pure I couldn't imagine world-renowned professionals doing it better. The sound filled the cathedral with rich harmonies and complex melodies winding and resolving and echoing. What had I done to earn this magic moment? The hair stood up all over my body. I felt a wave of gratitude to Mom for giving us an appreciation for this music. I had no idea what they were singing and playing. Some kind of Haydn. I would guess a mass from the structure of it.

Afterwards, it was dark and blowing and spooky walking back to the hotel. A Legend-of-Sleepy-Hollow fall evening. There were no streetlights and I was glad to have two couples walking and chatting in front of me to lead the way and dispel the demons of darkness.

By the third night of the Benesov Music Festival, a string quartet recital in a beautiful white and gold school gymnasium, people were getting used to seeing me in my cycling clothes, sitting in the front row. They now nodded and bowed in a friendly greeting to me and my Other Traveler.

I'M ALONE

I got a flash of looking down from my high wire. I was alone out there. My money was all that gave me entrée. My body was all that propelled me. As long as I kept pressing ahead I had practical issues to deal with. When I paused I faced my aloneness. Hanging in space.

I had that same feeling the first time I was alone on a highway many years before, the fear that I could slip between the cracks of reality and disappear. What am I doing out here? Non-directional panic. I wasn't doing anything well. Back at home my little cat had been put into boarding because the house renters had a dog. Brenda, I have let you down. Money was galloping out of my hands. I wasn't getting any fitter. I could end up just huddled in this hotel room, watching the rain outside and hiding until my money was all gone. My twitching eye kept reminding me that my whole being was panicked about something.

I couldn't go to sleep without help from Granny. She pointed out that I could only deal with was this particular moment. I had a comfortable bed and great duvet. I had almost-hot-water coming out of the shower. I had towels. I had a beautiful church outside my window. I was here in this room right now. I could enjoy it, enjoy being warm and dry, my Czech pastries, my Russian novel. And when I wanted to do something else I would.

Peace be with you Brenda. I felt my love and comfort leave my body and touch hers. Could she feel it? Did she get comfort from it?

HIGHWAY RIDING

I zigzagged on quiet back-roads from Benesov to Tabor, until the last 18 K. At that point it was getting dark so I decided that the directness of the highway (it was much more direct) was the only way I could get there before it was unsafely dark. But I wasn't happy. Highway riding is just getting somewhere. I truly missed the surrounding country life as well as the astounding quietness of the back roads.

The ultimate annoyance was from on-coming cars that insisted on passing another vehicle and barreling toward me in an unnerving way. It made me aware that wobbling during a gear change or a pavement crack would throw me off course a few inches and into — oblivion. Or, worse yet, permanent, crippling injury.

READING CRISIS

It was hard to keep stocked with English-language reading. I needed a new book in Tabor. I went into the organic labyrinth of streets radiating from the old town square, that wasn't shaped anything like square. The crowded shops were so old they looked like they were out of a medieval movie set. I was amazed to find a bookstore with an English-language section. In it I came upon A Lady's Life in the Rocky Mountains which reproduced the letters of Isabella Bird, an English horsewoman who traveled alone or with local desperados for guides in the mountains of Colorado in 1873.

It was a remarkable story of physical hardship, diplomacy, creativity and capability. She became my friend and hero. She was level headed and disciplined. And much to my delight I saw parallels with my journey. Isabella also described people trying to stop her from riding into the mountains and how she listened politely, thanked them and then followed her instincts. She recounted struggling for hours in the dark with snow so deep her horse could barely keep going and the relief of finally getting to shelter. She talked of help being there when she needed it and dangerous characters rising to the occasion.

In a note at the back I found out that Isabella was chronically ill and somewhat crippled. When I finished the book I mailed it to my mother, who also loved it.

SWAN LAKE

It was an overcast day. Completely still. Flat grey. No weather. The world was holding its breath. Riding along I turned my head to the right and there, on a pond, were two huge, white swans. Black beaks and eyes and then startling, flawless white. They were posed like ornaments, angled a bit toward each other and a bit toward me. Perfect. They were close enough to take my breath away, far enough away to be poor photo material. I knew all I could do was stop and look and absorb this gift to carry away with me as best I could.

Was it in response to seeing me stand there that they both moved? Slowly they glided forward. As they did they each left a little wake in the surface of the pond behind them. The elegance of the two tiny wakes made something ache inside me.

GLIMPSING THE WATERWORLD

A creek meandering between green banks, with trees overhanging, creates a world that is more than just beautiful. It is a secret, magic, tiny waterworld. I stop and gaze and listen to that lovely water-over-rocks noise. I feel a tug to see it closer, to enter The Wind in the Willows, to be in that place. I want to be silently part of the moss and the wildflowers dripping over the edge and rotting logs with fungus shelves that were home to tiny creatures. I want to watch the little pools where spiders run on top of the water. I long to be tiny and weightless, like the spider, to be in the water world without disturbing it. When you feel that pull, get off your bike and sit on the shore. Waterworlds are worth the time.

THE HUSBANDS

I saw them standing at hotel elevators, on street corners, in town squares: traveling couples. And too often I saw an understanding that it was fine for the husband to make a public display of his irritation with the wife. His patience was tried. What he had to put up with. It was part of the understanding that she would not escalate. She would not defend herself.

I only knew the words of those who spoke English: "Please Eleanor, not now," spoken as if to a child, heavy emphasis on the not, exasperated voice. "Sit here." Again, commanding. The male prerogative to control. And the females, somewhere in themselves, shrinking. They swallow. They brush aside the lessening with little gestures of oh dear, touching their hair, glancing sideways quickly, changing their facial expression as they launch a new topic as if this damage had never occurred. They close their mouths. They know how to do that, keep their mouths shut.

I thank my lucky stars that I am alone. Never did I feel as lonely as when I was back there, married. It was an awful feeling to pass a husband in the kitchen and feel isolated and lonely. The alone of by-myself was peaceful.

CZECH FOOD

The quality of Czech food was a treat after Russian food. The Czechs have many pastry shops and each pastry is a tiny work of art. The strudel is perfect. Light and rich. The bread is made in an enormous range of sizes and shapes as well as darkest rye to pure white, fluffy, cake-like bread.

In restaurants the food is German: sauerbraten, sausage, spicy meats, potatoes, and cabbage cooked many different ways. Most citizens of the southern Czech Republic speak German fluently and kept trying to do so with me.

In a standup fast food restaurant in Ceske Budejovicie I had delicious pork roast, mashed potatoes and rich, dark gravy. Hardboiled eggs are still the most common way eggs are served at breakfast but you can also get fancy crepes and omelets. There is toast in a few places. Czech coffee is made with the grounds left in the bottom of the cup. People only drink two-thirds. The total effect was somewhat muddy.

YIKES

After a sound sleep I woke in a state of panic about money. I had spent $2155 US in Russia and that didn't include phonecalls and Fed Ex-ing stuff back home. I wasn't going to make it all the way around the world. I would run out of money first. Granny? Where are you? She thought, as she often did, that at this point we didn't have enough information on expenses yet to come. She gave what was now her most usual suggestion — watch, remain alert, but there is no reason for our confidence to be shaken. Not with what we know at this point. Okay. What the heck. At least she knows what's going on. Was my eye twitching less?

ESCAPING EARLY FALL

I continued south through the Czech Republic, winding back and forth on secondary roads. I thought it would be fun to try cycling over the border, even though that meant over mountains. Maybe it is time for a test. Then I could pick up the rumoured cycle path that ran along the Danube River. That sounded pretty close to heaven. But it was getting cooler and wetter. I was uncertain. Fall was supposed to be a pleasant time of year here. Would it get better? I could only think of getting warm.

An airline pilot in Ceske Budejovicie said, "Get out of Northern Europe. The long-term forecast is awful. I've never seen fall this cold. It isn't going to get better." (After words: he was right. Europe was plunging into one of the coldest, longest winters in decades.)

Once that was established I consulted with everyone I could find who spoke English. Where, exactly, should I go for reliable heat and limited traffic? I also was thinking about ease of continuing my journey east from there, wherever "there" was. Most people shrugged. If they answered, they suggested Southern France.

The staff at the railway station did not speak or understand English. To compound the problem, they were impatient. The woman slapped a piece of paper on the counter and handed me a pencil and barked "Where?" I realized that trains from a small centre like Ceske Budejovicie would not go far. I needed a central railway point from which trains radiated across Europe. I wrote Vienna on the piece of paper believing that I could get a train to anywhere from there. This was one situation in which I paid for not knowing the local language.

The morning that I was leaving I wanted to dump my Czech currency. I remembered that I had been stuck with a large amount of Russian currency that no one, absolutely no one, outside Russia would cash. I didn't want that to happen with my Czech currency. I had a ton of Czech change.

I dithered about whether the doorman in my rather posh hotel would be insulted if I dumped my grubby pile into his hand. He had been kind and helpful to me about bicycle management but doormen can be snobby. In the end I left the hotel with my change.

The train station washroom was tended by an old man. He handed out wads of toilet paper for a small fee. A minute fee. He was organized and kept a clean, nice washroom. At first I held out my handful of change for him to pick out the correct amount. He was taking the smallest denominations. I reached down with my other hand, held his hand against mine, turned both of our hands over and dumped it all into his. Then I closed his hand over it, held both my hands up in front of me, palms facing him and smiled and pointed at him. He bowed. I bowed.

This man held down the lowest of jobs with dignity. We were pleased with the exchange.

SWITZERLAND
Winding through Europe

It took three trains to get out of the Czech Republic. One of the train rides was only five minutes long. My bike traveled on a different series of trains. I saw her parked on one of the train platforms at a station in the middle of nowhere waiting to be put on the next train. All by herself with a tag tied to her handle bar. Little international traveler bicycle.

An American couple, performing this odd train hopping with me, were confident that Nice, on the Mediterranean Coast of France, would be warm. That finalized it. And at first, they were right.

When I got to Vienna I was told that the only place I could get a southbound train to Nice would be Zurich. And the only way to get to Zurich was to get a train at one of the other five train stations in Vienna. And it was raining. But it was Sunday and there was little traffic and Vienna is amazingly cycle-friendly, wide boulevards that go on and on along the Danube and designated cycling lanes on the streets. So when I got to the next station to find that, no, that wasn't the right station either and that I now needed to pedal to yet a third station I was okay with having a chance to see a bit more of this lovely city knowing that my train south didn't leave until late in the evening.

When I got to the correct station it took an hour of back and forth between the customer service desk and the baggage department to work out a way to get my bicycle to Nice. Initially I was told it would take ten days. Flabbergasted, I negotiated, pleaded, tried to find the right person to bribe — being recently out of Russia — and finally threw myself at their mercy. The best they could do was get it down to five days. Fine. I gave up and checked my bicycle.

That left me four hours before the train left. I was weary and the station was crowded. It was a relief to no longer have to worry about minute-by-minute bike handling but there was nothing to do but eat and walk around. Anywhere I sat down in the station I ended up in the midst of weird street people. People hitting little kids, drunk people, people panhandling and groups of people with multiple-pierced body parts shoving each other and yelling.

Then, a miracle. On a rack in the minute English-language section of the station bookstore — a new John Updike. A gift. A miracle. Suddenly there wasn't anything the next 24 hours could hand me that I couldn't read my way through. He is such a genius. Describing everyday life, habits, thoughts, he shows us ourselves and people around us. He turns our sights on things that haven't quite penetrated our consciousness. Click, yes. Click, yes. How does he know these things?

The overnight train to Zurich left late in the evening. It was a lovely, modern train but the heating wasn't working properly and by morning I was chilled to the bone. The conductor spoke of there having been snow overnight down to 100 meters. Okay, I'm outta' here. Just in time.

In Zurich, a lovely old station, I ate buns and sipped three cups of hot chocolate to warm up. I lingered in my trackside bistro. It felt like an outdoor café under the giant skylight. I fancied myself the cosmopolitan traveler. A European. I heard echoes of the past humming around me in this old meeting/parting place. I felt the intensity of history crowded into this emotional narrows, layers of hellos and good-byes, dramatic and passionate through the centuries as clothes changed and social systems evolved. What famous people had big moments here? What no-bodies laughed and cried, feared and rejoiced amidst wars, plague, social upheaval. There I was, another atom spinning into the narrows.

Chugging through Switzerland by train, the country was so — Swiss. Green, alpine countryside and Swiss chalets gliding by the window. Jersey cows, beautiful, perfect, bovine Jersey cows. Inside the train, the obnoxious cluster of teenagers playing awful music was a blight that I had to keep mentally neutralizing. When do these damn kids get off? Why do I find them so irritating?

ITALY

Italy by train

Northern Italy — I couldn't believe it. I am seeing Italy. Right out there. Right out the window. I was loving every minute. It hadn't been part of any plan to take in Italy. But there was something wonderful about making the decision based on WEATHER. Maybe that was what had me cowed — my own audacity. Weather here not good stop heading south until I hit it warm stop will let you know when arrive stop. Ain't that just lovely? Just like the audacity to lie on my bed reading for days in Benesov, the audacity of weather-driven travel had me a bit spooked.

Now Genoa. Shakespeare knew Genoa. I sensed that the Mediterranean Sea was just on the other side of those buildings. The students were now mercifully gone and in their place the whole Fellini cast: the middle class mother over-controlling her brood; the aging, hair-died-jet-black, fuchsia dressed woman with a mask of make-up slipping down her wrinkled face and the burly man, unshaven, wearing a yellowed under-shirt. They were all on board now. The cast of characters acting out what Fellini showed us on the screen.

There was a nun two seats ahead of me. She was biting her fingernails with a vengeance. At that rate she'll be at her elbows by tonight. A lifetime habit of nibbling at herself. It was tempting to pass judgement.

Now, I had arrived at the famous gold coast. The playground of European aristocracy. Money, style, international jet setters, gold jewelry, gold tans, gold sun, gold beaches, gold bank accounts. Gold Coast. But outside the train window I could see that for every mile of gliterati there were one hundred miles of day-in-day-out just getting by. For every inch of beauty, a mile of shabbiness. Ordinary people, waiting for the train to pass. Hanging out the laundry. Being Italian.

Northern Europeans scorn the Italians. Sneer that they are disorganized, lazy, incompetent and thieves. So what? What do they care? They have the sun. And the sea.

I was surprised that the first glimpse of the Mediterranean felt like a huge moment for me. I craned my neck and watched for it to come into view. So much of our history, so many stories ancient and current revolve around this sea. Splendour and squalor. My eyes were popping.

The railway traveled west on a narrow ledge between the sea and the hillside, forced into the hillside one tunnel after another. It was Sunday evening. People were pulling on T-shirts and leaving the beach.

And over there, Africa. Bet I could see it if I stood on top of the train. Am I ready to take on Africa?

Shanties beside the water looked like those clustered around the Salton Sea in California, the lowest point in the continental USA. Trailers from the 50s, their tiny, curved silhouettes weathered into the landscape. Their faded tarpaulin porch-roofs and scrap lumber additions clung precariously to the flimsy dwellings.

Palm trees. Oddly enough I hadn't thought of palm trees in Italy. Similar vegetation, landscaping and economy to Southern California. An economy based on hanging around. It was like arriving in the California desert for holidays. The permanently brown sun-dwellers, casually slouched around the station in resort clothes welcoming the less fortunate to heaven.

FRANCE

Taking Granny home

When we crossed into France I felt like I was taking Granny home and I saw her puff with the pride so particular to the French. We were returning to the only civilized country in the world according to Granny.

I was flooded with childhood memories of this French grandmother. I remembered the little brass bell beside her telephone. When Granny decided that she had had enough of the conversation she picked up the bell, rang it and said, "I have to go. The bell is ringing." And she hung up the phone. People she had done this to would stand in her hallway and watch her do it to others. This did not embarrass her. A law unto herself.

The first thing a Custom's officer saw when he opened Granny's suitcase was her dirty underwear. Granny had discovered that it cooled the most zealous searcher. She always put it on top.

Granny got her mailman to fix the whalebone reinforcement in her industrial strength corset. She returned tomatoes to the store after leaving them in her kitchen cooler so long that they went soft. When she approved of the food in a restaurant she summoned the chef and chatted, one connoisseur to another. If the chef spoke French, they talked in French. An imperial style. No self-doubt.

OUTDOORS

The wonderful hot Gold Coast climate created a luxury lifestyle: open windows, meals outside, living in the garden. This showed up in the architecture: huge windows and glass doors opening to the sun, awnings, balconies, terraces, walled gardens, patios.

I felt one with the travelers who came, with wonder, to the sand, sun and sea. I noticed myself humming dream never dies, just the dreamer.

DOGS LIFE - A LA NICE

She came to the park every morning. This wasn't one of the high-class Nice parks full of designer dressed, be-jeweled, tanned, women. This was Nice low life. Old people and lower class residents who service and live off the trickle-down wealth that floods into the Gold Coast and supports shops, hotels, restaurants, coffee houses, antique stores, beauticians – all of the highest standards in the world.

She was probably in her mid twenties and she came with three dogs: a classic German Shepard, a classic Scottie dog – which seemed the oldest of the troop – and a puppy. The puppy was going to be a big dog but right now it was a roly-poly fur ball.

She arrived every morning around ten with the puppy on a leash and the other two off. They always went to the same bench. Throughout the morning her friends would arrive and plant kisses on both cheeks, which took a while when two or three arrived at once. These were not quick air-kisses, these were affectionate hugs and mouth-to-cheek contact and excitement and joy. Comfortable affection. All the dogs were greeted, patted and if one seemed to get less attention, they were brought forward to get their due.

Then everyone settled back on the bench and, while conversation continued, the dogs roamed freely around the group. When the girl threw a ball for the dogs, allez rechercher, she held the Shepherd's collar for a moment to give the Scottie and puppy a head start. When they lost interest she went and got the ball herself and tried again later.

They all got patted and talked to and scratched and loved. When the puppy got tired the girl would pull him up to her lap and cuddle and snuggle and scratch and kiss him. The dogs seemed so safe and so loved and so free of self-doubt that they just did dog things: hanging around her bench, tug of war with the collapsed ball, romping together, being dogs.

The Shepard, with the calm detachment of a big guy, remained a bit removed from the rough and tumble. He could be relied on to stay close, stay out of trouble and wander under the trees checking discarded things on the grass, sniffing the important places and watching new dogs that came into the park. The Scottie likewise had adult responsibilities, keeping an eye out, sniffing around.

And every afternoon the girl gathered her dogs together, put the leash on the puppy and started off. When the puppy needed to look at something, sniff something or go to the bathroom, she and the other dogs stood and waited patiently, never pulling the leash, until everyone was ready to get going again.

When one of them needed to check yet something else, the whole troop stopped again and waited even if they had only just started up from the last investigation. Eventually they were under way. Everyone kept together.

The Other Traveler and I came back day after day to enjoy this gentle loving and wished it would infect the world.

THE MARBLE VEIL
She lived in an elegant villa on the French Riviera. A villa built for Russian princesses. Grand staircase, big reception rooms, views of the Mediterranean and glass doors that opened onto a huge second story balcony over the sea.

She was just a head and neck with a blowing veil draped over her, as if the Mediterranean winds blew in through the rows of glass doors and billowed the veil. You could see her perfect features through the veil. Her regal nose, high forehead, perfect chin and mouth. And all of her, including her veil, was carved in marble. Solid marble. So the blowing veil revealed her features in the places where it blew against her face and between those places hung down in gentle folds.

How could this be done? How could a sculptor conceive the idea and then execute it so perfectly? Even touching her veil and her features it seemed impossible. The illusion was perfectly executed. It defied the senses. How long had she gazed through her stone veil, blowing impossibly gently, blowing forever?

Musee de Beaux Arts, Nice, France. A must-see.

LETTING GO OF THE SOULMATE
I had achieved one of my two life goals: my daughter had grown up lovely, capable and equipped to find happiness.

The other aspiration, to find a soulmate for myself, hadn't worked out so well. The quest had become entwined with dancing even though dancing partners had proven to be bad choices for life-partners. Over and over I had extricated myself from dancers, or been brushed off by dancers. Several times I resolved that I would just dance. Strictly dancing. And then, shadowing a man's lead, feeling his touch on my back, being guided masterfully through a twirl, a dip, a sway, at one with the music, somewhere at the back of my skull, a gland pumped hundred-proof hormones into my bloodstream. For a while I again believed all was possible.

The sound of the music brought it all back. Alone, in cycling tights, in broad daylight, music filled me with longing to feel that again. Have that again. And with a sense of failure that I didn't.

I felt a flush of yearning and anxiety when I thought that people at home were dancing without me. I had lost my place. I no longer existed. I was out of the game. Country and western music, Celine Dion, love songs, dance music. I heard it in streets and restaurants everywhere and it made my face flush. An instant flash. The yearning inside me stirred, leapt forward.

Aha, said the genie, the Jill-in-the-box – Aha. Gotcha. And you thought you could ignore me.

No. Not really. I was just taking time out.

Fool.

Yeah.

The French Riviera was full of fondling couples, gazing into each other eyes, sharing intimate moments and, all the while, looking beautiful. Movie-star couples making couple-dom perfect. The land of couple. I felt unattractive in my cycling clothes, lumpy thighs, no makeup, shapeless haircut and aging body. Unwanted.

Granny, widowed before I was born, showed me a new vision. She was complete without anyone else. It would have been laughable to image Granny as part of some greater whole. Granny was whole. She was a universe. She traveled, entertained, amused and was amused, managed a household, lived her life gliding through the galaxy like a stately comet in from the edge of The Milky Way. She was watched with awe and admiration as she sailed through. Granny didn't need a twin star.

Maybe that was the way it was going to be for me. I was going to go through life without a soulmate.

It was the beginning of feeling whole alone.

FRENCH FOOD

I had been a skeptic. I didn't believe it when people told me food in France would amaze me. What can they do with food that's so special? What can be better than a Coffee Crisp?

I'll tell you what they can do. In France, a salad of iceberg lettuce with dressing drizzled over it is like no salad you have ever tasted. I would ask, "What have they done to this? How can lettuce and salad dressing taste so good?" They serve thin slices of raw beef in a salad that is out of this world. Even the international food in France, such as the Vietnamese fast-food restaurants all over Nice, had better food than I had ever eaten anywhere.

Take French cheese toast. How do they make cheese toast to die for? They use freshly grated cheese and they've got goddamn white sauce under the cheese. The Russians, not to be anti-Russian, my dears, they would have plopped a cheese whiz slice on a piece of tasteless, state-produced white bread and have fried it in an inch of Mazzola oil. In France it was broiled to perfection, light, flavourful and lovely.

The care with fresh ingredients, the food displays, the eating settings, the French love of food was apparent everywhere. Want a good meal? An exceptional meal? Go and eat in France.

However, let it not be said that I went to France for a good meal. I went to France for sun. And with sun, they are also good. Bare skin and no bra does not scandalize the French. I could relax.

SIMPLE TASKS

It felt good walking to the laundromat with my arms full of dirty clothes. There was something grounding about these simple tasks. They pulled me into the fabric of the local life. Suddenly I was a local. I could remember that my Dad, after his retirement, enjoyed the day-to-day maintenance of the campground he had bought as an investment. "I like these simple tasks. I like changing the ice machine. I even like cleaning the washrooms."

Once at the laundromat I would have been happy to figure out the washing machine, soap, coins and buttons by myself but there was a laundromat manager. He took me under his wing and patiently led me through it all, got me the right change, got me extra soap. I became fond of him. He reminded me of Dad when he stood with his hands, in fists, parked on his hips like Dad used to do when we were hanging around the kitchen talking. He was delighted when I used my remote to take a picture of us standing side by side.

He was a neighbourhood institution. Many passersby stuck their heads in for a brief word, some lingered and a few even left him their laundry. He told them that my grandmother was Parisian and had married my Canadian grandfather. They showed delight in this news and had the good grace to cover any disappointment that my French was terrible. It felt like a heroic French ceremony when he kissed me goodbye on both cheeks.

Walking down the street with my clean, warm laundry I was grounded and content. Thank you Dad and Granny. Your lives have woven into mine – and become me and left me with gifts.

CORSICA
Island hopping
After six days walking the streets of Nice with Granny, savouring the scene, feeling overweight, undertanned, unglamorous and unrich, my bike finally arrived. I could see that the insane traffic in the crowded Cote d'Or made cycling completely out of the question there. So where next?

I was on my way to Turkey but I felt like seeing something else first. I had long known that islands were good places to cycle. An island is set apart from mainstream life and offers more peaceful riding because there's no through traffic. I also liked the satisfaction of doing the whole thing. So I took the early morning, high-speed ferry to Corsica.

Contrary to popular belief, Corsica is part of France, much to the chagrin of the Corsicans who blow up mailboxes in protest but are quite civilized about leaving tourists alone.

Once I was there, I considered trying to ride and hop the Mediterranean islands south and east to eventually get to Turkey by bike and ferry. That sounded like fun and offered the challenge of trying to get back and forth across the borders of two countries that are more-or-less at war with each other.

THEY KNEW
Like all tourist information offices in France and Corsica, the one in Bastia closed from twelve noon until two. Even though the ferry arrived every day at twelve, by the time I got off it and across the parking lot to the tourism office, it was closed and shuttered. So I ate lunch, which is exactly what the Corsicans were doing. For two hours.

Once back in business, the tourism man casually advised me to start my trip by cycling over the mountains that ran down the middle of Corsica. The other side would offer better cycling. So off I went. A mountain range wasn't getting in my way.

It was a long, hot, hard climb. The view of the Mediterranean became more spectacular and then paler as I climbed. I left the ferry town behind and then I left the houses that were perched beside the steep switchback and cycled up into steep fields. My water was running out but I continued to drink plenty — a bold move in the middle of no-where. I assumed I would find more.

And I did. In a rock wall beside the road, a concrete pool was being filled by a bare pipe above it, The cool, clear water overflowed and created a damp, mossy cavern. Was it just for cattle? Was it safe to drink? I mentally declared it quite safe, filled my water bottles, drank gulps down and continued up. And up, and up. Some of the switchbacks were steep, some required walking the bike a few feet. Then, the top. Marked only by a pull off, a flat spot between two hills and a view of the coastline far below on the other side.

I stopped in the pullout to catch my breath. I asked out loud, Where are the cheering throngs? The bottle of champagne? The confetti? Where is the television crew and the amazed announcer? Where is my public?

Not here obviously. This had to be appreciated for what it was: a solitary triumph.

Back in the saddle, I pulled slowly onto the road just as a Pugueot with three middle-aged Corsicans bounced over the hill from the other side. As soon as they spotted me they flashed their lights repeatedly and honked their horn. Blat, blat, flash, blat, flash, flash. Alongside they waved enthusiastically and grinned and cheered. And drove on.

They knew.

They were excited and proud for me. They were with me in my triumph. Did they know how much that meant to me? Tears of pride and joy ran down my cheeks as I coasted down the other side. They knew.

WADING IN THE STREETS

It started like any fall cloudburst: heavy rain, a bit of thunder, plenty of wind. The rain poured down so hard it was sheeting across the highway in rivulets. But each time it subsided a new storm would start. That was the first thing that seemed odd. Each seemed to have more rain than the last one. Three racing cyclists passed me on the way toward Isle Russe and then I passed them as they took shelter under a high hedge. When they saw the pattern of ever-escalating storms, they chose to just blast through with great rooster tails of water behind them.

Of course the travel information office was closed at 12:02 when I arrived and I was forced to eat a wonderful but expensive lunch for two hours, shivering in sodden clothes while I waited for it to open and help me find economical accommodation.

When I finally got settled, I pulled everything out of my panniers. The downpour had pounded into all the corners and clothes ranged from soaking to damp. I dressed in the least wet clothes I had with me and went out to explore town and buy food. The streets of Isle Russe had become rivers. Cars were abandoned where they had stalled in the middle of the road and inhabitants were bemusedly standing in shop doorways surveying the scene. The village was on the side of a hill curved around a Mediterranean bay. The river in the streets, stained by the ochre clay soil that gives the town it's name, had plenty of slope to keep it rushing through town. Where the torrent met a dead-end it turned and rushed off in the other direction. The rain eased up and stopped and the river in the streets kept rising.

The curbs were high so a step down into the water was a step into deep water. My sandals were as wet as they could get. I waded in and across with the teenagers. Most people stayed on the sidewalks and watched, but business continued as usual. Many shopkeepers seemed oblivious to the torrent tickling at their curbside. Booksellers were selling books, making change, offering suggestions. Banks were cashing travelers' cheques, counting money, phoning other branches. Other shopkeepers were standing at the doorways shaking their heads, laughing, raising their palms to the sky in stagey shrugs. I actually heard them say: C'est la guerre, the way only the French can.

The next day the fire department was pumping out the basements of businesses and inns and houses along the lowest point in town, the edge of the bay. By evening there were more thunderstorms and more rain. Now thunderstorms around the clock. Odd.

I couldn't get my clothes dry, I couldn't get warm, I couldn't talk the lady who owned the pension into turning on the heat and the pathetic dribble of hot water that came out of her shower was just an insult. I also couldn't get anyone to tell me if this was unusual. They seemed to shake their heads and shrug. No-one could tell me what was happening. No-one could give me a weather forecast.

Being cold was seriously debilitating for me. My body shut down. I had no strength, no balance, no stamina. I operated on will power, which was never fun. I stopped taking pictures. I stopped exploring. My whole life revolved around trying to get warm. I could not relax.

I gave up. I took a train to Calvi, to the only airport in Corsica and bought a ticket to Paris, the only place you can fly to from Corsica. While waiting for the flight I browsed a newspaper in the airport shop. I was able to translate enough to find out that some hurricane off the coast of Portugal had spun off a series of freak storms that flooded Corsica, washed out roads and bridges, cut off transportation and communication and showed no sign of letting up. Ah. That's what this has been. Love it. The earth's weather visited me. Visited upon me. And it was news.

SO I SLEPT IN THE PARIS AIRPORT

Doesn't it sound urbane? So casual. So world traveler. Paris was the only way to get out of Corsica and on to Turkey or Greece or anywhere goddamn hot. So Paris it was until I could get a flight, onward.

I flew into the domestic airport so had to bus across Paris, bike and all, to the international airport. I hoped to get a cheap charter to somewhere, an additional stop on my way to Turkey. The charter terminal was kind of a cheap, crummy terminal that was so unimportant that it did not even rate a bus stop. I got off at the adjacent terminal, walked down the sidewalk and through an underpass, turned left, through the parking lot and I was there. Easy. And by the time I did it for the fourth time I knew my way without asking.

No-one anywhere could help me plan my next move. To get advice on my options I would have to leave the airport, with my bike and luggage, and go into downtown Paris, in the pouring rain and find a travel agent. You see there is no Left-Luggage in the Paris airport any more. No left-luggage of any kind. Including leaving my bicycle with the information desk for a minute while I went to the bathroom. Non. Non. Non. I had to take my bicycle and my bags with me to the bathroom. A security ruling. Bombs you know.

I got fresh information chatting with travelers in the charter terminal. I found out that it was cold in the north of Turkey right now. And if I went to Greece I'd have trouble getting to Turkey from there. But there was no one to talk to about charters or cheap fares.

I was cold and tired. It was late. There were many hotels in the airport complex. Time to get some sleep and make decisions tomorrow. Off I went, with bike, to the first hotel. The registration area was packed with be-suited men. I overheard the desk clerk explaining to one man, in English, that his reservation must be for another hotel with the same name (there was one) because they had no reservation for him. And no, he couldn't just register there now because they were fully booked. No, all the airport hotels were packed with the international conference. Nothing at any price. If he didn't have a reservation at the other hotel he would have to go into the city.

Why wait around to be told that again? I straggled back to my dumpy charter terminal.

It was chilly in there because any time someone came or went the automatic doors opened and the wind and rain blew in. So there I was. Fifty years old, a fanny pack full of gold cards, trying to lie on a row of three molded chairs with all my warm clothes on and my hostel sheet over, then under me, then me inside it, and my towel on top of me for a little extra warmth and every time I needed to pee I packed up the whole works and took it into the bathroom with me until I decide to-hell-with-it sometime around 1 AM and just walked off and left everything I had sitting on the molded chairs with my bike leaning against it all. My own little midden in the Paris airport. At four-thirty AM cleaning staff started leaving and charter staff started arriving. The charter manager spoke a bit of English and I had lost any pride so I begged him for help. Which he gave me.

The old question loomed: could I have planned this better? What bad judgements did I make that got me here? At what points did I make them? Are there repeated habits I have that bring me to this kind of dilemma?

And the perennial question: how to do this story justice in the retelling.

WHY CAN'T I MAKE THIS WORK BETTER?

However hard you try when you are traveling, you do things wrong. Inefficiently, expensively, repetitively, badly. Your timing can be off. Your money badly spent. Your options closed down by fear. I did it all the time. And I berated myself for it.

And when a decision was pending, I held up high standards of performance for myself. What was the most economical way to get from Calvi to somewhere warm that would make it easy to get to Turkey in a few weeks, without doubling back, and where I didn't need to already have a visa and that wouldn't be too expensive to stay in and the roads would be paved but not have too much traffic? What would be the cheapest way to get there without exhausting myself with overnight travel? What should I do next?

When you stack up that kind of decision in front of yourself and are doing the whole transaction in another language, with your fully-loaded bike leaning against your leg, cut yourself a little slack.

Granny taught me that. You will rarely make the most efficient decision. And in spite of all the cheap flights, cheap places to stay, cheap boat fares that every other traveler gets, you'll never get these. You'll get expensive fares. Expensive fares with awkward connections. NEVER efficient and cheap. Never.

And that's life. And that's just fine. True life is going to include bad decisions, miscalculations, bad luck and questionable motives. And that's fine. So stop aiming to make it all work out. It doesn't. And what's so important about efficient anyway? What about ambling, meandering, browsing around, of taking time, wasting time, savouring nothingness, getting lost, doubling back, screwing up.

Listen, when the government is inefficient they cost us a few billion dollars and we have to put up with them insulting our intelligence about it as well. Whatever your choices, things will move forward, even when they seem to be going backwards.

You are flawed. I am flawed. Our decisions are flawed. Perfect and efficient is a human construct. It happens by chance. The mistakes along the way are full of possibility. Let yourself go with that.

AND THE EYE TWITCH?
So much for my theory of airplanes and lack of sleep causing the eye twitch. This time it didn't. At this point, the eye twitch only happened some days. Did that mean that I was acclimatizing to no structure? Or that structure, on-the-road structure, was creeping in? Oh no! I want to stay structureless, I want to float, untethered, in the zone of all possibility. Whatever. But it's nice to have the twitch fading.j6

BENIM GOGIA TURK

THE INFIDEL ARRIVES

Turkey had two big pluses: cheap and warm. Better yet, it was off the beaten path.

After 36 cold, frustrating hours in Paris I flew out of the grey, drizzle and into night-time Istanbul. Istanbul, Constantinople, a city of magic and mystery, a cultural crossroads – like St Petersburg – where east meets west – only this one more eastern – the home of amazing St Sophia. I had always wanted to see Istanbul. But Turks sipping coffee in the Paris charters terminal said that Istanbul was cold right now.

And I sadly admitted to myself that I was intimidated by its size, chaos, Muslim-ness. I was not ready to deal with this and a bicycle by myself.

The stories about Turkey had worked. I was concerned about being publicly flogged for wearing shorts. That would be hard to turn into an amusing travel adventure. I was nervous about Turkish men. What springs to mind about Turkish men? Harassment. Harrrr-assss-ment. In your face, aggressive, woman-demeaning, pushiness. Especially for you. You're so blond. Religious extremism. Barbaric laws. Mob scenes. It felt more manageable to get to a small Turkish city where tourists were common and where I could avoid megacity traffic congestion. I changed planes in Istanbul and heading directly south to the Mediterranean Coast.

I stepped off the plane at 2 AM into a warm, velvet-black night in Antalya. The Turkish Riviera. There was a hot wind blowing. I was warm. Yes. It had been a long time since I was warm.

I dealt with customs. I got my bike back and put together. I found a station wagon taxi amongst the amiably squabbling taxi drivers. Two of them muscled my bike in. Thanks to the advice of an Englishman in the airport, I found a medium-priced hotel with English speaking staff. They had room.

I was in. I lay naked on my bed with the hot Mediterranean wind blowing my curtain into the room. Warm without end. It felt like the world was my blanket. I knew I would like it here, whatever they did to me. Hot wind. I could live with this.

The next morning I consulted with the front desk clerk, Icud. He said, "It is pronounced I could. In school they used to tease me and call me "I couldn't". He had a soft, chubby body. Was he gay? I could imagine Icud being the butt of schoolyard bullies.

I asked him if I needed to cover my arms going outside. "My dear," he said, "Don't worry. They go naked on the beaches."

THE OWL USED BOOKSTORE

Meandering down a dusty back lane in the noonday heat of Antalya I saw an unlikely sign propped on a fence: Owl Used Bookstore. This looked promising and, being in English, that meant they would have English titles, right? And sure enough.

The rows of books were covered with dust, not fine, soft, indoor dust — I'm talking sand. Sand that had billowed in from the lane. Some of these book had not been touched by a human hand for a long time.

The owner was a huge man who played beautiful western classical music tapes and was knowledgeable about western authors. He had a couple of Turkish guide books, which I needed, plus plenty of fiction with appeal, which I needed just as much. I would finish my current book and trade it in.

But it was four days before I returned. In the meantime I had an attack of my allergies brought on by three days of Corsica/Paris wet and cold and 48 hours with almost no sleep. When the worst was over I ambled back to Owl Used Bookstore. I was more than ready to trade in my books for new ones.

He prescribed and brewed me some healing tea that was such a complex mixture of herbs I couldn't identify any of them. But it tasted wonderful and made me feel better. I had a second cup as I browsed through his titles. He approved of my final choices and he approved of the books I traded in. That was smugly gratifying. International snobbery. I stood taller. I was a reader of the finer literature of our culture. (Good grief.)

When he saw me crossing things off my list he said, "That is a nice pen."

"Thank you. It's nothing special." In fact it had cost me ten dollars but I was disappointed by how heavy it was and didn't like it.

"Could I have that not special pen?"

"Sure." I handed it to him.

As I headed back into the dusty lane from his dark room he stood on the steps and smiled. "Be careful not to die riding your bicycle in the land of the infidels." I would like to go back when I am there again. I like this big, learned man who wants to serve healing drinks to his sniffling customers and has a foot in both cultures.

Hawker #1:   Hello. Where are you from? Sprachen Sie Deutsche? Norwegian? (They ask in Norwegian.) Finnish? (In Finnish.)

Hawker #2:   English? Do you speak English? What language do you speak?

Hawker #3:   Please come here.

Hawker #4:   Step inside and see my beautiful carpets.

Hawker #5:   Tea? I would like to have a cup of tea with you.

Hawker #6:   Just a minute. Don't go yet.

Hawker #7:   Hello. Yes please. Coffee, tea, breakfast, sandwiches. Yes please.

Hawker #8:   Where did you get that jacket?

Hawker #9:   Please, wait a minute

Hawker #10:   What's the matter? Are you mad at me?

Try walking through that and resisting the generosity of their hospitality, the force of their wills, the manipulation of their international savvy. These are multilingual sharpshooters. With my blond hair they never, for example, asked if I was Spanish. In Rhodes, it escalated to:

I like you. Will you come and stay with me?

I don't know you.

Sit down, you can get to know me.

I want to go to dinner.

I like you very much. I want you to come and stay with me.

Thank you very much. I'm flattered, but I'm going to dinner now.

Please, just sit a minute. Do you like me?

I don't know you.

Then sit a minute and you can get to know me.

Thank you but I want to go for dinner.

This makes me so sad. I LIKE you.

Thank you. Goodbye. Maybe another time.

You try to think of yourself as the Girl from Ipanema (...tall and tan and young and lovely, the Girl from Ipanema goes walking and when she passes each one she passes goes Ahhhh.) That's who I am. The lovely, golden, beautiful girl from Ipanema. Leaving a trail of yearning and broken hearts behind me. Regally walking on.

It doesn't work that way. Their need tugged at my body and flashed in front of my eyes and collected on my shoulders until, weighed down and hacked up I fled to my hotel room and lay on my bed reading and hiding. From there I sent Peace be with you out to the street vendors and back home to Brenda.

Each time I went out I would say; This time I'm going to glide through, impervious. I will not be eroded or distracted. I will not be belittled; I will not blush or waver. So I did not look in shops, scan the rich goods and touch the exotic wares. I was a prisoner in the street, caged by my own protection from their pushing.

In Ephesus, amazing, awesome Ephesus, I successfully fought back, much to all of our surprise. Embrazened with several cups of tea to warm me from a chilly, early-morning start I was buzzing when I arrived at the tent village of sellers crowded around the entrance to Ephesus. I had decided this was the time to make some serious choices about Turkish gifts and momentos. There were several things I really wanted and there was a mailing kiosk right there. So I would look at all their wares before going in, think about it while touring Ephesus and then come out to make decisions.

Hello.

Hello

How are you?

Very well thank you.

Aren't those lovely?

Let me show you these.

Come and have tea.

Would you like coffee?

As I worked my way along the row of displays, I chatted and told them I was traveling by bicycle and didn't have much room but that I wanted to come back and buy after seeing everything. Word spread in front of me so I would be greeted at a kiosk with, "You are the lady on the bicycle."

Three quarters of the way around I saw a father call his ten-year-old son aside and instruct him to hit on me as I approached their tent. The father shoved him forward and gave him instructions and pulled at his sleeve — all at the same time.

The son said, "Hello. Would you like to see these things? What colour would you like? Would you like to try them on? Please step back here and let me show you others. Very beautiful."

Before I knew what I was doing I was poking at him with my fingers and pulling at various places on his sleeves and shoulders and mimicking him. I was exaggerating his and everyone else's wheedling. Hello, hello, please come and see these, are they beautiful, would you like to try my things, do you speak English? What colour are you liking? Hello, hello, please take tea with me. I like you. All the time poking, plucking, laughing, exaggerating.

For a moment he was shocked. Everyone froze. Horror. Then the boy grinned and then laughed. Then the rest laughed. We all laughed. It was a moment of cross-cultural insight. Of sharing the absurdity of what they were doing and what I was doing. They relaxed. They let up. I finished my browsing uninterrupted.

I vowed I would do that with street vendors from then on.

But I didn't.

I'VE HUNG THE LAUNDRY ON THE RUIN

Side (with the final "e" pronounced "ay") is a tiny but popular seaside tourist town on the Turkish Riviera. It has always been at the same place. For 3,000 years it has been at the same place. The Temple to Athena, on the beach, had once been a bold, white landmark, visible for miles from shore. Sailors used it for navigating. Now it was a few standing pillars and many more littering the ground.

New buildings have just been built in around the ruins. These people grew up in the ruins. They hang their laundry, with pink, plastic clothespegs, on rope strung between pieces of ruin while travelers pay money to come and gawk and take pictures.

The travelers sit at outdoor restaurants with wobbly tables placed among the ruins, stroll the shops, buy boat rides and stay in waterside pensions.

One enterprising young man had a beautiful litter of newborn puppies lying in the middle of tourist thoroughfare. He displayed a penciled sign on a small piece of cardboard to the effect that they did not have money to buy food for the mother so the puppies were hungry and would die. Would we please give them money for some food for the mother? Do you think they used the money to buy dog food?

JUST A LITTLE HELP TODAY, THAT'S ALL.

Stray cats in Turkey won't let you touch them. You never get to pick one up. But a calico kitten in Side didn't know this. It let me pick it up and stroke it and scratch it. It purred and meowed. It was still cute and not completely dirty yet. I felt I owed her something for the pleasure she gave me so I went to a restaurant (after fending off a drunk old hawker who dragged me into his kiosk for something that I never figured out) and asked to buy something for the little cat. They laughed. They scrounged around and found some fried fish scraps – mostly skin and bones but a bit of fish on it. They grinned as they turned down money. I knew they were humoring me.

I carried my scraps outside to my little feline. I wasn't under any illusions that I was saving this little cat, that I was making any difference in the big scheme of things. I was just a brief source of food for one day. All its other days the kitten would rely on whatever other sources it could find.

It dropped any pretense of being friendly as I pulled the fish off the bones and fed it. This was survival. It grabbed food out of my hands, it was ready to kill for it. It went on to bones and skin and fins. Nothing was being left. But the cat was small and took a while to chew it into pieces it could gulp down.

I left the kitten with its head on the side chewing, swallowing, licking the ground where the fat left a smear. A tiny life. No more and no less significant than mine. Just getting through another day. Vulnerable and struggling. I had played a tiny part in the food chain. I can save nothing.

Peace be with you little Turkish cat. Peace be with you pampered little Brenda at home. Grieving my absence and her loss of her home

THE POOL OF PAIN

I had seen it as a child in the faces of Auschwitz victims, staring at me from Life magazine. I felt it when the one I loved left me for someone "better." I was swallowed by it when my Dad died. That bleak, black, weight of sadness and pain and hopelessness. That shapeless heavy lump embedded in my chest bone that I couldn't soften with the heat of my hand and I couldn't loosen with sighing. The black cylinder that came down around me, shutting me in. I remember the dread I felt in the last fraction of a second when I saw the black cylinder descending, knowing what was coming and that it would last —

forever. Then my life was defined by that weight. It pulled me down so my shoulders dropped and my eyes drooped and my cheeks sagged and every part of me sank lower and couldn't be pulled up because I had lost the will to pull myself up. The hopelessness beyond why-me when I knew there was no answer to that question.

With time I had learned that my own pain and sadness took me places and taught me things that I could never learn any other way and for that they were beautiful and enriching. When they came I knew it wouldn't be a fun time but it would be a rich time.

But what about the pain out there? Traveling, it is everywhere. There are no borders on pain. There are no language barriers. There is no statute of limitations. And out there the laws, social agencies and standards are often so different from at home that we encounter pain we have never seen before.

The tiny, malformed kitten in Thailand that came from an undernourished mother and will never receive a full meal but will struggle to survive and have its own malformed kittens when it is still a kitten itself.

The old man in Moscow, who isn't that old but looks ancient and wears street person clothes. And he stands straight and still, alone beside the road, holding three beautiful, flawless gladiolas hoping someone will stop and buy them. All day, standing.

The Turkish man leaning into a rickety wheelbarrow that he is pushing along beside the highway. On it are huge wooden beams sticking far out to the sides. And he pushes ahead, bent over. How many loads has he pushed? What is he building? Against what hopeless odds?

The beautiful young girl sobbing and clinging to her boyfriend on a train platform on the French Riviera. Her parents are there, or an older sister and her husband quietly trying to console her. They also give her privacy to hold him again and kiss him again and say goodbye again. Her heart is breaking.

The Turkish men sobbing in the airport. Has there been a death? Three men, are they brothers? Cousins? They sit in the boarding lounge. They put their heads together and hold each other at the back of their necks, the back of their heads. Their sobbing is loud. They wipe their eyes with the back of their hands, say a few words and then lean together again in their misery and sob.

A pair of American sisters at the St Petersburg Hostel, Rose and Kathy. They were in their late fifties. Rose is a Russian history teacher from the USA, who had always longed to come to Russia. Her daughter had been raped on a university campus five years before and had contracted and died of AIDS. Rose didn't cry when her daughter finally died. It was later, at the grave of an aunt who had died at 59 that she sobbed, "Now I'll never get to Russia." Kathy said, "I'll take you to Russia, Rose." And there they were. Their husbands back at home trying to figure out what these women were doing.

On the road I saw the world's pain. I had no-where to go with it. It stabbed into me. I would wince and look away. I would sigh to try and let it go. It left me helpless and hopeless. What am I supposed to be doing?

Eventually I realized that like the force of life, this great pool of sadness and pain just is. It is part of the landscape, woven right into the wonderful. It is part of the beautiful and young and hopeful and new. All the abandoned buildings, bombed ruins, empty farmhouses, boarded up factories, all were started with hope and joy, now abandoned to rot and ruin. Just there. Beginnings and endings.

And when I accepted that as part of the world, part of life, part of my journey I could see the beauty of the pain. It unites us, this thread of sorrow. The shared connection of loss and fear. The connected pool of pain and sadness, binds us into a web of life and energy and being. This counterpoint to love and hope and joy colours it all the more brightly with it's contrasting black. The bitter with the bitter-sweet. The melancholy memory. The minor chord.

Together the beauty and ugliness, joy and sorrow, pain and pleasure make up the tapestry of life. Rich beyond comprehension. I could only sit and stare and feel and hear and comprehend the edges and know there was so much more.

Learning to feel awe at the beauty of sadness became a source of peace. It grounded me. It highlighted the poignancy of life. I could see it and feel, Yes, I understand, I have felt that. I no longer tried to shrug it off. It was in me and out there and back home and everywhere. Together in our pain

When I was able to make the connection to the pain out there, it bound me to the world I walked into and made the beauty safe.

THE BOAT PEOPLE
Graceful tour boats glide along the Turkish coastline, floating on the clear blue-green water. They had tourists dripping off them like boat people, only these boat people had food and credit cards, not to mention water. And their priority was getting tanned, not staying alive.

TURKISH MEN
Turkish men are beautifully lively. And they are beautiful. Dark eyes, thick black hair that turns white as they age but doesn't fall out. They look like Omar Sharif. I could take a fancy to these beautiful, dark-eyed men but remembered my friend Noah's travel advice: "Don't fuck the locals, Marg." Yes, that would be a problem. They wanted too much from me. A ticket to America. A new life. Opportunity. So, hands-off, I watched them. They have fun. They hug, kiss, slap each other's backs, holler across the street, laugh, argue, tease, drink tea, play backgammon, sit on restaurant patios until late at night. They like each other. The whole country is a men's club. It would be fun to be a Turkish man.

So I resented not being able to have unguarded conversation with them. I resented always being manipulated, wheedled, pushed. Come on you guys. How about just a conversation? Without an agenda?

At the same time, something was not working for these men. They fiddled nervously with their prayer beads, nibbled on little nuts and spat out the shells, chewed their fingernails. They seemed compulsive.

Whatever their problem it wasn't caused by shortage of things to wear. For every ladies' store there were twenty men's stores, each with a wide range of current fashions. Ladies' stores carried a few drab, shapeless items – unless they were lingerie shops. There were more sexy lingerie shops than I could imagine the population supporting. Are all these wives, in the secrecy of the marital bedroom, parading around in Victoria's Secret every night?

All the drivers in Turkey were men. They came barreling up behind me honking their horns, waving, swerving all over the road. Oncoming cars and trucks flicked their lights and honked, drivers leaned out of their windows and yelled things at me, grinning.

It took a taxi driver in Cyprus to teach me what was really going on. On my 4 AM ride to the airport he never stopped communicating with the few other cars on the road. He would pull up close to a driver in front. The driver in front would flick their rear lights. Pass me because I don't want to go any faster. The taxi would pull out and pass and then flick its lights, Thank you. The other flicked back or honked, It was nothing.

The road conversation never ended. They honked, tailgated, flashed their lights. It taught me to reframe the daytime headlight greeting. After that I waved and hello'd with genuine warmth. What changed? Me I guess.

TURKISH WOMEN

I kept thinking, there sure are a lot of guys around here. Of course there were women too. There just weren't many of them. I saw them on the streets and in the markets. The more I got away from the westernized, tourist locations, the fewer women and the more they were covered. Secret hair. They were beautiful. I wanted to take their pictures, make eye contact, talk with them.

A beautiful woman who did cleaning or cooking in the hotel in Soke wouldn't let me take her picture. Watching this, the young man who managed the front desk and had movie-star good looks, shook his head, rolled his eyes and said "Turkish women. They have a problem." I sat in the lobby with him for a while watching a strange Turkish movie on television. A woman was recounting a childbirth story. It was oddly surrealistic. The newborn baby was held up and laughed like an adult. It was kind of creepy. Again, he turned to me, waved his hand disdainfully at the television and said, "Turkish women."

It was interesting to watch how these men suppressed and controlled their women and then belittled them for internalizing it.

ON-THE-BIKE PROCESSING

"They" say that pedaling, like running, is a balanced bi-modal activity and, as such, balances the right and left brains. That may be. All I know is that on a bicycle, day after day, I pondered and reviewed all the hurts, humiliations, pain and miss-adventures as well as the joys and gentle pleasures in my life. My whole life in review. It meant I might be riding along grinning or in tears. Either felt right.

A HERO

One of the great thrills of cycling alone, out there, is to solve problems by yourself and fix things with found objects. My secret yearning to live my life with the resilience and creativity of Robinson Crusoe had a chance to be fulfilled. And I found out how smart I was.

My panniers, usually completely reliable, developed two separate problems. These required some creativity. One I fixed by improvising with some waistband elastic out of a pair of pants. The other required a bigger screw or a lock nut. I could figure that much out after re-tightening the screw twenty times in one afternoon. However tight I cranked it, it just kept working loose, in shorter and shorter periods of time. It meant that sometimes I'd look back and find the pannier hanging by one hook swinging precariously out from the bike.

I foolishly appealed for help to the man at the tourism information office in Side. He had taken a fancy to me. He wanted me to have tea with him. He put his hand on the back of my neck and shook my head affectionately, like he was my uncle. He wanted to drive me in his car to show me a great place that a friend of his had where he would arrange for me to stay cheap. He declared that he was going to take me to the waterfall for a real Turkish dinner.

He also believed that he had fixed the problem when he screwed the screw back in, tight. I tried to explain that it would come out again. That I too had screwed it back in tight several times and the road vibrations always worked it loose. He laughed heartily, pulled on it to show me how solid it was and said now it was fixed. Silly little woman, doesn't understand this man stuff.

The next morning, screw loose again, I stopped at a machine shop in a Turkish military town.

Inside I mimed my problem to two young guys and drew a picture of my screw and a bigger screw. Ah. Yes. They took me to a huge box full of every kind of screw imaginable. All used. All just thrown in there. Screws, bolts, nuts, brackets, rust and grease. We tried several. If it were too much bigger, it would split the plastic frame it screwed into. We pawed through. We tried more.

Then a third guy appeared. They told him in Turkish. I told him in mime. We pulled things out of my pannier so that we could see what it screwed into from the inside.

We tried one that was close but not right. Then he knew. He said in Turkish, "You need a lock nut". I knew that was what he said just from the look on his face and the sound of his voice. The eureka in there.

I said, "Yes. Smart man."

Back in the box of everything, he miraculously found one. And it fit my screw. He put it together, screwed it in and made the international sign of, there: arms out at sides, palms forward, a satisfied smile and shrug. Ta da. It was nothing.

It hasn't come out since.

THEY'RE SO FRIENDLY

Everyone says of the Turks: "They're so generous. So friendly." I'm not sure I agree with these assessments. Everyone said the same about the Irish. The Irish weren't friendly. They were servile and resentful. Obsequious and fawning as only the long oppressed can become. The tourists, wanting to feel welcome, saw it as welcoming. It wasn't.

Most Turks are hungry for our money and will say anything to get it. They would ask the name of my hotel to size me up. Who doesn't have an angle? Icud didn't. The Owl Used Bookstore man – pen notwithstanding - didn't. Everyone else was trying to get something from me. All the men I passed on the road calling out to me as I rode by, all the street hawkers, all the people in hotels and restaurants, pushing and wheedling. My friend, Noah, hit it on the head when he emerged from several weeks in the northern hills of Thailand: "I'm tired of being the tit they all want to suck on." Yeah. I know what you mean.

MY GUYS

I had paid too much the night before so I wanted to economize in Alanya, a touristic town packed with Germans and Brits on package deals that made it cheaper to be there than they could live at home — including airfare. Anyway, I wasn't on a package and I was tired of pushing my bike through busy streets and being turned down at hotels. The sign outside said hostel. Sure the front patio was packed with men but the beautiful Muslim woman in charge seemed comfortable so why shouldn't I be? However, after getting reassured that there was hot water for a shower and only getting a cold dribble from a bare pipe in a slimy shower room I wondered if this bargain might be more problem than it was worth.

My fellow hostlers included two dozen young men watching TV outside. A couple of them had no legs. There was a young man who didn't seem to have much more than a head and arms who swung himself along on a piece of carpet attached to the bottom of him and another man lying on a bench looking very sick. Oh dear. They all watched me and teased each other when I asked for something or just walked past.

The blanket on my bed was dirty. The lightbulb over my bed was bare and shone in my eyes when I tried to read in bed. There was no light in the squatty toilet. No toilet paper. It reeked of urine and the door didn't close properly.

So what's going to happen in the middle of the night? Do they fight? Do they gang up on women tourists? Where was the beautiful woman?

I alternately worried and read all evening. I was grasping at things to worry about. My mind ranged around and found thoughts to pump adrenaline into my body. I could feel the jagged lines bounce around in there. I tried to smooth them. Then my mind would light on something new that gave me a fresh jolt. Money and time were two, reliable, old favorites.

I was full of questions. What was going on with the guys in the hostel? What were road conditions ahead? A Finnish man and the desk clerk at another hotel in town had said the road and traffic further east were worse than the scary highway I had struggled along so far. It felt useless to fight it.

I kept fretting about going to the bathroom, in all its splendour, in the middle of the night. Then I'd fret about going back to it again later. The worry turned into feeling like a failure. A travel failure.

All I could do was read and doze with the light on.

Eventually the hostel became quiet. Someone came in very late. Didn't bother me. I was awake anyway.

I slept for three hours and then was right back at it, on duty. So I turned to Granny and had a wonderful consultation. I told her that I felt I had lost the spirit of fun and adventure that I had started with and had become a jaded traveler and not a very good one. Budget blown to hell, victimized by hawkers, unable to find a ferry to Cyprus because they had stopped for the fall, I piled it on.

She reminded me that it made it difficult when I tried to live up to the expectations of others. Nipper rode his bike fast and covered long distances every day. Patty, who had loved the Turks, saw all the ruins and was probably speaking Turkish within three days. Sonia loved to see me do bold, interesting things, not cower in fear of a squatty toilet. My travels were pale by comparison.

Granny reminded me that the only way to have fun was to figure out what would be fun for me. What would be fun for me next? Forget down the road, forget planning, what did I want to do the next minute?

Well, let's see. At the moment what I want to do is get up before dawn and head out and check the road and traffic and any time I'm not happy with them, quit trying — without feeling like a failure — and hit the beach or catch a bus or whatever other opportunity presented itself.

I was already wide awake when the pre-sunrise call to prayers sounded so I assembled panniers, bike, water, all and sundry, on the road in front of the hostel. My guys came shuffling from somewhere, some building behind the hostel up a driveway as I organized myself. They lined up in a row on the sidewalk watching me. I wanted to touch them. I wanted to say, "You are beautiful. I am sorry." I wanted to do something. I got on my bike and waved cheerfully and said, "Goodbye, thank you, goodbye." My guys waved and teased and were still standing watching me as I rounded the corner. There's that pain again.

That is what I did because that's what I felt like. And if I hadn't, I would have missed the best cycling I had in Turkey. Ah Granny, thank you for giving my adventure back. For helping me find my wisdom.

Again I was reminded that when I **was** fretting; going round and round; berating myself; gathering issues to worry about and piling them up; annoyed with myself for not solving something better/quicker/differently, I could drop everything and go to Granny. I could get her steadying hand, let go of the fretting and create a pool of peace for myself.

I could remind myself that I came out here looking for adventure and fun and and answers and I could find the humour. I could experiment. I could fail. There was no right way. I had no control. The learning could be painful. The process wasn't complete yet. Learning boundaries. Learning balanced self-care. Learning to let go of worrying. All big, lifelong things. A journey. That's what I came to find. This is what it looked like searching.

ON DUTY

There was a sparkling, new, Petro Ofiso station around the corner from the hostel. I tried their bathroom in the morning. It would be hard pressed to be worse than the hostel grotto. It was still dark and the city streets were quiet except for the occasional taxi. The drivers called out to me, flung their arms out their windows, palms up, in a gesture of what-the-hell-are-you-doing? A small police car was tucked in beside the service station and there were two policemen in it. Their seats were reclined and they were sound asleep. Snoring.

TURKISH CLUB MED

After dire traffic warnings and a fretful night, I could hardly believe that I found little traffic on the road the next day. It didn't seem like the same highway that had delivered an endless stream of trucks buzzing me for the last three days. The road went up and down but was easily graded. I was presented with one stunning Mediterranean vista after another. I was delighted to stumble upon my own, undeveloped, Roman ruin. No hawkers, no tour buses, just a grassy slope and a collection of aqueducts and stone walls clustered around a steep bay of perfect, aquamarine water, clear to the bottom.

Better yet, I arrived at Gazipasa, my goal for the day, by mid morning. The luxury of it. The bulk of the day left to explore and loaf. I cruised the town for lodging and the beach. But suddenly, after a morning of waterside travel, no beach in evidence. The town was hectic with Turkish activity. Most businesses had construction materials piled outside: brand new squatty toilets, rebar and lumber and pipe. Is that all anyone does here, build houses? Renovate? No seaside accommodation?

The town was small enough for me to wind my way through all the streets and see clearly that there was no beach. That's when I remembered that Lonely Planet had mentioned that this town hadn't been on the water's edge since Roman times. River silting moved it three kilometers inland.

Back on the highway I stopped into a Petro Ofiso station. Always reliable. The guys there — there was always a collection of amiable, eager-to-help, guys hanging around a Petro Ofiso — directed me to a wide, boulevarded street on the opposite side of the highway to the town. The boulevard was a brave attempt to create grandeur. Stunted palm trees planted down the middle and high curbs with sidewalks on either side wound down to the sea. A resort entrance. But the few houses along it had chickens scratching in the yards and docile children playing under clothes lines of laundry.

Even when I got to the water, it did not appear promising. There was a spit out to my left with a huge, industrial truck like a mining truck - wheels bigger than a man - dumping gigantic boulders into the water. It must have been building a breakwater or creating a road around the point. The beach ahead was a combination of smooth rocks and sand. A few stray dogs loping along. Scattered people. Not many.

There was a row of shabby-looking buildings on my right so I asked a young woman walking by if this was a hotel. She took me around to the front and walked me along the side of the cabins facing the beach. Suddenly I was surrounded by landscaping, lawn, actual green lawn, two huge swimming pools and a tidy row of porch-fronted little cabanas, new and neat. Was I still in Turkey? Inside each one a clean, spare room with twin beds, a good bathroom and a kitchen that was in a separate, outdoor room entered from the porch. Generous porches with tables and chairs. Very nice. A resort. A bit of comfort. A soft landing after the night with my guys in the hostel.

They did a nice thing with their swimming pools. Unlike the lip-edged North American swimming pools, with the water level several inches below that, these pools had a flat edge with the water right up to the top. It created a slab of blue water in the middle of the lawn. Lovely. Reminded me of that strange Chanel commercial that had us abuzz in the '70s.

Bathing-suited and loaded down with all the sunbathing essentials, I trotted off to the beach and settled in for an afternoon of reading, a bit of water experience, maybe a doze. It was noon and would have been insufferably hot if it weren't for a steady wind. I reminded myself to be careful about sun exposure during my first Turkish beachside lie-in. Ah yes, this was worth cycling to.

I have never been much of a swimmer. Like Art Buchwald, I view swimming as staying alive while in the water. But I wanted to immerse myself in this mythical sea, to be washed by the waters that had carried conquerors, explorers, traders, biblical figures and legendary creatures back through time to our cultural pre-conscious. I wanted to be watered. And the water was so warm there was no water-entry-shock. The huge, tugging, warm waves like a wave-pool. The continuity with past made them a spiritual experience. I didn't go in far, just enough to let myself bob up and down on the surging waves. Okay. That's enough.

For the first time in my life I was comfortable lying on my towel in a wet bathingsuit. Ah yes. I loved this. But I had only read three more pages of my Henry James novel when I noticed that the wind had picked up. Now the Med was solid whitecaps, the blowing sand was a stinging sandstorm and the last remaining couple on the beach were — as we say — beating a hasty retreat after rescuing their airborne umbrella.

I could see the palm tree fronds whipping about the way they used to in newsreels of hurricanes. It was time to go inside. Even so I was looking back over my shoulder at the waves as I headed in. Passing the manager, he said, "You are unlucky." I tried to tell him that I liked it and found this exciting and beautiful but I could tell that he thought I was making that up. And it is true that I was asking, what are these freak storms chasing me around the world?

One of the stray dogs was lying on its back under a bush in a hollow of the grass. All its legs were flopped out, its belly to the sky. Sound asleep. This was an animal that got fed and petted by tourists passing time, sitting on the front porches in their bathingsuits. The dog had seen storms before. This one wasn't worth waking up for. Possibly a perfect dog's life.

For the next two hours I lay on my bed reading and listening to the storm. What a luxury — inside comfort during a storm. If I were riding, I would have had to find shelter from this. Instead of struggling, I was clean, lying on a comfy bed with a great book and being entertained by the howling wind and whipping plants outside. Smug as a bug in a rug. Even at the distance of a full city block from the shoreline I could hear the waves pounding.

The adventure had returned. Once more I was feeling ready to play. All I had to do was: whatever I wanted! How simple. But not simple. A bit tricky. I particularly had to be careful that I wasn't being what other people wanted. I also had to watch out for my own tendency to plan. That trap. Driven by my own plan. Fun to create and a burden to execute.

After it stopped raining I suited up with my warm clothes and rain jacket for wind protection and went down to watch the huge, pounding waves on the beach. It was still heavily overcast except for the sun shining golden onto a band of water at the horizon. This created a dramatic, sparkling, mirrored streak over there with dark sea between us. Gradually the mirror traveled along the water toward me until, there, the sun was out, shining hot down on the beach. The wind was tapering off but the surf was building higher all the time.

I stood at the edge of the water, at the top reach of the waves, watching the pounding. Why was it so wonderful? Then I found one of the wooden beach beds — slats on two-by-four runners just above the waves' reach so I first sat there and then lay with my coat behind my head, watching and listening.

I watched each new wave pounding toward me, so close, but they stopped before they hit me. The thrill of seeing that wall of water gathering itself, coming in, bearing down on me and then stopping just short. Wave after wave until I was confident that none of them were going to come higher. And then one did. I was submerged. Glub, glub, struggle, thrash. I wondered if people were watching. It would have been funny to watch. I felt a bit sheepish as I walked along the beach until I found another beach bed further away from the edge and re-settled.

Two hours watching pounding waves, one after another. Restoring, contemplative, entertaining. I don't understand how it works, why the waves on the shore, are so calming. But they are and I am drawn back to them time after time.

GOT IT?
The pause at Gazpacho gave me a chance to remind myself of the value of being still. The value of listening to what is around me and working in harmony with that.

Could I stop thinking of plans and label those thoughts ideas? An idea would be less likely to trigger my urge to execute. Out there, my plans didn't work. There were to many unknowns, too many variables and systems that operate with a different kind of logic to mine. An idea, unlike a plan, can form and it can also fade as new options arise. A fluid evolution, letting go without anxiety. Creativity without obligation.

I wrote in my journal, "I may return to this issue." No doubt.

RESCUED
It was hot. Dry, still, ringing, hot. On my detailed, German map, the stretch of road appeared to meander along the side of the Mediterranean. And in fact it

did. But it also went up and down the side of the mountains as the road looked for footing on the steep slope.

I made it up to the first summit. A long, hot struggle. Curving along up there with the perfect Med far below and barely anyone around I was full of myself. Then fast down to a small village at the water's edge where I mailed a letter to my nephew Andrew. It was stifling hot down in the steep bay and there was no wind. Just pounding heat. Then, I started climbing back up. That's when I decided a closer look at the map was in order. It indicated that the last climb I had done averaged a 10 % grade and I was now starting into a grade of 15%. I frankly couldn't imagine a road being steeper than the last stretch, which, based on MY recollections of geometry, was more like a 45% grade.

My water was running low. I had only been eating fruit because I didn't want anything heavy in my stomach while I was working that hard. I was tired. It was noon and I had been riding since first light. I was using my lowest-low gear, the one I usually saved for Armageddon. I guess Armageddon had arrived.

My water wouldn't last long with me sipping every few minutes. Should I flag down a truck — which seemed to be about all there was on the road? Should I sit by the road and see who stopped? I didn't relish the idea of being in a truck with a Turkish man who then decided I was his.

It was too steep to ride. I could get a foot on one pedal but by the time I could get the other foot on the second pedal the bike was rolling backwards. And every pedal revolution would have required standing on the pedals, pulling as hard as I could. How long could I keep up that kind of output? And I didn't see the top of the hill.

I was even having trouble walking. It was hard to keep pushing the loaded bike upwards.

I was calculating how long it would take me to reach the top on foot. Would I have to sleep among the trees? It was warm enough to do that comfortably but were there snakes? The big and pressing problem continued to be water. Drinking water every three minutes now, it was disappearing fast. I had to get more water.

I thought about people I knew lounging in Calgary coffee houses deciding if they would have a second latte. At that very moment. Yeah, but I was in Turkey. They'd trade me any day. It was worth it. And the sweet, spicy smell of hot, dry, evergreen needles was heavy in the air. Intoxicating smell meant something on that mountain.

I pondered various scenarios. My legs were tired. I knew if I made it up this hill I didn't have another ascent in me. And according to my map there was another ascent. I started wishing someone would stop and give me a ride instead of just being useless dicks and honking and waving and yelling. (Yeah. Peace be with you too buddy.)

Then a car, going the other way, did a u-turn and stopped. The German at the wheel said, "I think perhaps you should ride some of the way with me. It is a very long way. I have been further up the road and it gets worse. I couldn't ride this road."

'Nuff said. I'm in.

Once in his car, bike in the back, I drank the rest of my water and felt sick —
hot and cold, nauseous, shivers. I didn't want to alarm my rescuer so I chatted
and ate some of my food, which gradually settled the problem. I had pushed
myself into some kind of overload/overheat situation. Good little body. It hung
in there for me while I needed it.

"I drove past you. I was on my way to the fortress ruin at Anamur. I
couldn't believe you made it to here. I ride mountain bikes and I couldn't ride
this road."

"Thank you. That's kind of you to say."

"Listen, this road gets worse. I've been past here. I've been further up. I
wanted to stop but I thought a woman would never accept a ride with a
strange man. It gets worse and worse. And it goes up a long way. I kept
worrying about you. Then I saw an old man with a long beard. A very old, very
wrinkled man. I know it sounds silly but it kind of felt like, well, like seeing,
sort of, seeing God. Beside the road. Giving me a message. He was telling me to
go back for you. So I did."

Thank you God.

ENTER MARK

Mark, of the rescue car, was in his mid-thirties, traveling alone, divorced. He
was on his way to the ruins of the huge Crusaders' fortress at Anamur, the next
town. He asked me if I would like to explore it with him. Anamur was the town
I was cycling to when he came along. Having been snatched from a grim
demise on the side of a mountain, I thought a ruin sounded as good as any
other idea. At that point I had lost track of what time of day it was. Evening?
We climbed for a long time. I don't think I would have made it in two days on
my bike. Then down to Anamur and the sea. There was a nice beach there so
we settled on some beach beds, under umbrellas and ate our food and chatted.

I asked, "What are you doing here?"

"I'm on holiday for two weeks. This is such a cheap place to come and the
weather at home is terrible. I'm from Germany. I rented this car today just to
come here, to this fortress. It is famous."

"What happened with your marriage?"

"Funny thing is it was fine until we got married. See we were together, you
know, not married but together, for fifteen years. My daughter was born.
Everything was fine. Three years ago we got married. I don't know why. She
wanted to. For our daughter. I could see that. But it was a mistake. Problems
started. We didn't have problems before that. Maybe we got married so we
could get divorced."

After eating and lazing in the sun talking about our lives, our histories, our
ideas on the way things should be, he asked, "Are you ready to swim?"

"Sure. Let's."

We struggled into our swimsuits just turning away from each other and
continuing our conversation.

"Myself, I would rather just swim without a bathingsuit on."

"Me too!"

"...but this place is too..."

"...there'll be Turks pouring out of everywhere. But I hate the feeling of a wet bathingsuit. I'd swim more if I didn't have to wear a bathingsuit."

Suddenly, all the old body-image issues flooded back: flabby body, white thighs, cellulite, droopy boobs, crepe-ie neck. No. No. I refuse to be tyrannized by the internalized beauty ideal created by someone else. By fashion designers for heaven's sake. Guys who don't even do women. And by teenaged models less than half my age, twice my height, chainsmoking and anorexic. I wanted to do this on my own merits. I am a world-traveling, fifty-year-old women who owns an advertising agency and has a daughter. I have more going for me than my skin. I simply must screen out those eroding messages.

And, I did. It seemed to work — much to my amazement. It helped that I had not felt those feelings for a long time so their caustic effect was easy to identify and easy to resent. For two months, while I had been simply riding along, I just thought of myself as a person. I was rarely aware of my femaleness. My priority was not female allure. My priorities were more like keep warm/cool, sunscreened and watered.

Well, it sort of worked. On and off something would trigger it again and I would go back to battle for my freedom. I am what I am. Anyone who doesn't like this person living inside this body might as well figure that out now. Flickers and darts of fear back and forth.

The water was warm — good ol' Med — and the waves were big. It was a bit much for my swimming skill so I was out of the water first. When Mark rejoined me on the beach bed he asked me to put sunscreen on his back. The sunscreen was very warm, almost hot. So was the skin on his back. It felt lovely against my hand.

"I forgot how nice warm skin feels. Warm skin."

"Ummmm. Feels nice to me too."

My fleeting urge to pull my hand away dissolved into lingering indulgence. I drew it out. I covered every centimeter from the hair on his neck to the top of his bathing suit. I savoured those tender places down his side that can be ticklish or wonderful. I rubbed it in well. I added another layer. I checked back to see if it was well rubbed in. And I saw myself feeling again those glorious feelings as hormones enter the blood stream and rush to relevant body parts. Mmmmm. But also, oh dear, let's not lose it here. I distracted myself with chatter.

"Traveling alone, I forget what it's like to just have casual conversation with someone who isn't, you know, being a pest."

"I'm sure for you, it is hard in Turkey. A blond woman, alone. Do you have trouble with the men?"

"Well the street hawkers are annoying. The other men, it's not like I have a problem with them. They are beautiful. I love the look of Turkish men. But the minute you try to just have a conversation they are trying to get you to do something, or buy something. They are so needy. They cling. They beg. It is just a drag. I'd give anything to just sit down and have a conversation – just chat, you know. No agenda."

It then seemed justified to ask for my back's sunscreening. And I saw the same thing happen to Mark as I thrilled to his touch and the little anxious question of where will this go?

"You have a nice back."

"Thank you. Yes, I like my back."

I lay in the sun, thoroughly happy and so glad to be off that mountain. Remember the mountain? This is all in the same day. Eventually we climbed up the slope to the base of the fortress wall that had towered over us on the beach.

"You must be in very good shape. Very fit."

"Uh, well, I ..." (feeling self-consciously aware of the size of my ass, which would be right about in his face at that point in the climb, and at the same time struggling to NOT be thinking of my ass and my shortcomings and my thighs.)

"I have to be careful of that."

"Of what?"

"Of giving compliments to women. They don't take it well. They turn it into...something...else..."

"Whatever. Thank you." (Blushing and relieved he couldn't see that.)

Exploring the ruin together, rubbing arms, his nearness, his touch, giving each other a hand up or down now felt charged and full of potential. We took each others pictures coming around corners in the ruin, sneaking along narrow passageways, clambering up steep stairs. We sat on a tiny bridge and threw breadcrumbs to the fish in the moat.

I wanted to put more sunscreen on his body. I thought of his touch on my skin. What would it be like when he touched my neck, the top of my leg, my... I blushed. I babbled. I moved closer. Then I moved away. The ruin whirled. Heaven only knows what we talked about. I was otherwise occupied.

As the sun lowered, we went back across the highway to the tiny restaurant where the car was parked. We had cold drinks that were served with giant flowers on the tray. We lingered. The restaurant owner put my bike together and rode it around in his parking lot. We took pictures of him. He asked me to sell it to him. Then the bus came and I fled.

The restaurant owner flagged it downs as he promised. There was a great flurry as he, Mark, the bus conductor and several other passengers wrestled off my panniers and the front tire to fit my bike into the luggage compartment. Price discussions, destination discussions, all hurried. I hugged Mark goodbye. I got on the bus and rode away. Whew. Was that ever fun!

TURKISH BUSES

Turkey has two kinds of buses: dolmas and modern coaches. Dolmas are little vans that carry local people and tourists without rental cars from one town to the next. For greater distances you have late-model highway buses, beautiful coaches. Some are double decker. All have rich upholstery, huge windows and insane drivers. However, that is Turkey and you can get a grand thrill sitting in the front seat of a top deck barreling down the highway taking ridiculous chances.

There is a conductor on these buses who helps with luggage and serves beverages and alerts the bus driver about who wants to get off where.

On the ride away from Mark the conductor offered me fresh figs. Then he stood with his hand draped over the back of my seat so it kept brushing against my hair. When he sat beside me I knew I was in trouble. He took my hand and held it in both of his. I laughed and pulled it away. He took it again. He asked me in Turkish and sign language, over and over, if I was married. His mime of a bride looking beatific as her veil was pulled back from her face was very funny. I played dumb for a while. Then I realized his perspective. I was either one of two things: married or his. I hate lying and resent people who push me into lying. I also hate to hide behind a man, even a non-existent one. But it was all he understood. Finally I said, "Yes, yes, I am married, yes veil over face, yes wedding ring, yes, yes yes."

He got up, went to the seat across the aisle, curled up and went to sleep.

THE ACCIDENT

On an all-night bus ride, I noticed a bright orange fire ahead through the inky black, pouring rainy night. Traffic was heavy and backed up to a crawl. We crept toward the fire. A vehicle, upside down, beside the road. Tires in the air. All of it engulfed in flames. A fireball. A few people were standing on the shoulder of the highway. Their hands were on their mouths. Rain poured down their faces.

Were there people inside? Being burned to death as we crept by? The people on the side of the road didn't look as if they had just stumbled out of an upside down vehicle — even if it wasn't yet in flames when they did.

Further down the road, ten minutes later, a fleet of emergency vehicles came from the other direction, converging on the spot. This had just happened. Dark rainy night, wet crowded road, Turkish drivers. People. Pain. Unspeakable agony.

There was no-where to put my feelings on the dark bus as we gradually regained speed and lumbered down the highway for several more hours. Over and over I groaned inside.

TURKISH FOOD

Breakfast was always the same: bread, feta – sometimes several varieties, olives, hard-boiled eggs, and sliced tomato. Butter and jam are served on cold bread, which didn't appeal to me. Tea was the common beverage and in places with many English tourists this was served with milk and sugar.

Turkish food was displayed in front of restaurants. You could pick the raw fish or kebob or rolled meat that you wanted cooked for you. Meatballs, donairs, barbecued chicken, lamb stew were all common and delicious. Their spicing is superb. Most places have salads that are like Greek salads — but don't tell the Turks that.

In low-end restaurants for the peasants you find things like greasy mutton soup for breakfast served with lovely white bread chunks.

Whenever you want something sweet they offer Turkish delight which I happen to hate.

WHAT DID YOUR MOTHER SAY?

It was the question asked in every culture, every language, every country. They heard that I was traveling around the world with my bicycle. Alone. "What did your mother say?"

"My mother said, 'Go for it Sweetheart.'"

And again, the reaction was always the same. "You have an amazing mother."

Yes.

And what happened to the other mothers? How did they become fearful and doubting? How did they lose confidence in their children's' ability to go out into the world and be fine? Why did they start holding their children back and teaching them to fear? Why did they hobble their daughters?

Where do mothers need to go to get in touch with their courage again?

BENIM GOGIA TURK

She was an English woman in her late forties. She looked as if life had been hard. She had grown up sons in England and a string of bad relationships behind her. At the insistence of her friends — You need to get away, — she came to Turkey grieving her father's death three years before. She had signed up for a tour and hated the tour and hated the other people on it. So she broke away and spent an afternoon sitting in a modest, outdoor Turkish restaurant across the highway from the fort ruin at Anamur. During that time she did little more than make eye contact with the Turkish owner. He was thirty-five. "He was old for a single Turk. Their families usually don't let them go that long without getting married. He was shy. Turkish men are shy. He couldn't talk English and I couldn't speak a word of Turkish."

After she left they corresponded for a year. There must have been some translators available.

Now they were married and lived in the restaurant where they first set eyes on each other. With their baby daughter. "He cooks the meals. He gets up with the baby. He adores her. She adores him. They spend most of the day together, father and daughter. He isn't like a Turkish man. Handling children is women's work. His father saw him walk in holding her one day and scoffed, 'That's women's work, don't walk around carrying that baby.' He said, 'She is my baby and I'll do what I want.'"

"I've learned a little Turkish. It isn't grammatical but I can get by. I visit with the local women and now that I have her, I'm in. But the Turkish men can be a pain. I just say, 'Benim gogia Turk,' which means, "my husband is Turkish."

Memorize that. Ben-im go-gia Turk. Use it when you travel in Turkey and wear a wedding ring. Men respect another man's property. Sometimes it is the first thing they ask you. You get in a cab, close the door, tell the driver where you are going and the driver asks, Are you married? Ben-im go-gia Turk.

INTO THE WAR ZONE

CYPRUS

Let's try a war-torn island

As I cycled east along the south coast of Turkey, Cyprus came into range on the map. Cyprus has been in the war news all our lives. Greek Cypriots, Turkish Cypriots, bombs, hostages. (Were they taking hostages in Cyprus or was that somewhere else?) War zones are to be avoided. Life insurance, any life insurance, is null and void if you knowingly go into a riot or war zone. But Russians holiday in Turkey and Cyprus. And expat newspapers in Russia carry ads and articles on the sun, sand, beaches, shopping and restaurants of Cyprus. A thriving tourism business. A warm island, closer to Africa than anywhere else I had been, exotic and begging for travelers. I'm ready. By fall there was only one ferry still operating, the high-speed ferry from Tasucu to Girne.

THEY ARE GENTLEMEN. WHY NOT?

After going through customs and drinking the little glass of tea they offered me, I hovered on the dock uncertain what to do next. There was a boat at the dock. Was it mine? No-one seemed to be getting on it. Eventually the chief engineer came along, asked me if I needed help and led me to the boat. Under his supervision deck hands secured my bike at the railing.

I then spent most of the two hour crossing at the helm, beside the captain. He wore navy bermuda shorts, white, short-sleeved shirt with navy epaulettes and an air of comfort with authority. We talked of the global positioning system they used for navigation, and of navigating the old way with charts and radar. Then we talked of politics, the strange storm two days before — he too thought it was odd — his career on freighters around the world, his wife and the fact that she and other women wouldn't want to go out at night without their husbands because Turkish men were such barbarians.

His crew, wearing matched yellow T-shirts, torn and stained, hung around the wheelhouse and joked with each other. One of them had the longest eyelashes I have ever seen, great, languid hoods over his huge brown eyes, curled up at the end. I mentioned this to the captain, who translated to the rest. You can imagine the hilarity that created. They jostled, laughed, teased, cracked open hazelnuts with their fingers and fed them to the captain and me. Then more tea. Then more.

I observed how well the crew all seemed to get along. The captain said. "Sure. Yes. Why not? They are all gentlemen." They seemed more like a litter of puppies to me.

Word came over the radio that the man who owned the ferry company was crossing in the opposite direction. We altered course a bit, much joking. There they were, another high-speed ferry, just like ours, coming on fast. The guys opened the door to the wheelhouse and blew our whistle as the boat came speeding up. Our captain stepped out to wave as they zoomed past and everyone over there, including the owner in a beautiful, silver-grey business suit, waved back. He was leaning out toward us, over the railing, giving a full arm wave. It felt like two carloads of neighbourhood boys, passing each other in the street and the boys leaning out the windows and hollering and whooping and bringing their heads back in, glowing with the thrill of just seeing each other. I too felt the afterglow of a lifetime of gleeful greetings, of happy meetings, brief glimpses, thrilled encounters. Timelayers of joy triggered by their amusement.

Before the end of the crossing, I moved outside to the stern. I was tanned. My arms felt long and strong and lean and muscled. Pampered by the crew, stared at by the passengers, I felt capable and brave. One of the Valkyries. Awash with pride and joy. Just thrilled. How I loved it. My beautiful little bike, my unfailing friend, tied to the railing, out looking at the world together. How blessed I was. Thank you, Universe, for this gift. May this moment be mine forever.

The light, powerful boat was biting into the water and pounding through the waves creating a double wall of spray at the front and a deep wake behind. I was alone out in the world. I was singing "...around the world I searched for you, I traveled on, when hope was gone, to keep a rendezvous..." I went out there to find my Other Traveler. And I had. And I would learn more and bond more with her as we continued, together, around the world. Around. All the way around. So much more for us to see. Now it all looped back to my inner self and felt like I finally understood something important.

Standing in the stern of the boat, I recalled when the idea had first come to me as I fumed about being on the downhill slide and losing value. The trip was just an idea. Just an example of what would turn that around. Thank goodness I got captured by my own example. Bless you Andrew for suggesting I mortgage the house. Thank you all for encouraging me. Yes. This is being alive.

They marched to their own drummer. Always had. In the fifties Tanju was a career military officer who dashed about in a racy sportscar and smoked cigarettes. His family was not wealthy but relished the prestige of generations in the Turkish military. Bilkis was a model in Istanbul. Her family was wealthy and religious. They were proud of that status and determined to seeing their daughter marry well.

Neither family was happy with the match.

Once married, both sets of parents set out to control the new couple — quite normal in a Turkish family. Their power plays were staged at family meals. Tanju and Bilkis decided to present a solid front against their families. Next time her family came to dinner and lectured the new couple, Tanju responded with, "This is my house. We do things our way here. If you don't like that, leave." They did.

Same scenario, other in-laws, shortly after. Same result.

That took care of that.

In the twenty years since, all the other family marriages have gone bad, ended with divorce and terrible money messes, custody battles and recrimination. Tanju and Bilkis are now held up as the family pets by both sets of in-laws. This is how a son-in-law should be... Here is the perfect wife for my son. Write that one down newlyweds.

The other interesting thing about Tanju and Bilkis is that, in spite of a military career, Tanju is an artist. Has always been an artist. He painted in his office for years and participated in officer art shows. (You mean that there were enough army officers who painted to have showings of their work? Sure.) He painted battle scenes from history, he painted military and political heroes, he painted ships, and he worked mainly in oils. But at some point since then he has worked in every medium and painted every kind of subject.

Now, retired from the army and living in Cyprus where he and Bilkis have a tiny boutique of imported clothes, jewelry, household decorations and gifts, Tanju paints watercolor. (You know it suits this place.) Sunny scenes of Turkish houses, gardens, patios, flowers, the sea. Beautiful, light, warm paintings that are popular. He is known all over Turkey and his paintings sell well.

Their house is furnished with an array of Turkish furniture and art and objects from around the world. The living room has a sunken fireplace with a ring of low, built-in seating, marble floors, old rugs, artifacts from India, white window shutters that were all closed with no windowpane in evidence, just window openings.

Their teenaged son and daughter, both on the verge of university, hang out in the kitchen with the cats and parents. Tanju and Bilkis cook together. Everyone chats and drapes their arms around each other and leans their chin on someone's shoulder while talking. This is a house of love and indulgence. This is a warm, happy dad who shares daily tasks and enjoys people, his work, his cats.

Watching one of his kittens give the other a bath, on the kitchen floor, Tanju laughed, "Look at that." The bath-ee was in ecstasy. Eyes closed, head up, neck exposed. "Sometimes these turn out badly and they fight. But this one looks okay. Look how he loves that."

Bilkis went to the hairdresser to get her blond streaks fixed. They both insisted that I spend the afternoon there and stay for dinner. Tanju played Turkish music on his state-of-the-art Japanese sound system. Then the amazing score from the Christopher Columbus movie Conquest of Paradise. I had not heard it before. I was moved to tears. The sadness of conquering a paradise. The music said that. I heard pain, sorrow and beauty. I think of Christopher Columbus setting out on a voyage of discovery, and I think of my voyage of discovery. And of pain everywhere, always.

As in my journey, the pleasure of each note could only be enjoyed while it hung, in the air. A mere vibration. Then, gone. All I could do is savour the sound of the next note. Seemed trite. Can we learn to not hold on? Not fear the loss of the note? Can we learn not to manage the next note? Can we Tao-of-Pooh the notes that drift past us?

In every country there are brave travelers who have transcended their cultural imprinting and become citizens of the world. They remain true to their souls. They can teach us all about courage and thinking for ourselves and living by what we believe, in spite of pressure from the ethno-centric around us.

Go to Girne in Turkish Cyprus and visit Blondie's in a lane just off the main street. Tanju and Bilkis will be there.

YOGA ON THE ROAD

I had enjoyed yoga, on and off, since learning it from a book in my early twenties. I particularly liked doing yoga after exercise. My reward for exercising. The exercise warmed my muscles and bathed my system in raw energy and oxygen. Then yoga smoothed this energy into soft waves. My body loved the flexibility and smoothness that carried over between sessions.

I would have loved to do yoga after each day of riding but conditions were against it. I wanted a bath even more. Yoga covered with layers of road-dust sand-blasted onto my sunscreen did not appeal. I was often very hungry by then too. So I was more interested in the lower levels of Maslow's Hierarchy when I came off the road. And once they were dealt with I needed to wait a few hours before doing yoga and by then I was asleep.

Even on days when I didn't ride, I was often in accommodation that had such a filthy floor that the thought of lying down on it, even if I put a blanket down first, made me recoil.

So I didn't get much yoga on the trip. But when I could, I fit it in at the start of a non-riding day. An hour-long present to myself. And on those occasions I experienced, for the first time in twenty-seven years of yoga, the pleasure of giving it all the time my body liked. Each posture performed slowly. After each posture I would lie or sit, and just be inside my body, quietly watching and feeling that energy flow and echo. It felt like the re-bounding waves inside a waterbed mattress after you pick up a corner of it and then let it drop. Waves of energy radiating out, rebounding off the sides and passing through the outbound waves as they echo back in and out at the same time.

I became more attuned to this energy. Arms raised above my head, I would put my palms together, lower them down in front of my face, down to my chest like an eastern prayer. The currents of energy around my hands passed like a shadow over my face. Eyes closed I could see them and feel them. That's my life force. That's what separates me from being a dead body. I was listening to my life force.

To spoil myself I would finish with twenty minutes of sitting quietly with my eyes closed feeling that energy ebb and flow in my body. I would relish that and rest on my breathing. Some call this meditating. I'm reluctant to do so because I'm really bad at meditating.

ANOTHER CARLOAD OF CHEERLEADERS

I passed some English tourists, two couples in the middle of no-where. They were eating on the patio of an open-air restaurant perched on a hill overlooking the sea. They cheered and waved encouragement as I pedaled by. When they overtook me twenty minutes later, one rolled down the window and said, "Do be careful".

I replied, "Thank you, Love. Of course. And you too," which they thought was terribly funny.

They went one way, I pedaled the other, along a road beside a winding beach covered with plastic litter at the high water mark. On the opposite side of the road were rock cliffs eroded into smooth, curved shapes. A Gaudi cliffside. No one for miles. Not much that I needed to be careful of out there.

OVER THE MOUNTAINS

It looked simple enough on the map. (So often that is the case.) East along the north coast of Turkish Cyprus. Then, over the hills that run down the middle of the island and down to the south side.

The road along the shore was paved but single laned and wound up and down the natural contours of the landscape. That meant steep little hills and roller coaster rides down the other side. The scale was like a small kiddies' roller coaster. Short and steep. Then a sharp turn and another sharp turn. The road wound around low, desert hills and rocks and olive groves with few signs of human or animal life. I had the road to myself. How nice it would be to swim naked. But Turks do have the ability to materialize out of the ground or air or rocks. Sure enough, I'd just get my clothes off and from out of nowhere would be a grinning Turk. Just couldn't risk it.

The climb began at the little village of Kaplan where I turned inland. This was a poor, un-touristy village. Dark houses that looked like they were built out of mud. Dirty children in raggy clothes. They all held out their hands and ran alongside, chanting in Turkish. One cheeky child grabbed the back of my bike and dragged backwards. Never a nice feeling and worse when struggling up a hill. I wasn't making much headway without the kid hanging on.

But I finally cleared the town and the kids and was into continuous, long, hard climbing. And my water supply was running low. A middle-aged English couple came inching down from Kantara, a famous monastery at the top, in a small rental car. I waved them over, which on this narrow road means they stopped in the middle, and asked if they had any water I could buy. They didn't but they had a can of Fanta that I could have free. They said I couldn't possibly make it to the top. They had been coming down, in a car, and it had taken them half an hour. No one could make it up on a bike.

I thanked them kindly and kept going. I ate my Mars Bar. Sometimes I walked and sometimes I rode, depending on how steep that spot was. Then down came a pickup truck, not a common sight in Turkey, carrying two men, a German and Turk. They had some water, so I refilled my bottles.

Now I had plenty of water and I could see the top. I was confident. Even if the road wound around further than was evident before the summit, I would still get there, eventually. I had plenty of time to send peace to Brenda, Sonia and the ragged children in the village back at the bottom.

I was riding when I crested the peak. Happy, proud, relieved. Invincible. I refilled water again at the mountaintop restaurant, sat beside the fountain while I ate a perfect omelet and started down the other side.

The south face was the side that the tour buses used because it was better graded and had corners that they could negotiate. From this vantage point I realized how high I had actually climbed. The coastal plain and Mediterranean looked far away, stretching out below me. But down was lovely and I covered it quickly until the last 5 K, which had the nerve to include a few, mild uphills. Practically my undoing at that point. I found accommodation in a beautiful, new pension that was just short of completion when the owner died, leaving his widow to cope with an unfinished source of income and a young daughter.

In the middle of the night, I stepped out onto the huge deck of my apartment. It hung on the side of a hill, just above the Sea, with Africa just over there. I looked up at the amazing Mediterranean night sky. So different from the Canadian starscape. So black. So many stars. A vivid slice of moon. There were clear constellations everywhere. No wonder people living under these constellations made up stories about them. How else can you explain those patterns that, surely, had to be planned? A warm wind was blowing softly out of the blackness. A delicious combination: black and warm. I wanted to stay there forever.

I'm at the Mediterranean. The centre of our cultural heritage. The home of our early history. Someone called it The Cradle of Civilization. The highway of commerce, cultural exchange, warfare, not to mention the backdrop to the myths that underscore our sense of life before history. I am here with all of them who have ever been here. They have seen this night sky. They have felt this warm wind. Thank you for letting me come. It is an honor to be here with you.

DO NOT PUSH THE RIVER

Remember the Zen wisdom we discovered in the 60s? Do not push the river. Sure. That makes sense. It won't work. It couldn't work. It would sweep you away. Whether you push with the current or against it, pushing the river is pointless. So why do we spend our lives pushing the river of life? The river of inexorable unfolding.

I have been pushing. I do it all the time. I make a living doing it.

Now I'll stop. I just won't push it any more. Now, armed with this new/old insight, I'll stop. I'll move with the river. Float.

But.

We never resolved how we could accomplishing anything if we truly didn't push the river. Do you get out of bed? Do you get out of bed when you don't feel like it? Do you write an assignment? Phone a friend? Draw your next breathe?

Over the years since, I still haven't resolved it. If I don't push the river how do I make a living? Can I live like the lilies in the fields? Fat chance. Riding and trying to buy tickets on planes and boats and getting my bike on with me and trying to find places to stay I came to the following conclusion on the river-pushing issue: it is fine to set out to cross, divert, swim in, drain, drink or do whatever to the river. But when the goal becomes a source of fear, it is time to reconsider, get creative, read the conditions more quietly. Stop pushing. Explore what is instead of imposing The Plan. And I can't remind myself too often. As an Aries, it might be my life work to keep balancing my planning/goal setting with - being.

LESSONS THE WAVES TEACH

I am captivated by the waves. Little baby waves just barely curling their lips against the shore and grand, pounding dramatic surf rolling in - one relentless volley after another. Pound, wash. Pound, wash. The sand or rocks clatter and sift back down the slope of beach when the water recedes. Then the next one.

The exhilaration and comfort of walking in the waves, right where they meet the shore, never gets boring. Feeling waves surge up against my legs and lift me that last little bit, then try to pull me out and suck me down. Up and back. Up and back. The repeated pattern that never ends. It is reassuring. Lulling. Here is the place that no-resolution becomes okay. I kept watching for resolution, listening for it but the waves never finish and they taught me that. Sometimes my trip looked like trekking from one wave site to the next. Always drawn back for another wave lesson.

PLAN B: THE KEPT WOMAN PLAN

I waited out the two-hour bank lunch-closure by treating myself to lunch at an expensive seaside resort catering to Europeans, Brits and Americans. This was a Club Med situation. Package holidays. Chefs on the patio whipped up salads and burgers to order for patrons in bikinis and suntans. The beach was littered with wooden beach cots and foam mattresses. A beach-boy dispensed towels and holiday-ers slouched around, reading, getting sunburned and groping their partners. It was lovely to see that affection. I saw a very old man staring at the waves and holding his wife's hand in both of his while she read beside him. I saw a giggling couple on side-by-side suncots, she running her toes up the inside of his leg — up and up. Kissing, nuzzling, staring into eyes, all ages, shapes and sizes. I liked this place.

The hotel was next to the Cyprus demilitarized zone. At the edge of its beach there was barbed wire that went down into the water and on the other side of the wire was a row of bombed-out high rises that had probably been hotels themselves on this perfect stretch of Miami-esque beachfront.

It would be an indulgent treat to relax in the resort for a couple of nights until my plane flew me back to Turkey. But it was expensive. I caught myself musing about the possibility of finding a wealthy man, a tanned, silver-haired shipping tycoon, an Omar Sharif, who would take me into his suite of rooms and finance my every whim. And if the chemistry was right, who knows? This is the nineties for heaven sake. What's the big deal?

However in the course of eating lunch this man didn't step forward and identify himself so I thought I'd better see if there were insider rates or deals or something. I asked the waiter if he knew of an economical way I could stay at the hotel for a couple of days — being a cyclist with limited funds and all.

Next thing I knew, he brought over the chef, a little man who spoke French and looked French but I never could figure out if he actually was. It turned out that he had a spare room, in staff quarters, that I could have for a couple of days. Free. "He doesn't want any money. For two nights, no problem." (There's the tip off. No problem is always a tip-off.) Okay, sounded like a deal to me. Over we went to have a look. He showed me a single room with an un-made bed in it, men's clothes strewn around and blinds closed.

I tried to ask if he slept there. He seemed to say that the hotel was very busy and when it was he stayed in the hotel. Then he seemed to say that he was only there from 11PM to 7 AM. Hmm. I didn't like the sounds of this. Anyway, this guy didn't look like Omar Sherif and this was no luxury suite. (Of course in theory it is all the same thing, just the price tag is different — as that old joke used to say.) He showed me how the key worked and handed it to me.

We went back to the waiter.

"Is that his room?"

"Yes."

"Does he sleep there?"

Again vague conflicting comments about when the hotel is busy. "You see the hotel is very full. But it's no problem, he comes to work at eight o'clock in the morning and is in the hotel all day."

"Then he goes to the room and sleeps with me?"

"I guess so."

"Look I need to be clear here. Does he think I will sleep with him?"

They chatted among themselves then looked at me, the waiter shrugged,

"Yeah."

I handed back the key, bowed to the chef, "This was a kind offer but I do not feel comfortable accepting. Thank you." He bowed as only Frenchmen do and I walked off.

Okay so much for the Pretty Woman plan. Now I think I'll take on negotiations with the front desk. See how far I can get with them.

Well I didn't get far but at least paying my own way I'm my own person. (Is that the lesson I'm learning?)

Up in my second-story room, very nice, I sat on my bed, took off my sandals, listened to the wind rattle the shutters. I noticed that the bed bounced gently up and down and thought, "Hmm, an interesting construction technique. Build the building kind of flexible so that it blows in the wind. That'll be nice to go to sleep to." It was only the next day telephoning a friend in Calgary that I found out it had been an earthquake. Quite pleasant.

The next morning breakfast was truly a marvel. Hot food, cold food, Turkish sausage rounds, tiny spicy sausages, fresh tomato, hard boiled eggs, two kinds of scrambled eggs, at least ten kinds of bread or buns, toast, six different packaged breakfast cereals, jams, chopped fresh fruit, whole fruit, yogurt, six different cheeses, four or five kinds of cold meat, and a huge water-side deck.

The weather cooled during the day and I moved my reading from the beach cot to the lobby. Once there I got into conversation with a retired American medical doctor. He looked like a cross between Picasso and Dr Spock. He was also by himself. Smart, interesting, well traveled we decided to have dinner together that evening. Is this someone who will grow into a place in my life? Certainly would beat the hell out of the financial disasters I've had a habit of linking up with. Not to mention the intellectually challenged. What fun to dress up in my new ankle length sarong and enjoy stimulating conversation and a lavish smorgasbord.

However, one of his remarks over dinner flicked the switch: Yoga probably isn't doing you any harm, although no-one will ever prove that it contributes to your health. Aha. One of those. I was cool, I was calm and polite but I made it known that I have little respect for the medical profession's approach to health. We disagreed.

After dinner we stood on the patio overlooking the beach and enjoyed listening to the waves and watching the lightening. But the chairs were wet from the rain and I was feeling I should get packed to be ready for a long, early taxi ride to the airport the next day.

Still amiable, we shook hands, expressed our pleasure, quite sincerely on both parts, for each other's company. Contrary to travelers' usual exchange, we good-bye'd without asking for the other's address. And that felt oddly liberating. Good-byes and closures are so fraught with — well, trying to soften it somehow and thereby not doing what we have to. "I'll call you." It was a nice gliding away to not even touch on that. No holding on, no making more of it than an interesting dinner conversation. Nice.

Back in my room, alone, I mused that it had been quite a little adventure there. I was glad to be alone. Glad not to have to bend or distort or cover up what I believe in order to accommodate the world view of someone else. Tomorrow, up at 3:30 AM to get to the airport in time for my flight. How did I get so lucky to have all these lessons just tumble, gently down on me? Guiding, nurturing, healing lessons? Where were they coming from?

MERCEDES TAKSIS

All the taksis in Cyprus are Mercedes. This is a small geographic area with a small Turkish population. A beautiful, woman professor of engineering that I got chatting with in the bank, told me that the economy is artificially supported. There are three universities, some luxurious big houses, an airline, tourism — the only visible industry — and Mercedes cars everywhere.

She said the universities are populated with rich kids from all around the Mediterranean. And I saw them in their luxury cars and designer clothes and air of smug satisfaction, that speaks of young and moneyed regardless of race or culture.

LUGGAGE SECURITY

Leaving Cyprus the luggage is laid out on the tarmac. You pick out your own luggage and indicate it to the crew who then load it on the cart and put it on the plane. My bike wasn't among the suitcases, it was over to the side. It always tugged at me to see her alone, working her way along a production line and being picked up by impersonal handlers.

TURKEY RE-VISITED

ANOTHER TASTE OF TURKEY

I had cycled east along the south coast of Turkey. From there I had made the leap south to Cyprus. I could only get to the Greek side of the island by leaving Cyprus and returning from somewhere in Greece or a neutral country. Cyprus wasn't worth that much attention but I wanted to stay in a warm climate and I ruled out Africa because I only had a three-week window before I needed to be getting on to New Zealand on business. With Africa I didn't know where to start.

So I caught the one cheap flight on my whole trip. It appears that the flights inside a country are the cheap ones — as long as the country isn't Canada or New Zealand. I flew to Izmer in the northwest corner of Turkey and cycled down the west coast. I had grieved about each country when I left and was delighted to be going back, street hawkers and insane drivers and all, back to Turkey.

THIS IS WHAT ADVENTURE LOOKS LIKE.

I rode south from Izmer with a blessed tailwind. The strongest tailwind so far on my trip. It was a pleasure to be spoiled by that. I was feeling more relaxed in Turkey since Cyprus. I was more tolerant of the attention-demanding men and the grubbiness. I waved at the honking drivers and the beautiful young Turk sitting on a tractor talking on his cell phone. He interrupted his conversation to call out the usual, "Hello, hello. Where are you from?"

I stopped for the day in a town that was so small it wasn't even really a town. Just a few houses scattered around, a little store with Turkish junk food and this restaurant with rooms built on the roof. The sign said, "Motel". Another sign said, "Restaurant". This was not a prosperous business. Two men and a woman. All late thirties, all handsome. Very little English.

I got a corner room with windows on two sides, which was nice. But the room was spare and grubby and the toilet had no toilet seat and no tank. I flushed it with a pitcher of water that I filled from the stained sink. However, it was cheap and I was ready to stop cycling for the day.

I was in early enough to stroll down to the waterfront. There was a fenced army camp at the beach but the giant custodian came up behind me on a tractor and invited me in through the gate. I could get down to the water's edge from there.

When he noticed me trying to entice a cat to come and visit he called to it. The cat trotted over to him and, much to my amazement, he picked it up by its head. He just reached down and wrapped one giant hand around its head and picked it up. And even more amazing the cat then rubbed against him and purred. Buddies. It was touching. Hoss from Bonanza. With a cat.

Once I was settled on the stone beach watching the wavelets lapping and writing in my journal, the gentle giant came up behind me with a tiny cup of Turkish coffee offered, in one hand, in front of him. In the other hand, Turkish tea, in its little clear glass cup on a metal saucer. There was no way that I could drink it without getting seriously wired but I felt badly demurring. I mimed my heart pounding as I said, "No thank you." He went away. I groaned a bit internally wondering what this was the start of. And sure enough he was back a few minutes later.

This time with a cup of Turkish yogurt drink. I'm very fond of that and showed how thrilled I was and drank it down and had him take a picture of me sitting on the beach drinking it. I thanked him and the dear man had the good graces to go away.

Later I strolled slowly along that water-meets-beach strip, explored a rock hill that went down into the water and eventually started back to the "Motel". I was feeling mellow and pleased with myself. I had finally got a bit tanned and felt I wasn't looking totally ugly without makeup. I had bought a couple of wrap-around skirts in Cyprus and enjoyed strolling in a skirt. I pondered whether it was like the first skirt ever tied around a waist. I liked that continuity with human evolution.

A little dog, built like a corgi, with long soft ears, was barking and snarling at me as I walked back from the beach. He looked menacing. But his bark turned to mushy excitement when I leaned over, slapped my thigh and called to him. He couldn't get enough of my stroking and scratching and patting and ran along beside me tugged the end of a stick I was carrying and licked my feet for goodness sake. It's been a while since I have had my feet licked.

Two men, an old man and a younger one, were selling lemons beside the road at the highway. There weren't any cars going by and no other people around. The little dog seemed to be theirs, so we "talked" about the dog and I took their pictures. I would have liked the picture of them just as they were, standing around, joking with each other, their eyes alive. Like most Turkish men, they were beautiful when they were "at ease". Wearing their picture faces with their chins pulled in, stiff and solemn, all the sparkle and character disappeared. It frustrated me that I couldn't stop that without catching them unprepared, without asking permission. That felt rude.

I tried to buy a lemon and they insisted that I just take one. I thanked them, bowed. They, as usual, tried to get me to stay and talk even though neither of us knew each other's language. The older man wanted me to sit on his crate. He put his jacket on it. I smiled and waved and strolled on.

There was a small, roadside store across the street from the motel where I bought a snack and played with their little cat. She was a calico like mine at home and seemed to relish being stroked and scratched. The couple watched bemused as if they had never seen anyone do that to a cat before. He asked how old I was and then a few minutes later, as if he had picked the wrong question, asked where I was going. I was feeling fond of them and their little cat.

While I ate dinner amidst a swarm of flies, one of the men at the "motel" kept trying to talk to me. He knew three things in English: "chef" (pointing at himself), "madam" and "no problem". He kept trying to ask me questions. We didn't understand each other, but he wouldn't give up. Finally I laughed, picked up my book, bowed and walked up to my room.

As I often do after a day of riding, I fell asleep at 6:30 PM and woke again three hours later. I had been up since 3:30 to get to the airport. So I put on my light and read. I was lying on my bed, at the bottom of the bed, actually, because the bare ceiling lightbulb was shining right in my eyes the other way, and just getting ready to go back to sleep again, when "chef" came to my door and knocked. "Who is it?"

"Madam, blah blah blah" in Turkish.

What do you want? (But I knew there was no point in talking, we did not understand each other.)

"Madam, blah blah blah." in Turkish.

He kept knocking and over and over saying "No problem, Chef. No problem. Madam."

"I don't want to talk."

"Madame, (many madams, many no-problems", pleading tone.)

For long periods I said only "Go away," and then didn't bother saying anything.

"Madam," and a string of Turkish.

I was irritated. He was there for twenty minutes.

When he left I had a sense that it wasn't the end of it. I got up and put on my shorts and a second T-shirt. I tried reading. I could hear him and the woman arguing downstairs.

And sure enough, footsteps in the hallway again, stagy sighing with exasperated annoyance, knocking on my door. All the same stuff. Madame. Chef. No problem. And lots of Turkish.

Then I tried tone. "Go away" firmly, annoyed. "Leave me alone."

I decided an angry tone was now in order, forget about the words, we needed an angry tone. I yelled, "Go away. Policia. Go away" (And wondered, Is that the word for police in Turkish?)

I repeated that litany a few times, remained silent for extended periods, gave up on reading although I continued to hold my book in front of me. I felt my rage building.

Again he left after twenty minutes he left and took up arguing, more loudly, with the woman downstairs. It was now after midnight. I might need to bail out of this place. First, I would try getting help from the couple at the grocery store across the street. They had been pleasant while I played with their cat. If I couldn't rouse them, I'd sleep beside the road. It was too dark for me to ride and I didn't have a light on my bike.

Fighting downstairs was escalated again. A row.

I was thinking: "I left home for adventure. This is what adventure looks like. And I'm up for it." I was aware that my body was flooded with adrenaline and my heart was pounding. Fortunately my dominant feeling was rage rather than fear. I was furious. Who does he think he is?!?

When next I heard footsteps in the hallway I had to fight the urge to open the door and attack him with my bare hands. Much sighing and groaning in the hallway. Then I heard keys in a lock. I knew it wasn't my lock but it was close. I heard moving around. Was he in the room next to mine? Was there a door between? A peephole?

I was lying on my bed, head at the bottom, book in my hands. I lay still and listened. I listened with every fiber in my ears. I could almost see those tiny filaments straining for sound waves. I looked over at the wall. I heard shuffling in the next room. After four or five minutes of scarcely breathing I silently swung my legs over the edge of the bed to tiptoe over to the wall and go over it carefully, inch by inch.

Just before my bare feet touched the floor, I heard a noise behind me. I swung around to see chef standing on my balcony outside my window, inches away.

I have no recall of climbing onto the bed. I only remember being up on the bed, frantically trying to get the window open. (Was I planning to push him off the balcony? I was certainly ready to fight.) The window wouldn't open, probably a blessing for both of us.

Three hours of adrenaline was ready to go to work for me. I was screaming and purposefully screwed my face into rage knowing that the words meant nothing to him. I was flinging my arm out to point aggressively off the balcony.

"Get away from me. Get fucking away from me. Go away. Go. Now. Get off. Fucking get off."

He put his fingers to his lips in a shushing gesture.

"No. No. I won't fucking shush. You get away from me. Go. Get off. Getting fucking away."

I was screaming.

I was ready to go down fighting but I assumed I would win. (Back at home a friend said, "Very good Marg. And how kindly would the Turkish courts look upon a Canadian woman who killed a Turkish man?")

Next he pointed at my ceiling. I paused to look over my shoulder at what he was pointing at. The lightbulb? So I clambered off the bed and hit the lightswitch still yelling. Then I turned and went back to the window. He was gone. I heard him open the balcony door in the hallway, close and lock it, and with his stagy sighing, (What do you have to do to get through to these women?) he walked back down the hallway and downstairs.

My body was throbbing. I heard every unintelligible syllable of their downstairs fighting. I heard unidentifiable sounds. One was like a golf ball bouncing on a table. Then furniture scraping along the floor. Water running? A shower? A toilet flushing? That adrenaline is amazing stuff. Should I just pack up and go? My ears were ringing.

Two hours later I was still wide-awake and they were slowing down downstairs. Eventually all was quiet.

What was with the light? Some kind of religious thing? Saving energy? It didn't make sense, especially when I noticed the light was on all night in the hallway.

I asked my Turkish contact at the Canadian Embassy in Ankara what that was all about. He said, "He wanted either you or your money or both. You are just lucky that he wasn't drunker or didn't have a friend with him."

"What about the light?"

"That was nothing. That was trying to save face when he saw that you weren't going to co-operate. He tried to use that as an excuse for being there. He would believe that any woman traveling by herself would be promiscuous."

Think again pal.

IT'S NOW

I had spent much of my life contemplating the nature of time. Faced with an unpleasant three-hour exam or four-and-a-half minute piano recital, I would contemplate how to leap-frog that time period and be looking at it from the other side. Done. It should be possible.

Ephesus is the ultimate ruin. It is the last word in antiquities. It must also be a time travel entrance. It shifted my perceptions of yesterday, today, history, then and now. Ephesus bent time around on itself and smacked me in the face with all-now-ness. My sense of time melted. As I walked the streets of Ephesus, English, French and German tourists were taking each other's pictures, consulting their reference materials and listening to entertaining guides with amusing inside stories of Roman and earlier Greek life there. This city was built 3000 years BC! We haven't even made it to 3000AD yet.

This is reputed to be the last home of the Virgin Mary. Paul's scolding letter to the Ephesians, reproduced in the Bible, was written to these citizens. This is the neighbourhood where they walked, talked, sinned, did business. This is where they went to bed, tired or satisfied with their spouse or someone else, and did what we do in bed — worried about performance, thrashed against insomnia, elbowed the snorer. This is where they squabbled with neighbors or shared makeup or sports stories. This is where they got exasperated with their kids and hoped something would smarten them up. This is where they complained about incompetent politicians and shook their heads over yet another stupid political move. There is no difference. This is not the past. This is now. They are us.

Some trick of time travel has replaced their toga'd population with our shorts and tank tops and put cameras in our hands. The mind's eye can see the editor's trick of holding a scene and changing the people in it in a few frames. They were here a moment ago. What changed? What made this different? Just let me think about this a minute to get my head around it.

Time has been the only variable. This is the place. These are the things. Their street. With their chariot wheel ruts in it. Their public toilets and their astounding Library of Celsus. Ephesus spreads as far as the eye can see. And more, a whole mountainside, was still being excavated. I could see it covered with continuous tenting along the hill.

The same thing happened at the Roman coliseum at Aspendos, just outside Antalya. I missed a performance of La Traviata by one day. Standing room only. A 19th century opera performed in a 200 BC coliseum to an audience in 1996. And the audience did just the same thing it did in 200 BC: gossiped, compared clothes, raged about the tall oaf who just sat in front of them, worried about the kids, longed for the performance to begin, fretted that they hadn't bought a drink, continued their domestic bickering — or took a break, distracted by the excitement of the occasion.

This is the coastline where Anthony and Cleopatra were meeting on the shores, plotting politics to protect their passion and driven by the urge to couple. This is where the wealthy Cleopatra fumed about Anthony's politically correct marriage fearing that it might jeopardize their relationship. This is where she offered to finance his wars in order to retain his loyalty and love. This is where they eventually committed suicide in despair. This is woman-who-loves-too-much. This is tabloid material. Sex and politics in bed together. Cleopatra fumes as Anthony weds. Tony and Cleo in love retreat. Cleo hands over cash to keep Tony's love.

It is us. It is now. We are one.

Maybe time is linear because we can't deal with it all at once. But somewhere time exists concurrently, all bunched up in the same place. And some people may know how to get there from here. And maybe Ephesus is an entrance.

THE BOYS BACK HOME
I phoned my nephew Andrew at home the next night and was delighted to find my dear friend Noah also there. In spite of being my nephew's age, Noah and I are fast friends. We talked, we gave each other comfort. Noah said, "What you are doing is more profound than any of us did traveling. A woman, alone, in those countries. No wonder you need a safe hotel from time to time." Such a comfort. "I love you Marg," as we signed off. My guys.

CHECK-IN 9 AM

As usual I was on the road at first light. I started the day heading inland to get further south on the western coast of Turkey. And the terrain proved to be hilly. Long, big, highway hills. Fortunately not much traffic. But each hill seemed insurmountable. I was tired. I wasn't getting in my stride or hitting second wind or getting any boost of retro-rockets. I was dragging myself up each hill and dreading the next one. Finally I coasted down into landlocked Soke, a very Turkish town, which means nothing western. No tourist amenities. But there was a hotel for traveling Turkish businessmen.

I had been on the bike since sunup at 6 AM. It was now three hours later, just nine. Businessmen were checking out. I checked in, climbed into bed and slept until noon. I woke proud that I knew to stop riding. Some days 26 K is enough.

INSIDE A TURKISH TOWN

In Soke, I stuck out. People said that Soke was a prosperous town. That was hard to believe. It looked like a hovel. There were horse and donkey drawn carts in the streets. This was the only place I had kids following me asking for money. Two of them got bold and pointed at my fanny pack, worn against my tummy. Their fingers were inches away from it. That was unnerving and I pushed them and snapped No, loudly. At the same time a man passing in a car called out to them and they backed off.

I saw mostly men on the streets. And only men in the dark little holes where they loved to sit around greasy tables smoking and drinking tea and playing backgammon and whatever other board games and gossiping. They often carried their prayer beads as they walked along. These beads were in a loop bigger than a bracelet, smaller than a necklace, with a string of a few extra beads on the side of the loop. They are beautifully proportioned and looked smooth and nice to touch.

I saw men sitting in a circle around an outdoor hub of faucets, pants rolled up, washing their feet. Then they stepped into wooden clogs and, carrying their shoes, suit jackets draped over their shoulders, they walked into the mosque looking penitent and reverent.

Women didn't seem to have time to sit and play board games and pray. Women worked and carried groceries. They got driven in the back of open wooden carts pulled by tractors out to the fields to work in the cotton. Huddled in these carts they were tightly shrouded in baggy clothes, wrapped against the morning cold. They would work in the fields all day, seven days a week.

There were a few stores in Soke. And like all Turkish stores, half their merchandise was cleaning agents. Laundry soap, handsoap, dish soap, floor cleaner, counter cleaner, tile cleaner, toilet and sink cleaner, disinfectant, aerosol spray - all of these in numerous brands and sizes. I saw laundry draped on many balconies. I shuddered to think of cleaning perfectionism in that dust bowl.

But the serious retail action took place at the market Saturday mornings.

A huge concrete square, completely empty when the market folded its tent, was thick with stalls and sellers and customers and children, so dense you couldn't see through to the far end. You couldn't even see into the middle. Fresh fruit and vegetables, dried fruit, fresh fish and shellfish in kinds I had never seen before, children's clothes, baby supplies, men's clothes, women's shoes and boots, pots, pans, bowls, utensils, furniture, pictures and ornaments, spices, herbs, honey — life. Men and women selling. Many of the women who had their hair covered were smoking. They often had leather fanny packs for making change. The fish salesman was as entertaining as an auctioneer chanting, cajoling, boasting, nagging, humoring.

TWO KINDS OF CHILDREN
On weekday mornings the Soke busses disgorge schoolchildren in uniforms. All Turkish students wear uniforms. The Turkish child population breaks down into students, wearing uniforms, and workers. There are three million children between the ages of five and fifteen in Turkey who never attend school. I saw them shining shoes, working in stores, selling buns in the street. They didn't wear uniforms. The differences will increase as they grow older.

SAY THAT AGAIN, GRANNY
I had a guilt attack about the food I was eating, money I was spending, time I was taking. It was like being hit by a meteor. Whomp.

Granny pointed out that this was neither a perfect nor a logical trip. It was chaotic and random. Justice was a human construct that occurred randomly out here. So was any sense that things got better. I wouldn't necessarily get stronger, richer, slimmer, more enlightened. I wouldn't get more secure. Things would change. That's all that was for sure. She seemed okay with that. So I guess it's okay.

OFFICIALDOM
The ferry from Bodrum to Marmaris cost one million seven hundred and fifty Turkish lira.

"Could I have a receipt?"

"This," holding up a piece of paper.

"Yes but that's the ticket and they take it away."

Dumb look.

"The ferry man in Didyma took my ticket. I need a receipt to show I paid this after they take my ticket away."

He waved the ticket at me.

"He'll take this away."

"He has no reason to take it. You show it. You get on. It is yours. You keep it."

On the dock at the ferry check-in next morning a woman reached to take it:

"I want to keep this."

"No we need to take this."

"So do I. I need it for when I go back to Canada as a tax receipt."

"We need it to get the money from the tour office that sold you the ticket."

"He told me I could keep it."

"I don't know why he said that. It is the only way they pay us. We give them the tickets, they give us the money for them."

"I would like a receipt. Could you give me a receipt?"

"I will photocopy this."

In Russia they charge for receipts and write them out on grubby scraps of newsprint.

THE GATEKEEPER

I went to the customs desk at the hydrofoil terminal in Bodrum to cross to Greek-controlled Rhodes.

"Madame, too early. Three-thirty."

I watched him visit with his friends until three thirty-one and then went back.

"Madame, too early."

"You said three thirty."

"Four o'clock, madam too early, four o'clock."

He visited and smoked until four.

I waited until others started through. Then I followed.

THE SHE-COLOSSUS
OF RHODES

CROSSING AN UNFRIENDLY FRONTIER

Rhodes is the only Greek island I could get to from Turkey. Relations are
strained. But Rhodes is so close to the Turkish mainland everyone involved
seems to have made an exception. I loved to see entrepreneurial initiative over-
rule centuries of bad blood. I wanted to get a taste of Greece and to enjoy the
cycle-ability of an island where food and lodging were reported to be cheap
and the traveler had access to great history, architecture, scenery and beaches. I
also went because Andrew said I would love it. (Prague, obviously forgotten.)
Pulling into the Harbor at Rhodes, our hydrofoil was dwarfed by huge cruise
ships and private yachts. The French Riviera yacht club had met its match.

THE COLOSSUS OF RHODES

The Colossus straddled this harbor entranceway. It had been one of the Seven
Wonders of the Ancient World. So long ago that I thought maybe it fell into
the mythical category. Was it real? They say it was. They say it was more than
30 metres/100 feet high. Isn't there anything left of it? No, they say it is long
gone. Not even a stone fingernail resting on the bottom of the harbor? A lock
of hair? How can something that big de-materialize? They laugh. No. Nothing.
I don't believe them.

PLACES TO STAY

It was dusk when I got off the hydrofoil, cleared customs and headed into the
gigantic walled city, the old, frankly touristy part of Rodos Town. (The island is

Rhodes, called "Rodos" by the locals, and the city is called "Rodos Town.")
Even at dusk, it still thronged with people shopping up and down the winding,
cobbled streets jammed with stores and restaurants. But I had no idea where to
find accommodation and I didn't like being out after dark with my bike. I was
tired.

On impulse I stopped a passing couple. They were wearing comfortable
shoes and sweaters and they looked as safe as two people can look. I asked
them about places to stay. It just so happened that although they were visiting
from Holland they had a friend in Rodos Town who owned a hotel and they
would take me to his gold shop. (Oh dear, what now?) And there he was, a
couple of blocks along. He had wound down his hotel for the season but gave
me the key to the front door and sent his lovely daughter to help me settle in.

A tiny hotel to myself. Easy walking to the market, the history, the
architecture, the food. I liked Rodos. For two days I got my bearings and
enjoyed strolling around without my bike in hand. She was safely locked in my
hotel.

Then I set out to cycle the perimeter of the island. It was dark and all was
still as I rode the deserted streets and found my way out of the city. After the
glory of a dazzling sunrise across the water beside me, traffic built steadily. So I
was pleased to see it virtually disappear once I had passed the turnoff to,
Lindos, a popular resort half way down the east coast. At that point the lack of
shoulder didn't matter, I had the whole car-lane to myself.

It was hot, which I loved. I stopped at a brand new bakery on the edge of a
village that didn't quite come to the highway. There I met Nicki. She had lived
forty years in Toronto, ten of them supporting a frightfully violent husband.
Finally she left him, raised her two boys herself while working in factories and
now, sons grown, she has remarried and returned to Rhodos. This is where her
new husband wanted to retire.

She refilled my water bottles and we talked international girl talk about men
and women and life and courage. We had fun. We liked each other.

Later that afternoon, at just the right moment, after 72 K of riding, a seaside
restaurant appeared out of no-where. Nothing around. Nothing for miles. Just
this restaurant between the road and the sea. And it had a sign that said
"Pension". Hey, this is good. It was unbelievably cheap. My room overlooked
the water. The owner told me the story of her husband courting her, a story of
shy near-misses.

The waves were pounding in. Huge, heavy, relentless waves that sent spray
into the air and seemed to shake the earth. The sun caught the spray in a row
of airborne water-diamonds. I watched and listened and felt them and loved
the foreverness of waves, again, and noticed that I didn't ponder any more why
they draw me. They just do.

CLIMBING EVERY MOUNTAIN ON YOGURT AND HONEY

The next day the road was level for the first hour of riding and then I headed up into the hills. The hills got steeper, bigger and rockier. It felt like I was working my way up some giant steps. A cool front had moved in and the sky was low, dark and threatening. It was still early in the day and I was a bit chilly and I had more climbing ahead. I needed a boost. I stopped at a restaurant perched on a dramatic point over the road with the Med far below. When I heard that the climbing had just begun, that settled it. I ordered Greek coffee. The famous Greek coffee.

But I also wanted something to eat. The young woman suggested yogurt and honey. Sounded a bit lame and healthy to me but she was convinced I'd like it — and was she right. This yogurt was so rich and smooth and wonderful. Not like yogurt at all. Think ice cream. The honey was clear and thick and golden and full of flavor and was poured over the top like a rich sundae. One of the restaurant cats sat in my lap and licked yogurt off my spoon, much to the annoyance of the owner and the delight of the young woman and me. Coffee and treats and cats. Beat this. Leaving was not easy.

As it was, I was glad I had chosen to fortify myself. Even loaded with coffee I felt lame. I felt like the caffeine never seemed to kick in. The problem was, I would climb and then go down again, climb again and then down again. It was a never ending string of mountains, up and over, up and over. Visual drama, rock cliffs, picture-perfect views, little traffic — and more climbing. In a cleft in the mountains I asked tourists going the other way if I faced more climbing.

Yes.

One more climb?

Pause. More than that.

A lot?

Yes.

I...see...Thank you.

I prepared myself to spend the rest of my life climbing these mountains.

I was so tired by the time I pulled into a place to stay I could barely walk. But feeling like a hero, of course. Always like a hero. A she-colossus. One of the Seven Wonders of the World.

IN TRANSIT

SINGAPORE

I was keynote speaker at the annual conference of New Zealand Public Health Nurses in early November. But I wanted to get a look at Singapore on the way there. Just the word "Singapore" conjured up exotic images and international allure. It was also a Southeast Asian anomaly: clean and organized. I wanted to have a look. So I booked the flight while I was meeting with Canadian Embassy officials in Ankara, the capital of Turkey. Then I flew from Ankara, changed planes in Istanbul and then on to Abu Dhabi and Singapore.

I loved even just touching down at those exotic names. I loved phoning home and saying, "I'm flying to Singapore tomorrow." And sounding casual. I hear that some travelers get jaded. Maybe they just don't phone home enough.

It was raining when I got to Singapore and I was only going to be there for three days so I checked my bike at the airport and took a taxi into town planning to "do" Singapore on foot.

THIS IS EXACTLY — WHERE?

It was the only time I couldn't figure out where I was. I knew I was in the biggest bed that I had ever been in, in my life. It was a daunting task to get the whole thing slept in. I knew I was in a luxurious hotel. Consciousness returned slowly.

Now where am I? I was on a plane recently. I flew for quite a while. So I'm not in Russia any more, no, no way this is Russia. Not this kind of luxury. And I don't think I'm in Turkey.

Am I in Hong Kong? I don't think so. I don't think Hong Kong was in my plans.

Malaysia? Thailand? Indonesia? None of those seem to ring a bell.

Where was my plane going? That last plane I was on? Why can't I remember?

The dispossessed. The international traveler who doesn't know where they are any more. Finally I got up and looked out the window.

Singapore!

I'm out in the world. I could have been anywhere. It really could have been any of those other places. I am half way around the world for Chrissake. This is the best.

Much as I hated to limit my luxuriating in that bed I couldn't wait to get out there walking around in Singapore. How many songs and movies and stories take place in Singapore? And now it was part of my movie.

INTERNATIONAL FEAST

Singapore caters to affluent tourists. I was in a mid-range tourist hotel and breakfast and dinner smorgasbords were sumptuous. Breakfast included the western standards: eggs, bacon, sausages, toast, french toast, cereal, yogurt, croissant, buns, pastries, cheese, fresh fruit, scrambled eggs, Eggs Benedict. Plus, on the same spread, they offered Asian dishes: rice, noodles, soups, spicy sausage, stir fried vegetables and meat, exotic seafood and shellfish, things I could not identify. Likewise at dinner there was a huge spread of both kinds of food cooked to perfection.

Exotic oriental food was everywhere in the streets and malls. The food was unlike that in any western Chinese restaurant. Sometimes it was hard to tell what animal parts were on the plate. Fish, unusual vegetables swimming in broth, being gobbled down all over town. The locals didn't eat rice with these meals but white rice was available everywhere.

The only eating problem in Singapore is when to stop.

MY MOVIE

I was learning to accept that I did not have a partner and probably never would. I wrote to my sister, "Whatever force is directing this movie, it is probably the only movie I'll be in. I want to live it fully instead of regretting that it isn't a different movie."

AIR CONDITIONING

I finally got to a truly tropical country and was faced with dreaded air conditioning. The hotel and the stores were chilly. I could not turn off the air conditioning in my hotel room. I resented having to choose between carrying a sweater and shivering. I came to the tropics to be hot for heaven sake. So I was happiest walking the streets in the warm rain. I loved the luxury of being wet and warm.

DOWN TO THE MALL FOR REFLEXOLOGY

I was warned not to be lulled into manicures, pedicures and facials "out there". The sanitary standards were just too shaky. Well my toenails were a mess. And I had promised to treat myself to pedicures, as required, all over the world. No point in traveling on a bike with nail polish remover. Plus, traveling alone, I got touch deprived. It was a nice opportunity to have someone touch me, without my wanting to hit him. (Hers never pushed me to that.)

Singapore was full of multi-story malls. Most of them were open in the middle with walkways around the succeeding stories above. These walkways had rows of shops around them: restaurants, professional offices, clothes, art, jade, gold, precious stones, porcelain, wicker, furniture, linens, specialized health centres and reflexology.

I went in, washed my feet at the little stand, and reclined in one of the contoured chairs in a row along the wall. It induced instant relaxation. The reflexologist wrapped each foot in its own warm, tiny towel. He watched me carefully. The other reflexologists watched me. The other customers watched me. One of those westerners thinking this is a soothing foot massage? Well I had had reflexology before and knew that it could feel like ground glass in your feet. I was able to do that trick of relaxing under the discomfort that his fingers probed and emerged feeling refreshed and rejuvenated.

Up a couple of levels, I browsed some embroidered Chinese linen. Table clothes and napkins with blue flowers, pink or yellow flowers. They were so cheap I felt sheepish nabbing them up. I bought sets for everyone I know. The proprietor bundled them up and I trotted over to the post office and mailed them home.

The next day I had a facial at a hairdresser in the same mall. It was fun to watch how the hairdressers there carried on the same banter and had the same gestures as hairdressers everywhere. Turkey, Calgary, Paris airport, where do they all learn this stuff?

After our facials the woman on the other side of the curtain was leaving at the same time as me.

She said, "You are tired."

"Yes, I fell asleep."

"I know, You were snoring."

We giggled. We admitted how embarrassing that was, being caught snoring while having a facial. International beauty sprees. Just the girls, being the girls together. It felt nice to share this humbling self-exposure with someone from another culture, another country, another world.

"I was hoping you'd invite me up for a shower."

The guy seemed nice. Pleasant, friendly in an unpushy way, trustworthy. Grounded. We met in the tourism information office inside the famous Raffles Hotel. It was like a city within a city. Neither of us could find the even-more-famous hotel bar where the Singapore Sling was first created. Armed with fresh directions we went off together.

He owned a software company in the Midwestern USA and, from time to time, went out into the world to sell. He taught courses.

I remained composed when he took my hand and said grace over lunch. Some people like that sort of thing. After all, if you are going to believe in something, it is more admirable to live that belief instead of backgrounding it. Right?

It was fun to talk business and sales and travel and teaching. I had a good time. I took him to a tiny shop where he could buy postcards of lovely pastel paintings of the colonial buildings in Singapore. The Oriental shop owner had spoken to me with genuine regret about those buildings sinking into decay.

Then I said goodbye.

"Don't go."

"I have an appointment to have a facial."

"Can't we go up to your room?"

"Why would we go up to my room?"

"I thought you'd invite me to have a shower with you or something."

"Uh, I, uh, try not to do that with married men."

"Oh that. Oh I can explain that easily enough."

Yeah, I'll just bet you can buddy.

I fumed for days. I wished I had been rude. I toyed with phoning his wife but suspected that the slippery little weasel would get around that by saying I threw myself at him and was now getting revenge for him spurning me.

The son of a bitch. I still wish I'd taught him a lesson at the same time that I know those guys don't learn lessons. Mostly I resent that I had misread him so completely. Shit.

Dearest Father Almighty, thank you for our safe journeys and this bounty you have placed before us. And for this blond chick who might suck my cock after lunch.

HOME ON THE OTHER SIDE
OF THE WORLD

NEW ZEALAND

I wanted to include one of the "down under" countries in my trip. It was important to get to the southern hemisphere. New Zealand won hands down. New Zealand was the more manageable size of the two down-under countries. Plus, my sister and everyone else who had traveled there loved it. And New Zealand's high population of out-door, enthusiasts created the impression that drivers and services would be cycle-sensitive. Added to that, I had established a couple of business connections that, if they proved fruitful, would pave my way for getting back and teaching workshops and, of course, riding some more.

I flew Singapore Airlines to New Zealand. Do it for yourself some time. Singapore Airlines.

GOING HOME

What does it mean to go home? Even people who have never experienced a loving home are drawn to the idea of going home. What are all those layers of images, feelings, impressions, hopes, fantasies that we conjure up with the phrase going home?

The clouds parted and right there, just below them, was the shocking green that only happens in wet climates: Vancouver and fluorescent green Ireland. The sea was covered with whitecaps. Waves pounded on the rock cliffs, oddly silent from the airplane window. Tufts of mist were caught on rocks and crags along the coast.

The sight gave me a swelling, bursting feeling in my chest. My eyes filled with tears. Land-ho, after hours over an expanse of endless ocean. I was going home. I was going to a country where I had never been before and it was home. It was green, English-speaking and had a dollar currency and a British Empire heritage. Little did I think that would ever draw me. I was also sad to be leaving the height of adventure and going into the tame. Always that dot on the other side of the yin/yan circle. The pull of the opposite, counterbalanced from within. The richness of the contrast.

Off the plane in New Zealand, all the comfort and ease of a shared language and heritage surrounded me. So easy in customs. So easy at the tourist info booth in the airport. So easy chatting on the shuttle bus.

But for days after arriving I fought the urge to start every conversation by asking, "Do you speak English?"

GOING HOME FOREVER

The Maoris are not indigenous to New Zealand. They know that they have only been home in New Zealand for the last 300 years. They came from over the sea. No-one remembers where.

At the northern tip of New Zealand there are steep hills rising straight up out of the water. Not quite cliffs but steep. This is the big finger of land that points north to the rest of the world.

Sticking out from the side of the finger is a small, rocky point and just above the water, grows — or struggles more like it — a diminutive tree, bent and weathered. Maoris believe that when they die their souls go down into the ground and travel under the ground to that northern tip of New Zealand. Then their souls rise up through the roots of that tree and out the top of its branches to return home. Back to the forgotten homeland.

I felt the echo of other homelands wash over me as I stood and looked at this forlorn little tree with such a big job. It was a nice time to be alone with my thoughts, as so many traveling opportunities are. Alone I could feel those feelings echoing inside myself and touching off other feelings and images and thoughts and just be with them. Alone allowed me to feel it all. I knew that if I tried to talk about this, like describing a dream, all the richness and subtlety would drop away, all the wealth of things I could not capture in words, gone. Home.

THEY DIDN'T WANT TO GO HOME.

I chatted with two Australia women on a deserted beach. For four weeks they had been following their whims, their biological clocks, their inner spirits. The next day they returned home and immediately back to work. They dreaded it.

Living as travelers, they had learned a healthy pace. They learned to follow their instincts, to be in nature long enough to be nourished by it. They slept when tired. Ate when hungry. Trekked when curious. They had learned to enjoy mellow spaces between what they did. This would be no more. They knew that they would be forced back to an artificial pace. An imposed schedule, imposed priorities, all in a rush. They were grieving the loss of their freedom.

It would be so easy to end up pushing the river. Not going outside every day. No yoga. No aimlessness. No thinking. How do I prevent that? What can I hold onto from this trip? How can I stay changed?

300,000 YEAR OLD TREES

They are giants, like the redwoods are giants. And they are thousands of years old. They have a strange, primitive look to them with a tall, bare tree trunk and then a tuft of branches and leaves at the top, like a little duster. A giant duster. They were aggressively harvested by white settlers. A lumber goldmine. And burned down to get them outta' there for farming.

Then, when farmers worked the new land they found old Kauri trees that had fallen in swamps and bogs. The odd thing was that they had all fallen in exactly the same direction, sometimes a whole forest lying flat. The mystery was, what happened to these trees? Why were they lying down, all in the same direction? It has been suggested that a huge tidal wave swept them over all at once. Maybe an above-ground meteorite explosion. Who knows.

Carbon dating now indicates that these trees are 300,000 years old. And still workable wood. They are the oldest workable wood on the planet. Next stage is fossilized wood, which is 100,000 million years old.

ROAD WORRIER

I was intimidated about cycling in New Zealand. Too many hills. All steep. Even the small ones were steep. And the wind was a relentless gale — 70 kph plus, day after day. So I was spooked.

Each new country did this. Anxiety about the problems this one posed. People tried to dissuade me from riding in each place. Citizens in every country believed that their drivers were the worst in the world. Then, after overcoming the anxiety there, the next country had me thinking, "Yeah but this place has real problems." I worried until I started to ride.

I watched this in operation, the bisected ant-hill of worry. The worry was not productive. It held me back. It filtered my perceptions and clouded my judgement.

Often I eased in on an experimental basis. I'll just try a little riding. As an experiment. A test. I can stop any time. Shortly after: Hey, this is manageable/fine/great/awesome - whatever. Experiments not only got my own worrying off my back, they also got everyone else off my back. It's okay. She's just going to try it.

GENUINE NEW ZEALAND

The people in New Zealand had not yet grown an impersonal public relations veneer. Have a good day spoken with dead eyes by someone who doesn't give a damn about your day just doesn't happen in New Zealand. Kiwis made eye contact. They genuinely engaged with me. They shared some of themselves in a quiet, caring way. Gentle and genuine.

SUNSHINE ARCHITECTURE

As in Ireland, New Zealand architects have a healthy respect for letting in sunlight. Buildings have many large windows and most of them can be opened. I saw office windows open in downtown Auckland. The whole, big pane turned sideways so that one side of it jutted out from the building, five stories up, and the other side disappeared inside. Every sunny moment accessible.

ON THE MARAE

The Public Health Nurses Conference was being held on a Marae, a Maori meeting house. They dot New Zealand. People gathered on a Marae (you say "on" not "in" or "at") for several days and ate and slept together while settling a problem or burying the dead. There were specific traditions to be observed going onto a Marae and the father of one of the Maori nurses led us through them.

We waited at the edge of the property to be called on. A woman in Maori dress with a tattooed chin, chanted at the door, her hands tremoring at her sides. Rangi's Dad responded on our behalf. We gradually walked closer as this exchange continued back and forth. Inside there were long speeches in Maori and English, chanting, singing. We are coming together to be wiser together and we are being blessed to fulfill our purpose.

At the end of the first day of sessions we were bussed to dinner and returned to find the floor of the big, main room now covered with foam mattresses. Each had a quilt and pillow. There must have been fifty of us sleeping in the same room. Rumour had it that a night on a Marae was a sleepless one. I felt a reluctance to sink into that vulnerable state of sleep with so many people around, but the women settled quickly. All was quiet, just a few snores and a light left on at the end of the room.

SAFE HAVEN

Finally I got up the nerve. I went out there and rode and I came to terms with the hills and the wind — sort of.

I learned how the wind whipped around the contours in the landscape and around trees and bushes so that I was ready for it when it hit me full force after emerging from behind some windbreak or when it whistled down the wind-tunnel in a narrow valley. When I turned a corner and got hit by the wind head on, I learned to stay cheerful, philosophical, flexible. I learned to work with it. Cross-winds sometimes necessitated walking for stretches when I was blown off the road or blown into the traffic coming up behind me.

I learned to appreciate the beauty of the landscape and the warmth of the sun even if I was being blown to pieces. I continually reminded myself that I didn't need to rush into the wind and fight with it. I could relax and enjoy the good parts of the moment.

There it is, the not-to-be-pushed river.

But, whatever I did in my head, what a pleasure it was to get out of the damn wind. After a day fighting a gale, head on, I felt not only tired and dispirited, I felt like I needed comfort. I needed a home.

And, as my mother would say, The Lord will provide.

When I pulled up to Mac and Mo's Bed and Breakfast in Coopers Beach I was ready to stay a while. Mac was a retired fisherman and his forearms showed it. Years before, when he had complained to Mo that he couldn't get reliable hands on the boat, she said, "Why don't I come and be your mate?"

Off they went at 2 AM, night after night and they fished all-day. Mo got so that she could pretty much keep up with Mac. She pulled the fish off the row of hooks and laid them on trays as Mac reeled in the lines. They off-loaded at the dock at 10 or 11 at night and went home and fell into bed and got up at 2 AM and started again. Day after day until the weather was bad. Then they slept.

"Wasn't it cold out there?"

"Sometimes."

"How did you keep warm?"

"I cuddled up to him."

Now they run a bed and breakfast together. Mac does all the cooking. Always has. Hamburger, mashed potatoes, steamed cauliflower, zucchini, canned peaches and ice cream. To keep a leg of lamb tender, Mac cooks it covered, for five or even eight hours as low as 150 degrees.

On the livingroom radio set, Mo provides weather reports, three times a day, for all the boats in the area.

"Do you ever do the weather report, Mac?"

"Yeah, sure, sometimes. But they like to hear Maureen better 'n me."

Mac and Maureen also deliver milk twice a day, six days a week to neighbourhood houses and stores. They initially took it on to hand it over to one of Maureen's sons but he lost interest and they liked the early morning ritual and it didn't take them long so they just keep doing it. And they smoke fish and grow garden vegetables and help neighbors build things and solve problems.

They also monitor marine calls for help twenty-four hours a day. I asked Maureen how they sleep with the radio on. She said, "It's like having a baby in the next room. You only hear the things that matter."

And when a boat disappears, their livingroom becomes the search headquarters. The police move in there and the work goes on around the clock until they find them and bring them in.

"Someone has to do it. The guys are counting on us. Because we know these waters and we know the guys, we can help them out. The guys appreciate it. They know there isn't much money in it so they bring around fish from time to time."

Mac and Maureen are an institution. "We're good mates. We like working together."

What better harbor to pull into for a few days of comfort for my body, mind and soul?

That's where I noticed that somewhere out there I left the eye-twitch behind. Rode away from it.

THE FOOD BLANKET

I was turning to food for comfort and warmth. It's no wonder I needed comfort. I had been harassed by Turks, caught in thunderstorms and gales, scaled mountains, entered a city with blood all over my crotch, dragged my bike up stairs and over gravel, I had been thwarted by Russian bureaucrats, dragged off the train in Poland and still forged on alone.

I eat chocolate? I need comfort? Fair enough. Right on. It's like when one is nursing a baby. That was not the time to aim for Vogue body craziness. So I went with it. Mars Bars, Coffee Crisps, Mackintosh's Creamy Toffee, even chocolates.

As a result, I was getting chubby. That wasn't what I wanted. I wanted to go home from this amazing trip looking trim and tight and svelte and a million bucks. And that means skinny. I love skinny. I tried to find other ways to comfort myself. I could see that adventure needed to be balanced with comfort. If I got comfort by staying warm and sheltered at Mac & Mo's would I need less chocolate? How long would it take? I didn't stay long enough to find out.

LESSONS THE WIND TEACHES

Little soft zephyrs, howling tugging gales, moving air. What is it? What makes it move? Where is it moving to? Confronted by a relentless headwind I pondered over and over what was making my day so difficult, what made me feel so victimized. Just moving air. It was rushing to somewhere that there was less air or the air was colder, or thinner or something.

It carried new weather patterns and new temperatures. It changed the patterns in the sky and altered the light around me. It was huge. It affected me enormously but had no will, no intent, no collective consciousness. It just was. I may try to characterize wind in order to deal with it, but there was no character there. It just happened.

SAILING WITH MOM AND DAD

In New Zealand you are always close to the coastline but you rarely get a road that travels beside it for long. It wasn't a priority when roads were built. The shoreline was, and still is, unstable land, usually farmland, high above the sea. Chunks erode off and drop into the sea all the time. One way to get my fill of the sea was sailing.

Russell is a holiday town on the northeast coast. A friend of mine honeymooned there. Small, full of boats, history and places to stay. I sailed off Russell on Pip and Oliver's yawl. Like Mom and Dad, they had been sailing for years and worked smoothly as a team. Oliver, as my Dad had, sailed from boyhood and knew his boat, tides, currents and winds instinctively. Pip was completely comfortable crewing, as was my mother. I noticed the effortless teamwork as they cast off and rigged the sails. My voice caught when I told them that it was like sailing with my Mom and Dad.

It was a dramatic, dark, windy day. I loved the feel of the waves lifting the boat. And the silence. Just the waves slapping the hull. When I took the helm I wondering off course, the wind blew my hair and jacket, the boat leaned in the wind and tears ran down my cheeks. I love you Dad. I love the sea. I love the sparkle of the sun on the waves. I love this old technology. All over the world, sailors catch the wind. I am on the top of the world now, down at the bottom. My life circle, connected to my parents' lives, connected to human civilizations, connected, flying free, complete.

FEELINGS

A travelogue of camcorded locations doesn't dazzle anyone. It has been done. You can always see it better on Discovery Channel. But to be touched inside, to savour, to cry and laugh and gasp and open yourself to the feelings that are evoked by the world around you, that is a journey for you and your Other Traveler. Whether it is around the world or a commute to downtown, all the journeys are richer when we live the whole rainbow as we travel them.

RIDING ON THE OTHER SIDE

New Zealand traffic drives on the left side. Got that? Not complicated. It's the opposite side of the road. You just switch. But the body doesn't just switch. The problem is like the problem of getting on an escalator that isn't working. The body has been trained to flow into the movement of an escalator so that when you step onto one that is turned off, when you need to treat it like stairs, the body isn't convinced. So you get that funny, flat feeling when you step onto the stationary escalator that reminds you the body has it's own memory. It still assumes forward movement. However many times you learn to prepare your body carefully for that non-movement, it has its own plan. You are not accessing that body memory.

Just so, switching sides. It is fun to watch this body memory at work as a million impressions, habits, gestures, assumptions and perspectives surface on the other side. Turning signals seem inappropriate over there, (which arm do you use?), shoulder checking leaves you not sure what you are looking for and going around a round-a-bout the opposite way throws several layers of assumptions out the window. "Everything is the opposite. Just do the opposite to what is natural." But now nothing is natural and I can't remember what the old habit used to be. I was messing with automatic pilot and it was not accessible the same way memory is accessible.

I had stepped into a mirror and found complicated, underground wiring. It taught me how deep the roots of automatic pilot go.

LESSONS FROM LANDSCAPES

Sometimes a scene was so perfect that it nurtured me just to see it. A pasture below me with a hill at the other side, a little creek cutting through it, a willow tree, some rocks that the sheep have nibbled around so it looked trimmed and cared for. All covered with a layer of vivid green. A bit of wind barely sweeping the willow branches. Perfect. To be carried with me forever.

When I stood quietly, alone, leaning on my bike, watching this piece of the world, I opened myself to it and could feel it becoming mine. I rested my eyes on places in it and felt them in my body. Felt it everywhere in there. My body sighed, relaxed, rested.

I'M READY FOR YOU

By New Zealand I was savvy enough to see trouble coming. The Bed &
Breakfast owner pulled up at the ferry dock and offered to carry my bags up the
hill to his place. It was noon and he had the earmarkings of an alcoholic —
purple-veined nose, stale-alcohol breath, slurred speech, cavalier toss of the
head, theatrical gestures of bon vivant. Oh dear. Where was the wife?

It turned out she was playing tennis and he didn't know when she would be
back. So I locked the bathroom door when I went in for a bath. I usually didn't
bother. He knew I was going in for a bath. Surely, in a civilized house, it doesn't
require a lock to keep someone out of the bathroom? Surely a sane adult who
knows I am having a bath doesn't require physical restraint to stay out? This
time, a tiny doubt. Click, locked.

And it didn't surprise me when I heard him try to open the door (rattle,
rattle, shake, rattle) as I sat in my naked glory in the bathtub.

When it didn't yield he said, through it, "There's all kinds of bath salts and
soaps and things. I can show you."

"Thanks, but I've found them and I'm fine."

But I wasn't fine. I was fuming. Who does he think he is? Should I say
something? Ignore it? Rage at him? I was annoyed that the incident now
preoccupied me. The idiot didn't deserve a nano-second of my brain time.

When I emerged I said, "It is just as well I locked the door. If you had come
barging in while I was in the bath I would have been furious."

"Oh," he scoffed," I was just helping you find things."

Thanks buddy, I don't need your help.

EARTH OVENS

When I was a child I pretended that I was a woman of some ancient, nomadic
tribe, somewhere, who squatted on the ground to cook. What did that do for
me? Why did I like that? It felt so right. Squatting in a friend's basement I was
really on a hot, windy plain — in African? I felt connected to something
timeless. Patting flat cakes on a stone. Putting them on the fire. I feel that same
connection when I cook on a campfire.

Traditional Maoris' cooking was in a pit. A flat-top pyramid of logs was
arranged above it and large stones were placed on top of that. The logs were
burned hot, heating the stones that gradually fell down into the pit below.
Then the wrapped food was placed among the stones and it was all covered
with earth and left several hours to cook.

Some Maoris still cook their Christmas turkey this way.

Touch the earth domesticity, or what? I want to build one in my back yard.

NO SOUP, NO COOKED VEGETABLES

The food in New Zealand still carries the taint of English cooking: starch and
grease. There are tearooms everywhere but they aren't quaint, little spots with
linen tablecloths. Some are like a corner store with a couple of tables in them
but more usually they are tiny restaurants with a small menu of sandwiches,
fries, meat pies, sausage rolls, pasties, muffins, scones, buns, dessert bars and

pie. A few have yogurt and fruit. In the spring, even if the weather is cold, none of these places have soup. In fact I found it impossible to get soup, my favourite cool-weather meal, without going into a city.

Unfortunately the bread in New Zealand is also disappointing. Not much flavor, texture or variety. Think Wonder Bread.

You can get Marmite in all the stores and for those of us who love it, it is a godsend. What the heck is Marmite? Yes, well Marmite: thick, salty, paste made from fermented soybeans. It is spread thinly on bread or crackers. Sort of like concentrated soy sauce. You hate it or love it. Now you can get it in North America. Before that, New Zealand Moms used to mail giant jars of it to their children who were "away". Awesome on toast with peanut butter.

MOTELS

I loved cruising along, Aha, motel. Yessiree, just what we want. Motel. Looks like it'll do the trick.

The price included room and breakfast. What's the price without breakfast? What time is breakfast served? What time is the sun up? If I sleep in and decide that I want breakfast before I leave can I pay for it then? (In Russia there would be a problem with that. There would be a rule.)

Nice little 1950s rooms with twin beds, chenille spreads, arborite or veneer furniture and hot water bottles on the beds. No bathtub. Except for the most expensive hotels, bathtubs are rare in New Zealand accommodation. A luxury that I missed.

There is no central heating in motel rooms, hotel rooms or houses. Even a house built last month does not have central heating. And windows are left open all the time. In New Zealand they live in fresh air, whatever the temperature.

I was beat when I pedaled into Dargaville. I cruised looking for the centre of town and couldn't find any accommodation. But I did find a couple jogging and they owned a motel further down the road. With a bathtub. Just go in. The door is unlocked. We'll be back soon.

No sooner did I get under the overhang of their roof when another marvelous rainshower blew in. Apricot light from the setting sun slanted in under the clouds, flooded the garden golden. Dripping, golden, rain-bowed garden. This must have been the sixth squall of the day and the first that I was sheltered from. But I still had to stand outside and watch. I knew a bath was waiting.

NOT THAT AGAIN

Listening to music in the hotel dining room, I hear a song that I have waltzed to. I love it. My soft underbelly. A wave passes over me, sick with longing. Fear, doubt, yearning, a poisonous brew. I'll have to find a way to deal with this.

Ballroom dancers imposed rigorous standards of slimness and prettiness on women. They talked of women's clothes, bodies, weight, current partner, past partners, partner squabbles, inflated opinions of themselves, petty, spiteful, shallow nasty dissection of the surface of everyone. People are dying out here folks! Not to mention that we are all going to grow old. Do we simply cease to exist at 80? 70? 60? Our surfaces are going to wrinkle and shrivel and spread and drop. Are we then without value? Non-existent? What about some inner issues?

I so desperately wanted to go home different and was afraid that I would not. Different in what way? No longer afraid of the dancers' opinions? Never self-doubting? Consistently guided by my inner wisdom? Calmly floating above the pettiness? Would I ever be able to glide in, dance and glide out, without getting any on me?

Sitting there in the dining room I remembered Granny's lesson: that the here-and-now is all that I can influence. Those bigger changes don't happen because I make a decision to change them. I can only change the here and now. I felt myself relax. At this moment I am sitting in the hotel dining room in Auckland eating perfect carrot soup and looking at the rainstorm whipping outside. What could be nicer? This is now. I can relish the music and the bittersweet layers of memory and emotion that it touches off in me. Where it will take me next, I'll see next.

BACK TO THE UNIVERSE

Even on the road I could lose touch with the universal truths that were brushing up against me, what business calls The Big Picture. When I was repeatedly rushing to appointments I only thought of business. When I was cold I only thought of getting warm. But when I was on a bus for a couple of hours and I plugged in Conquest of Paradise on my Walkman, I immediately returned to all my life lessons, all my gentle insights, awareness of the pain, beauty, magic that wove through my journey. I could sit for hours, looking, through my tears, out the bus window. I was reconnected with the web of pain. Sad and happy and grounded.

MAGIC ALERT: IT CAN HAPPEN ANY TIME

It would have been nice to sleep in. Drizzle and cool and dark overcast. But I wanted to catch the ferry to Paihia before the roads got busy and I wasn't happy with the place I was staying so I suited up and headed out.

As the tiny ferry pulled out of the harbor a pod of thirty-five dolphins swam alongside, jumping out of the water beside us. They would surface on the side of the boat and dive down under the bow. The young skipper said they were playing with the boat, bow riding. They ride the pressure wave like underwater surfing. He said the dolphins were usually in the bay somewhere and people pay $85 to go out and watch them, if they could find them. I just leaned over the side in the rain and watched. They were fast and strong and knew this game.

Mac had said that he and the other fishermen were protective of the dolphins. "I would always help out a dolphin in trouble." In the summer they would take their children out with them and park them on an island to enjoy the day. They would swim with the dolphins, scrub them with brushes. "The dolphins like that. They like the attention."

NEW ZEALAND SKIES SPEAK

Over and over I saw dramatic skies that didn't seem possible in nature. Some skies looked like they were lighted for a movie. I entertained the possibility that El Greco might not have been imagining those boiling grey skies in his paintings. When I looked straight up into the action-packed clouds they seemed to pull up, away from me. Did that really happen? Was it an optical illusion? Why did it happen? Who could answer that?

I saw clouds so black that no light penetrated and they turned the landscape below dark and brooding. Yet between those clouds, brilliant sunshine made the ground below jump forward in contrast. The high winds sent the clouds ripping across the sky fast enough to be alarming, or funny. And below them the sunbelts and black belts whisked along as well. It made the landscape ripple as the highlighted view leapt forward and then dropped into darkness. All moving so fast they created a zooming feeling, like fast, time-lapse photography happening around me.

I WISH I COULD DO THAT

They hear I am traveling on a bicycle, alone. They hear I am out to discover the world. I am fifty. It is time. Their faces become wistful. They all use the same words: "I wish I could do that."

Where does I-wish-I-could-do-that come from? What do we wish we could do? Walk away from the stuff that we expend energy acquiring and looking after? Being free? Free of what? Becoming explorers? Following our instincts? What holds us back? Do we make it harder for ourselves than it needs to be? Dare we risk grabbing for fun? Adventure?

People magazine doesn't showcase a spirit quest. Movies give us action heroes not inner heroes. We don't have many stories of people who successfully attained peace and wisdom. Where do we turn to get inspiration when we wish we could do that?

HARD WORK

I felt chilly, battered and tired. I had been on the bike four and a half hours. I plugged in my Walkman to give me a lift. A great ABBA song. Yes, music helps. I forget that there are parts of this that are just hard work. I forget that.

JOY AND BRUCE SET UP HOUSE

Looking for a telephone to call ahead about an appointment, I came upon a caravan campground. These are common in New Zealand and follow a pattern. They are usually close to a beach but not necessarily on the beach. There is an open field with picnic tables in it and a central building with kitchens, laundry room and bathrooms that have showers. These are spotlessly clean. Then on a bench of land above this is a single row of simple rooms. Bunk beds without bedding, a table and a chair. You use the washroom below.

This one at Whatuwhiwhi (pronounced Photo-fifi) was newly built, still a work-in-progress. Joy and Bruce decided they wanted to work together and set up something that they could continue doing into retirement. So they built it from scratch. While it is still getting going they live in a Quonset hut that will eventually be for tools and maintenance machinery. Now it is big and sparkling, brand new metal. One big metal room, fully carpeted, with a television, king-sized bed, kitchen along one wall, open shelves, windows on the ends and things stacked up tidily.

"When it rains you can't hear each other talk."

GEARS

I learned that cycling in New Zealand's brutal terrain, it was best to go down to my lowest low gear when I started to struggle, not wait until things got worse. Then I needed to avoid the impulse to try and power up the hill because the hill would probably be long and possibly get steeper at the top. So I was best to focus on not hurrying. This was critical. It kept me out of the anaerobic zone, as did rest stops.

I also learned that I love the elegance of highest gear. Just gliding along with maximum efficiency. A tailwind worked nicely with this, but then find me a time when a tailwind doesn't work nicely.

WILDLIFE

I entered the lives of the animals as gently as possible. I so much wanted to see them, to get close to them. I didn't want them to be afraid of me. But I knew they would be. I would have given anything to be able to touch the lambs. Once in Ireland I had picked up a lamb after extricating its head from between two poles in a fence. However soothing I tried to be, it was terrified of me. But later the same day I was rewarded to find a pet lamb at a restaurant, eating the plants in the garden. It was quite happy being picked up. I could feel the lanolin in its thick coat, with the oddly tiny lamb beneath it.

I wasn't so lucky in New Zealand, so I studied them from afar. Sheep sociology justifies the expression "like a bunch of sheep", although cows are just the same. One sheep decides danger and the rest buy in and one decides it's safe now, we can stop running and the problem is forgotten. Often Mom gave the signal. Mom knew all. Mom was the Source and it was perfect just to be around her. Lambs loved to slide in under her belly to find a teat. They slide in on their knees, like a home run, with their heads turned up. They probably didn't give up this pleasure voluntarily.

There was a lamb by the fence. Mom, further back in the paddock, saw me and called the lamb over to her. The lamb positively frisked over with glee. Ah to be so thrilled to be called by one's mother.

Then a second mother, with twins, eyed me suspiciously as I approached. When she lead them off the two bounced around her bumping into her. There seemed to be some clubby joy in just being together. I didn't like the thought of them being separated.

I unwittingly frightened a pair of birds that looked like quail, from a roadside bush. They took off more or less in the same direction but they both ran in loops. So they would run on a course away from me but toward each other, bump into each other, turn and run away from each other and then loop back toward each other until they bumped into each other and ran apart again.

Over and over, in a flurry, they bumped away. I felt badly for causing their panic but caught myself giggling at how badly they fled.

I was appalled that the farmers were cutting off the tails of cows. They left pathetic ragged stumps that the cows twitch ineffectually to try, hopelessly, to ward away the insects. Whose stupid idea of animal husbandry was that? It bothered me so much I stopped watching cows and watching cows had always been a favourite pastime for me.

On the northeast coast of the South Island I stopped beside the road to watch the wild seals below. They were sunning themselves on rocks that went down into the sea. The pecking order was actively at work with ongoing squabbles and hurried escapes. Some of it looked vicious from above. A few stayed out of it by napping in less desirable real estate, far above the crowded water's edge. They slept through. Others ended up pursuing and being pursued into the water where they darted effortlessly in contrast to their awkward land lumbering. What a joy just to witness these creatures living a seal life.

In trendy downtown Auckland the shops and cafes had giant windows that were left open even if it was raining. The birds flew in and out. No-one seemed to notice. I saw a sparrow perching on the edge of a pan of rice at the steam table in a health food restaurant. Head into the rice and then it flew straight out the window over and over. The young man working there made a lackadaisical attempt to shoo it away a few times. Unsanitary? Probably. Wonderful? Uhum.

On a highway that curved up and down like a low roller coaster I came upon a mother bird, bigger than a quail but the same shape. She was surrounded by a cluster of chicks so compact that they looked like her skirt. The chicks were smaller than domestic chicks, each a tiny fluff ball. It looked like there were easily a dozen of them, is that possible? And they moved perfectly with her. When she darted forward they did too and stopped on a dime when she stopped. Collective conscious.

Anyway, they were crossing the highway. They set off and then stopped in the middle of the first lane. I had already stopped to watch and reduce the pressure they felt from me. I was holding my breath. I gasped, "Oh no, don't stop there. Keep going, Keep going." If a car had come over the little hump in the road they would have been nailed without the driver even knowing what they had done. Stop, start, stop, pause, rush, stop. Miraculously they made it and scuttled into the undergrowth, a mother and her skirt. I stood in awe. They were so beautiful. I was touched to have seen them. I wanted to touch them. As always, I was left hungry for some more.

MORE WILDLIFE

It was a magnificent morning. I'd been on the road since first sunlight and, being Sunday, traffic was light. It was warm. What more could I need? It was still early when I approached Hawera, a town behind Mount Egmont.

I saw a man standing at the racetrack stables, just standing looking out at the morning and at me, hands on his hips. I turned, nodded, said good morning as I usually do and turned back to the road.

That man doesn't have any clothes on. The sun was slanting low behind him so he was backlit but when I glanced back he had turned sideways and displayed the tattletale silhouette of an erection. And oddly enough he seemed to have a big brimmed hat on his head with what looked like netting that the sun shone through around his face. Right enough. Naked as a jaybird.

I turned back to the road ahead and just kept riding. Well it was harmless enough. A bit irritating to have him in my face but I had the sense that he was as startled as I was. We do have our oddities don't we?

However as I got further into town I developed a sense of responsibility. What if there were problems of someone exposing themselves to children in this town? What if there was a serious sexual offender? What if no-one had any trail to the guy? I began to feel it was my duty to provide this link. Damen Runyen would say, solid citizen.

I explained at the police station that I wasn't concerned about this matter myself but I wanted to pass it on in case it provided some useful information to them regarding a bigger problem. The policeman wrote it all down. We both agreed that people have weird habits and who were we to mess with them or ask awkward questions. But he would take a mosey out there and see what was going on and who was around.

SHELTER I

It had been a strenuous riding day. Roads got busier as the sun rose in the sky and everyone else got out of bed and hit the road. I hate it when that happens. Some flat terrain and then hills, down and up again to cross gullies. The wind kept building and after six hours I was worn down. It was warm but the wind was fierce and cold. I was pleased to be settled into Carlyle Motor Camp early in the afternoon.

I had the thrill of doing my laundry in a wringer washing machine there. Hand laundry didn't cut it, let me tell you. I was able to get out some of the dirt but plenty stayed in. So everything got gradually greyer and grubbier. Now I could do laundry. I remembered my mother doing laundry in a wringer.

I remember the dangers of the wringer. This device could suck you up from across the room and roll you flat into a cookie before you could say jack robinson. I had never operated a wringer myself.

Kids playing house couldn't have had more fun. I time traveled back to the forties and became post-war woman. Then, I became eternal woman hanging my laundry on the clothesline in the wind. All the women, all the centuries they have stood in the wind hanging up clothes to dry. My connection to forever.

But once finished I wanted a sheltered place to sit outside and write. And it was the kiddies' play area that provided it. Built into the inside of a horseshoe-shaped hill, the grove of trees was sheltered behind the contour of the windward hill. It had a tiny, children's picnic table in the sun and out of the wind. Around me, tall pampas grass and evergreens and behind me swings, a boat made of logs with a steering wheel and throttle lever settled into the bark shavings, beside it a lookout fort. Child heaven and my heaven. I could sit in there and write and watch the vegetation a few feet away bending and flapping while I got the occasional light zephyr. If I stepped a few feet outside this magic place I was tugged at by the wind.

A pair of beautiful tiny birds landed in front of me on the grass. Grey bodies, red heads, dark brown wingtips with a startling, bright yellow dot mid wing. Tiny, tiny. Many amazing birds thriving in New Zealand.

Life was rich and full. The wind spoke of letting go. Of passing change. Of the fact that I control nothing.

I wrote in my journal: I am in N Z. I am plotting a new way to live and earn money when I go home.

SHELTER II

It was an interesting day from the start. Just as the couple at the seal-stop had predicted the day before, the wind had shifted and it was cold, windy and raining when I woke. East wind. At first it was fine, misty rain but it was dense and persistent enough to have me soaked through in an hour. I was wearing my rain jacket with the hood pulled up over my helmet. Hands, face and around my neck (Oh no!) were soaked by the rain. Likewise, I was soaked from the hips down. And inside my jacket I was wet from either leakage or perspiration. It all had the same effect. Cold and wet. The temperature was dropping.

The first 15 K of the day's ride was along the rocky coast with waves pounding beside me. It was gorgeous and would have been breathtaking in sun and heat. In fact, it was breathtaking in the mist and drizzle with the high-saturation colour of an overcast sky. But I couldn't appreciate it and that irritated me. I tried to take a couple of pictures but I was too cold.

I went through two short tunnels where the steep hills humped over the road and down to the water. Both were single-lane with separate tunnels for each direction of traffic. In the second I had a huge transport truck ahead of me and a car behind. Exiting, I waved my appreciation to the car driver for not trying to overtake me in the tunnel. As the road widened and the car pulled alongside the passengers waved and smiled supportively. Thank you. Yes, that helps.

After an hour I put my hood under my helmet which cut down on the wind whistling around my ears but it was too late. My hands and feet were already goners. I was slow and unhappy. Every pedal was a struggle. And I passed a sign saying 182 K to Christchurch, not 132 as I had thought. Hmm.

I minimized moving anything but my pedaling legs. If I moved my head it reminded me my neck was cold. Moving my fingers reminded me my gloves were sodden and cold. Opening my front bag drenched everything inside. Every movement just rubbed more cold wet stuff against my recoiling body.

I started the first of three climbs to get over a mountain range. I was slow but decided I could quit any time. I also decided that it was a tea or coffee day and I needed it soon. I dreaded downhills. They super-chilled me. Climbing to the second summit I came to a road-crew.

One of them rolled down his truck window as I pulled up. No cars, no buildings, just the road crew and me.

I have two questions. What's the forecast and how far to get a cup of coffee?

He grinned. The forecast is not good, This is going to get worse. By this afternoon, thunderstorms.

And the wind?

Well, that's not good either. It is moving around to the south. (South, as in Antarctica.) You're heading straight into it and it'll get stronger.

For some reason that gave me a perverse going-into-the-worst thrill.

And a cup of coffee? I was preparing myself to not be disappointed if he told me it would be 10 K to get a cup of coffee.

He said, 60 K to the next cup of coffee.

Sixty. Six-tee. I couldn't belief it. But I couldn't risk not believing it. When hypo-thermia threatens, throw yourself at the mercy of the locals. Farmhouse here we come.

No-one was home at the first one and by the time I got to the door I could taste it. The house was lovely, a lonely little place with a lawn tennis court and a croquet court. Civilization just like, what Kiwis call, back home.

The next place I came upon was weird. It was a large, rambling combination of buildings sort of attached to each other, with some junk cars out in the back. The front area looked as if it might have been a highway restaurant in a prior life. Now it was deserted and I could see a jumble of plywood and discarded furniture in there. But an old Land Rover parked at the back gave me a feeling that there were classy adventurers in the area. As I pulled up I had second thoughts. It was looking very beat up. There were three freshly killed young rabbits on the doorstep. Repulsion and Charles Manson flitted through my mind.

I knocked tentatively and rehearsed a benign request. On the other side of the glass door, walking toward me was a huge man. His hair was shaved to half-way up the sides of his head and above that he had an unruly mane of red hair. He was carrying a gun as he walked toward me. "Hmm. This will be interesting."

However, I had a sense that it was okay. There must have been subtle cues that balanced off that apparent danger.

"Would it be possible for me to buy a cup of coffee from you?" I was standing dripping and shivering. No explanation was necessary.

"Sure. Come on in by the fire." There could have been whips hanging on the walls and a stack of Pop Sadism on the coffee table and I would have gone in to be by that fire. I peeled off wet layers and spent the next hour standing in front of the fire turning front, side, back, other side, front again, re-arranging my clothes draped on chairs and piles of wood to try and get some of them dry.

He had two boys, about seven and eleven and they were making paper airplanes and flying them with great skill. It was lovely to watch. He and his boys lived up there, one learning by correspondence and the other bussed into the school in town. They would have made a wonderful photo essay, this off-centre, mountain family, but taking pictures would have spoiled the gentle relationship we were forming.

He was cleaning his rifle and explained that he didn't eat much meat himself but on a lovely rainy morning like today he enjoyed going out and shooting rabbits to feed his dog and cat. I liked that. That he appreciated the beauty of the rain. He had nice values, the solo dad. Limited eye contact but nice values.

I felt a little awkward because no tea was forthcoming. Finally I asked if he felt comfortable if I made it. He said fine but the "siz" would have to boil. The "siz" is the weird little hot water tank that New Zealanders have mounted on kitchen walls. So his sons fired up the siz and I returned to the fire. Eventually he put away his rifle cleaning gear and did a bit of general tidying and then made a pot of strong tea.

I was enjoying all this, particularly being in front of the fire but after three strong, honey-sweetened cups of tea, I had no more excuse to hang around. My gloves were still soaking and the wrists of my jacket still wet, but off I went. Now bigger drops, serious, steady rain. But the tea had taken effect. Without milk in it, it was hard on my stomach and made me feel like I was going to throw up. But I really didn't care. I was travelling well. I could envision myself leaning over to the side, being sick, and just keeping on pedaling. That's how casual caffeine made me. I didn't need my lowest gears any more. I had plenty of energy. And I simply wasn't cold. Wet? So what? I was fine. Awesome.

I entertained myself with the mental movie of an unfolding relationship with the perfect man for me. I shamelessly engineered every facet to match me and my situation to a T. It was fun and satisfying and entertained me for several hours. In the first town I came to, (yes, he was right, 60 K) I bought soup, cookies, snacks and then paid $60 to get the only motel room with a bath - a family suite: two bedrooms, huge lounge (livingroom) and dining room, big working kitchen and a bath. The bathtub was teeny but I could get most of me submerged in hot water if I left my legs out. Later I worked at the table and watched it continue pouring outside. The space heater in the lounge was drying my things. I start tomorrow, whatever it brings, with bone-dry clothes. The tea probably kept me awake later than otherwise but I was relishing every moment of being inside. Who cares if I'm not sleeping. I'm warm and dry.

THE MILKY WAY PERSPECTIVE

I was tired of climbing hills so I decided to walk and stretch out my legs for a while. I wanted to listen to the wind instead of my panting. I wanted to watch the hills instead of staring down at the road surface as I labored, bent over my handle bars. The hills looked like they were covered with green velvet. That's the only reason that I noticed the flowers. They were growing on a pile of gravel beside the highway. Periwinkle blue flowers, low and close to the gravel. A little ground cover. And beside them, tiny bright orange flowers. A passing car wouldn't know they were there. I wouldn't have noticed them on my bike, struggling up the hill.

There they were, just quietly growing there. They had a toehold in the gravel. Seeds had sprouted. They bloomed and their blooms got covered with fine dust from the passing cars and trucks. Then it rained and they were washed off again.

I stopped and leaned on the seat of my bike looking down at them. I knew that in the whole scheme of the universe I was no more significant and no less significant than these tiny highway flowers. And together, they and I, were no more and no less significant than the Milky Way — of which we are a miniscule part.

The whole thing is big. Very big. And, from a subatomic perspective, very small. And it doesn't mean anything. It just is. And I just am. And we are nothing and everything.

THE PERFECT ROOM

Windy Wellington is what they call it. A cartographer said that on really windy days they tie ropes from one parking meter to the next to stop pedestrians from getting blown out into the traffic. I think he was joking.

It could also be called Steep Wellington. It rises sharply up from the harbor that it curves around.

Victoria House was a huge old house, on the hill overlooking the harbour. It was a bit pricey but well worth it. My room was a second-story addition at the back, on big stilts. Three sides of the room were windows. From corner to corner, from waist-height to the ceiling, I saw the hills of Wellington fanning out around me. Lights at night, sunshine in the daytime, the beautifully landscaped garden below. Wrap-around view.

The room was small and almost completely filled with my bed (four pillows!) plus a bedside table with reading lamp (yes!) and a little desk. Just outside my door was a large modern bathroom with a huge, square bathtub and clean towels every day.

This was nice. This was just fine. This I could stick around for. The owner's son, in his twenties, was a strong cyclist. He had cycled from the ferry at the top of the South Island to Christchurch, about 360 K, in one day. Oh dear. He laughed and admitted that that was pushing it. I did 200 K once and that didn't leave me any reserve for another 160. It's okay Marg. There will always be stronger people than you and that's fine.

A GIRL AND HER BIKE

I had to leave my bike locked to a tree in a small downtown Wellington park. There were crowds of people around, sitting on the grass eating, meeting people, sunning themselves. I had errands in and out of buildings, up and down escalators. I felt like I had left a baby, alone, in a baby carriage on a downtown street.

My cycling mentor at home had helped me buy her when all the bike shops tried to push a mountain bike on me. He took me to a cycle shop where we picked out a basic lady's bike. Then he had them strip it down and put on the equipment that I needed for touring. She was my friend from the moment I got on.

Returning from my errands I saw her standing patiently under the tree where

I left her. My eyes filled with tears. My girl. I'm back. I'm so proud of you. Such a pretty, little thing. I won't leave you again. It's just a bicycle Marg. No, she's not just a bicycle. She's my friend. My trusted companion.

AUTO TOILET

Tearooms did not have bathrooms but every town had well signed public toilets. These were usually clean even if they aren't heated. They had toilet paper in good supply. Kaeo was a small, grubby town but their public toilet was a sight to behold. The usual modest, orange street sign on a lamppost gave no hint of what this toilet had to offer. It was freestanding and designed with a combination of odd angles. Even the roof was pitched higher at one end than the other. It was fabricated of some tempered, enameled metal.

I stepped inside and pushed a button marked "close." A panel door slid closed, a light turned on, music started playing and I started laughing. I sat on the toilet and toilet paper was dispensed into a recess in the wall. I got up and it flushed. I put my hands into another recess in the wall and water sprinkled down on them, then a squirt of soap, then more water. Then the water shut off and warm air blew into the same space. I was done. I pushed the "open" button and the panel slid open, light went off and music stopped.

Don't I need to do that again? What more can I do here? I didn't want to leave this tiny building at my command.

PUB HOTELS

Sometimes the inevitable flashed hints of its arrival. Movie trailers. As I cycled south from Dargaville on the crosswind flat, I saw a pub and thought, There's always a pub. Even if the town has no gas station or grocery store or post office, they have a pub. Does that mean that altered states of consciousness are more critical to life than food? No. It means they make more money. Off I harumphed.

By the afternoon I was in an amazing Kauri Wood Museum and chatting with a couple about accommodation in small towns. They advocated staying in these pubs. Cheap and everywhere. And sure enough by the end of the afternoon when I was tired and ready to stop head-winding it, the closest town had no motel or hotel, only a pub.

I have developed a healthy respect for drunks and their pushiness, so I approached this with caution. I stopped at the local police station to ask what they thought of staying in the pub. The on-duty officer felt that I wouldn't have problems on a Tuesday night. He knew the owner and said he would look after things. Okay. We're going in.

Long ago this had been an elegant hotel. Now, a faded beauty, the regulars were quietly playing pool. The owner took me up to a small room overlooking the back yard and a treed gully behind. The shared bathroom was down the hall, down eight steps, across the landing and, immediately, up eight other steps. The toilet was in one room and a bathtub in another.

There weren't any locks on the doors and my door didn't even close properly. By now I had twice experienced only a lock between me and a man trying to get in — the Turkish chef and poor, stupid, drunk David. I valued locks.

Postscript: a quiet, uneventful night. Breakfast early in the morning in the huge hotel kitchen, just the hotel cat and me. As arranged, the owner slept through.

THE CLOSEST CALL

I had been warned of the enormous danger of this trip. Sonia had overheard some of these remarks and I wanted to neutralize them. Standing in our kitchen at home I said, "Look Honey, you are hearing people making worrisome predictions. I believe these are alarmists. I believe I'll be just fine. You know I manage fine wherever I am. You and I know how to take care of ourselves. But I want you to know that, if the very unlikely should happen on this trip, and I don't come back, I want you to know that I've died happier than I've ever been in my life."

"Yeah. I know. And I know you'll be just fine."

In Russia and then again in Turkey the hysteria escalated. And those countries had their challenges alright but I never felt that my life was in danger. It was in New Zealand that I almost bought it.

It was mid afternoon when I was riding into Christchurch. Christchurch is a big enough city that my route had to be carefully planned to stay away from heavy traffic and major highways. I asked advice as I approached and kept updating my plan, which was working well. Traffic got busier but I was on a backroad entrance.

Then I hit a round-a-bout. There were no sidewalks, no alternatives. Into the round-a-bout I went constantly scanning, turning my head back and forth looking behind, in front, to the side, back behind me, scan, scan, scan. Crossing one of the exits a woman came from behind me and decided to pass in front of me. She looked out her side window at me, met my eyes and turned in front of me. I jammed on the brakes, put down my foot and couldn't believe she hadn't hit my front tire. I felt shaken. In fifteen years of riding I've never come that close to a fast moving car. She knew I was there and just decided to whip around me. Because I wasn't going as fast as her, she calculated that I wasn't moving at all.

My heart was pounding. I had to get out of there. I looked back over my shoulder and got up on my pedals again. I had one more exit to cross to get out. And sure enough, here came another one. Again I saw her coming and this time I was ready to throw out the anchor. This one was even closer because she was heading for me broadsides and had to take a car-rocking swerve to get around me and still get out of the exit.

You guys are nuts. You are crazy. It is two o'clock in the afternoon. Where are you going in such a goddamn hurry?

In my motel room I opened the Christchurch newspaper to read how many cyclists were being hit in the round-a-bouts. Yupper. I'll say. And we just missed, by a hair, increasing that number by one today.

I'M BACK

I had traveled the North Island in three separate jaunts, each time returning to Auckland and staying a couple of weeks to attend to business. By the time I returned from the South Island, Auckland felt like home. I had friends in the hotel who greeted me at the front desk with "She's back! Hey you look great. What happened? Where did you go? It's great to have you back." I dashed in and out of familiar shops and businesses doing errands. "Hello stranger. You've been away." Yeah but I'm back.

I knew I could get sushi combo at the foodcourt on Queen Street. I knew the second hand book store and could go straight to my favourite New Zealand authors for a local perspective and good reading at the same time. I knew where the banks were, fresh fruit, stationary, post offices, treats and movies. I was back. It felt great and it felt like a cop-out. I was settling in and habits were taking over. I was losing the edge.

GRANNY UPDATE

Somewhere back in Turkey Granny had suggested that, faced with a decision, I choose the option that felt like fun. She suggested that that was as good a way as any to choose what to do next. The only way. The important thing was to only choose the next fun thing because these preferences change quickly. It had proven sound ever since. Now if I could just keep doing that as I moved into the gravitational pull of responsibility, I'd learn a whole batch of new things. But could I?

She told me that there would be a narrows as I left New Zealand and again as I re-entered Calgary. And there would be turbulent winds, chaos and distractions there. She reminded me that I had the tools to sail through them calmly, stay in touch with my instincts, stay flexible and not panic. And she was right. And I would.

A NEW PLAYGROUND

KOREA

After two months of riding and selling communication workshops to health care organizations in New Zealand it was time to meet my sister, Kath, in Korea, where she was teaching English. She and I were spending Christmas together.

Korea meant winter weather and traffic volumes that prohibited cycling, but the thrill of meeting Kath in a foreign place was too good to pass up. Our meeting seemed an impossible maneuver. Two tiny humans, traveling in opposite directions, half way around the world and meeting in a place neither of us had been before. And finding each other. Like threading a needle on the other side of the Milky Way - by remote control. So I was leaving English speaking "home" and going back into exotica.

SOMEONE TO MEET ME

By the time I got to Korea, I was used to snaking my way through customs into airports. I knew the drill. Get local currency and maps and work out transportation to wherever I was going or just ride off. Most other people had someone to meet them at airports. I liked to watch those blips on the emotional landscape. Sometimes they were restrained, or, worse yet, forced. But usually they were just bone-naked glee. Absence of decorum. Emotional water bombs. Occasionally I felt sorry for myself that no-one was there to meet me but I was so pre-occupied by practical details that it didn't get much airtime. Now, someone was going to meet me. Maybe. Someone I loved enormously.

To get to the Seoul airport in time for my arrival, Kath had to take the first early morning bus from Namyangju. But the busses only started running at 5 AM so we had planned that if she wasn't there by the time my plane arrived I would proceed to Left Luggage. I would sort the cold-weather-non-cycling gear I wanted for winter in Korea. This would occupy me until she arrived.

Inching my way through customs I tried to protect myself from disappointment. She might be there. She might not. And that was fine. She would get there eventually. Either way was fine. It was okay to meet her in Left Luggage. We'd have two weeks together. Just fine.

Inch, inch and finally out through the doors into an ocean of Korea faces lined up behind a barrier. The doors slid closed behind me. I was in a cordoned off space between the door and the faces ahead. Four people deep, fifteen feet ahead of me. A wall of people that went twenty feet in each direction. All staring at me.

I scanned quickly but felt awkward scrutinizing the crowd. I knew that if she was there and if I stood in that space, she would see me. Should I stand still? Should I parade myself along the row to be more visible?

Then I had a nasty thought: What if she isn't here? If she isn't here. All these people will see that no-one is here to meet me. However hard I look for her, no-one. How embarrassing. How humiliating. Public abandonment. I stood in one spot feeling lost.

"Marg. Marg. I'm over here."

I wept.

SLEEPING

A Korean hotel room is bare linoleum with a big cupboard like an oriental armoire. There is also a low mirrored chest. You sit on the floor to see yourself in the mirror.

The floor is heated. That's how the whole room is heated, through heating pipes in the floor. It makes for a pleasant place to walk and sit down. There is no static electricity.

Inside the cupboard are piles of heavy quilts. You can put as many as you want on the floor as bedding and as many as you want over you as blankets. Even with the two of us we never felt short of bedding. Then a hard little quilted cylinder to put under your neck as a pillow. We slept well and happily.

KOREAN DISHES

A Korean meal is guaranteed to have two things: many small dishes of different things and more kimchi than you would want in a lifetime. Kimchi is fermented cabbage. It is made in giant clay pots. Most apartment balconies had several kimchi pots on them with weights on the lids. If there are people, there are kimchi pots. When a Korean comes to visit, they bring a gift of kimchi.

Some kimchi is extremely hot, some tastes like sauerkraut. A restaurant meal includes at least four different kinds and sometimes eight. Breakfast, lunch and dinner and even with a western meal Koreans, will have a little kimchi on the side. I'm not aware of any other culture that has a food obsession parallel to this.

Live fish were displayed with pride in tanks outside restaurants and patrons pick the fish that they want. In spite of Korea's terrible history with the Japanese, many restaurants served Japanese dishes, more expensive than Korean food.

Whatever we ordered in a restaurant, Kath and I got a mountain of dishes. Some would be wonderful and some we didn't like. We tried them all. Deep fried, boiled, hot, cold, crisp, soft, it was always an eating adventure. Seaweed, squid, tiny spicy meat dishes, raw vegetables grated in vinegar, noodles. We got rice if we asked for it.

For people whose stomachs recoil at the strange and unknown it would be an eating nightmare. But we plunged in and tried everything knowing we were going to waste the things that didn't work for us. And that didn't matter because there was more than we could eat anyway. We tried all different ways of saying "not too much", but clearly we never did say it. So we just had fun with what we got. One of our frustrations was that we would find something we loved and not know how to get it again. We would ask the name of the dish, repeat the name at another restaurant and received blank looks.

LONGING IN THE STREETS
Western culture is so pervasive that even in a small town in Korea you are likely to hear western music piped into the street outside a CD shop. I would be walking along, pleased with the dinner ingredients I had bought from street vendors, watching the meticulously dressed and made-up Korean women and listening to the distinctive singsong cadence of the language when, out of somewhere, Celine Dion was weaving into the oriental streetscape: You're everything I need - because you love me. Then there was the wave of sadness. The empty longing. The reaching for - what?

THIS IS THE BEST WE CAN DO?
We were on the ferry back from Cheju, Korea's romantic honeymoon island. For the five-hour ride we lay on carpeted floors and leaned against walls. There was no furniture. This particular crossing was cold. Cold enough that the crew broke out blankets. We didn't catch on until the blankets were all gone but some neighbors realized our plight and kindly shared one of theirs.

Kath was sick during the whole crossing. Diarrhea and throwing up. Now imagine this: the squatty toilets didn't flush. Got it? Diarrhea and throwing up for five hours on a cold boat with toilets that don't flush. Hold that image.

Returning from one of her trips to the bathroom, Kath deadpanned that this could be considered the low point in the trip. We started giggling.

"And to think that we have luxury houses somewhere." That did it. We howled with laughter, tears streaming down our faces. For a while, any sentence we uttered sent us off again.

THE WATER CURE

I couldn't carry volumes of vitamins, potions and medicine with me on this trip. I had some Bach Flower Rescue Remedy, some anti-histamines, a first aid kit with painkillers, antibiotics, an anti-inflammatory, pills for dysentery, the critical stuff. None of which I used. But my most useful health support came from bottled water. My pre-trip advisor had suggested that the oxygen in water would act like a mild antibiotic, combining with free radicals released from invading organisms and flush them out. It worked so well that I continue to use it with great success. (Note to the medical reader: my amateur explanation is probably full of holes. Don't hold that against it.)

The weather was cold. The heating in Korea hotels was not able to handle it. I felt a cold coming on. I drank bottled water all day. Sipping constantly. I drank eight liters of water in one day. I would ease off gradually when the crisis passed. I didn't get sick. Over and over I fought off sickness. Although the overnight flights were hard on my body I seemed able to rally after a couple of days of antihistamines and litres of water. I never had a digestive upset and I never got a cold.

Back in Calgary my doctor said, "I've never known anyone to go on that kind of trip and not to have problems with sickness or injury. Never. You had a guardian angel looking over you." Yes. The water. And Granny.

PARTING PLACES

In Korea the dead are buried under grassy mounds. The mounds are on hillsides and mountainsides. Sometimes they have gravestones, sometimes not. These mounds are always hollowed out of the side of the hill at a nice vantagepoint. So the side of the hill kind of comes around them, embraces them. And in the middle of the semi-circle is the mound covered with grass. The mound is still almost attached. It may be three feet high or quite grand and wide but the proportions stay the same. Often there is just scrub, trees, wildflowers and nature on the rest of the hillside.

One site had stone steps set into the side of the hill and then a cleared path straight up the side of the hill, with a newly planted row of evergreens on either side of the path. At the top, big gravestones and two mounds and a beautiful view out over the mountains and valley below.

What a peaceful place to come and remember someone resting there. What a lovely place to rest forever. Another leaving place.

POWER AND MEN

Of course Kath and I talked about men. We felt that neither of us had ever been in our power, empowered, and at the same time, sexually involved with a man. We weren't talking about in-our-power as in bossy. We were talking about in-our-power as in adult. Capable. What did it look like to flirt and be self-sufficient? What did it feel like to calmly draw boundaries that kept his stuff off you? Are there men out there who are comfortable with that? What is our role in making that happen? Will we ever stop asking?

Trudging up and down hillsides, along busy streets, on subway platforms, this topic could be picked up and put down without preamble or closure. It just hung like that invisible haze of staph germs that hover over the table in an operating theatre, waiting for us.

MEDITATION REVISITED

Korea provided peaceful, stone Buddhas as models for meditating. Grounded giants. Everything about them: posture, face, hands, all still.

I bought a postcard of a giant, stone Buddha and used it as a bookmark. Before meditating it reminded me what serene and grounded look like.

They helped me become a stone Buddha. Straight back. Effortlessly balanced head. Rooted. At rest. Connected to all of it and floating free of any of it. I could draw down the golden light of universal love. It streamed in from the universe, where it always existed mixed in with anger, sadness and pain. It distilled from the universe and streamed into the top of my head. Then, when it circled through my body and out through my feet it returned to the universe and bound me to it. I was now like a pearl strung on this continuous strand of energy. Held there. All this felt plausible, natural, comfortable and good. I was woven into the forces swirling around me. The Buddhas were my teachers.

FACING THE MUSIC

Kath and I discussed my return to Canada. We talked about ways to protect me from panic attacks, over-work, sleep deprivation and frenzy — in other words, life as I had lived it for years. They say that most of us live that way. Chronic sleep deprivation.

Calgary pushed all my buttons and it specially would this time when I had a long list of things to accomplish to get the first cycling guide book finished, designed, printed, promoted and sold. I also needed to sell some communication workshops to keep me afloat until the books were generating money. And I needed to buy and learn a new computer, put together a homepage, create two slideshows and do all the miscellaneous practical things of life. And I had to move. Tenants were in my house and I was out of money. It made me buzz just writing the to-do list.

Kath and I concluded that the trip would be pointless if I reverted.

Granny concurred. She felt that I was putting undue pressure on myself to have an infallible twenty-five year, global, financial plan and strategy in place for my new cycling empire. It was fine to just nurture my dream, step by unfolding step. Seemed as good an approach as any when the plan was coming from within.

PARADISE FOUND

KOH SAMUI, THAILAND

Christmas was over. Funds were low. It was time to go home. But I had to get some heat before returning to the true north strong and free.

It took a Russian-calibre struggle in Korea to acquire an airplane ticket to Bangkok. Multiple phonecalls and eventually meeting the travel agent in a restaurant, in Seoul, on a Sunday, eighteen hours before the plane left. The final price was only disclosed in the restaurant and had to be paid in cash - a great wad of won. I was off to tropical Southeast Asia.

MAKE WAY

Kath and I had parted the day before to give her time to return to Namyangju for early morning teaching. At the airport, the Korean Airlines clerk stepped out from behind the counter and, in limited English, told me that the bike would have to be boxed. And that there were professional boxers just over there and I would go and get it done and bring it back.

Fine and dandy. He was right. These were professional boxers. I paid 500,000 won for them to build a box around my bike. The bike could then have survived being dropped from a five story building.

Now, you understand, I had a huge, sturdy box with a bicycle in it and panniers boxed separately, and I needed to get back to the Korean Airlines counter. Fortunately my boxers loaded my boxes on an airport trolley, sticking out either side. I was off across the terminal.

In the meantime, the terminal had become busy and crowded. Meticulously dressed Korean men and women were now in a thick crowd. In a flash I decided there was only one way to get through — at full charge. I cranked up the trolley and hollered, in English, Make way...bicycle...coming through...make way... as I charged on, leaving a scatteration of people in my wake. But I made it.

Back at the Korean Airlines counter, "my" man once more came out from behind the counter. He looked at the box, chin in hand. He pondered. He shook his head. "Box too big."

I smiled. I walked over to him and draped my arm over his shoulder. Slowly and quietly I said, "You sent me over there (pointing) to get a box. You said they give me the right box. I paid 500,000 won for this (pointing) box. If it's too big, you change it."

Ponder. "Is okay".

Who did that? Why did it feel so good? Was I being mean? I hope not. I wouldn't want something that much fun to be mean.

JUST SNAPPING OFF THOSE DECISIONS NOW.

It was the kind of change that early in my trip would have got me dithering with self-doubt. I intended to go straight to an island called Koh Samui, in the Gulf of Thailand, for my last three weeks. I would settle there, do some editing and a bit of riding — island advantages you know. Warm, cheap and enough tourist activity to give me the comforts I needed to write — comforts like electric lights through the night.

That was the plan. I would arrange getting there when I got to Bangkok. Friends had told me that you first catch the train in Bangkok and then the boat further south. It was five PM when I wheeled my bike out of customs into Bangkok airport. Once more I was in beloved heat.

But the first thing I found out in the airport was that there was also an airport on Koh Samui. And flights from this one to that one. Thirty-five minutes and you were there.

Say no more. Who cares what the price difference is. Muscle my bike around Bangkok to wherever the train station is? Hassle rush-hour traffic? Negotiate a train ticket? Sleep on the train? Then get from the train station to the ferry dock and go through it all again? With my bike all the way? Forget it. Decision made. Why did I fly to Koh Samui? Because I wanted to.

Unfortunately the next flight wasn't until the next morning. So I had to arrange for a hotel close to the airport for the night and transport to the hotel and back again to the airport in the morning. Still easier.

Left Luggage was the glitch. Left Luggage was full. My bike wouldn't fit in. I had enough experience to know what it would be like to take my bike along on this overnight jaunt. Expensive and physically tiring and it would limit my options of conveyance to the hotel, which meant it would take longer to get there. The situation called for shameless begging, pleading, wheedling.

The guy went back into his luggage room four times. Each time he came out and said, "No room." On the fourth time, when I offered to go back in and help him re-sort stuff, he relented.

EPIDEMIC OF INDOLENCE

They say that when you freeze to death you just get tired and want to lie down and rest and you drift off to sleep and it feels mercifully wonderful. It is a bit like that in Koh Samui. Whatever your state of mind when you arrive in Koh Samui, within 24 hours you can feel yourself sinking into indolence. The damp heat, the warm water, the cheap wonderful food, the massages on the beach, the English and German tour groups drinking by noon, the liveliest activity being getting tanned/burned — that's Koh Samui. Reading a book is a big project. Two German couples took to visiting every afternoon while sitting waist-deep in the water along the beach. They sat with their beer like a semi-submerged cocktail party.

How many hours can you lie in the sun? How many massages can you have? How early can you start drinking? I saw how quickly indolence became boredom. Thank heavens I had a book to edit. Watching me by the pool, other guests thought I was frightfully ambitious. Ambitious hell. I was just staying conscious.

TRAFFIC

You aren't going to ride your bike here are you? These drivers are nuts. They're all over the road. Trucks wandering from one side to the other. You won't last an afternoon. Ah, this again.

Certainly the traffic was an interesting mix. Scooters and motor bikes could carry three people, one holding a pissed off rooster, someone else holding a baby, and piles of wares for sale. Scooters were often driven by young children or by drunk, sunburned tourists with their trophy Thai girl on the back. Add in tiny cooking foodwagons, dogs, chickens and taxis with people standing on the running board. Trucks were reckless but they were also used to sharing the road with this moving zoo.

The roads were concrete or dirt. The concrete often had a sharp lip on the edge that needed watching and the monsoons left huge, sharp-edged cracks where sections of concrete had dropped into a wash.

Yea, it was chaos out there. But the weather was warm and being warm I felt anything was manageable, so I rode.

FOOD HEAVEN

Fresh fish, delicious fresh fruit shakes, curries, Chinese food, chicken, beef, pork with rice on the side. More kinds of fresh fish than you've even heard of cooked to perfection. Koh Samui was an eating paradise. Travel guides warn you not to eat raw food like salads but I did and never had a problem.

Western tourists crave western breakfasts so a chain called While You Wait, has become popular serving pancakes, sausages, bacon, eggs, toast, muffins, danish. Otherwise breakfast was unbuttered toast; hard-boiled eggs, omelets and fried potatoes that were almost like the western equivalent.

THE MERMAID

Betsy and her four-year-old son, William, joined me for a week at Nara
Gardens. Her husband worked in Bangkok and she fled the traffic, crowds,
noise and smog for a holiday at Koh Samui. She was a marine biologist. She
loved the water life in the tidal pools of the Northeastern United States. She
was like a mermaid in the water. So was William. He was friendly and chatty
and believed he was smarter than his self-effacing mother. It was hard to watch
his power building at her expense.

We spent several days chumming around and usually sat together for meals.
After they left I wanted to tell this woman that she was beautiful and strong
and intuitive so I wrote a story about a mermaid who knew that her life
depended on being near the water. I mailed it to her in Bangkok.

THE TEAPOT SHOWDOWN

During dinner with Betsy and William, I ordered hot water. Trying to explain to
the waitress that I wanted the water hot, I said "In a teapot," and made
motions of pouring from a teapot. I received two empty teapots. So I asked for
two bottles of water instead. They came straight from the fridge just as I was
leaving so I decided to take them to my room. Standing beside the table trying
to pick up the two bottles in one hand, plus the book I had brought to read
while I ate, my room key and my sunglasses, the water bottles, wet with
condensation, slipped out of my hands and landed on the table. The two
empty teapots bounced off the rattan table top onto the deck where they
broke. Oh dear.

The waitress watched all this. I turned to her and said, "I'm sorry." Off we
went.

In my room I was just out of my clothes when there was a knock at my door.
Back into my clothes, and over to the door.

Yan, a waiter, said, "You break teapots."

"Yes. It was an accident. The water slipped out of my hand."

"You have to replace them with similar quality."

"Well Yan I haven't got time to take from my writing to go out shopping
for teapots so why don't you go out and replace them and I'll pay for them."

"You pay."

"Fine. I'm going to bed now."

No sooner was I out of my clothes than there was again a knock at my door.
Back into clothes, over to the door, this time a waitress.

"One million baht."

"You've got to be joking."

"One million baht, you break teapot."

By this point I was angry and didn't happen to have one million baht on
me. "I'll deal with it in the morning. I am going to bed now."

The next morning at breakfast Betsy and William had just arrived when Yan
came over and asked amiably how we were. I was surprised to hear myself say,

"I'm kind of annoyed Yan."

"Why?" he shouted straightening up.

"Look this whole thing is very unfair."

"What you want?"

"I want to not pay for the teapots. Your teapots aren't worth one million baht. Broken crockery is a cost of your doing business. I pay one million baht a night to stay here. It's not like I did it on purpose."

Sudden change: "Oh well, fine. If you didn't do on purpose."

"Of course I didn't do it on purpose. That's madness."

He made a gesture of sweeping something off the table. "I thought that you just broke them."

"For heavens sake Yan, why would I do that?"

"No problem. Settled. You don't pay."

"Thank you."

Would I have done that — before?

SPIRIT HOUSES

There is a spirit house outside every business and most homes in Koh Samui. It is the scale of a birdhouse on a stick but looks like a tiny Thai temple. The more elaborate the building, the more elaborate the spirit house. If you renovate the house, you need to renovate the spirit house. A hospital or airport would have a spirit house with many wings and much ornamentation. The spirit house is often graced with offerings of flowers, oranges, water, perfume, necklaces or shells.

Former residents reside in the spirit house. It needs to be more inviting than the real structure or the spirits will take over the real one and create problems. A monk helps you site the spirit house correctly so that it works.

You cannot just take down and throw away an old spirit house. Like a nuclear plant, it needs to be decommissioned. This again requires a monk. Under his or her direction the spirit house is taken down and put under a banyan tree inside a Buddhist temple complex. I saw these trees with piles of old spirit houses under them.

I asked my travel agent if it would be okay to take a photo of her spirit house. I asked apologetically if this was an inappropriate request. Insensitive and sacrilegious. She said, "No, not inappropriate because you have asked. That is respectful. And that is all that is required. As long as you approach with respect."

Later, when I wanted to photograph the spirit house outside a hospital, I approached, stopped, stood in front of it with my palms together and bowed. I told it that it was lovely and I would be honoured to have a picture of it to take home and show other people how lovely it was. I asked if that was all right.

Then I stood openly, waiting. Nothing. Is no response the same as okay? I waited. It felt okay.

THE CRACK IN PARADISE

I saw women working on construction sites. I saw a woman carrying a dishpan full of sand. A blue plastic dishpan. One load of sand after another. Do you have any idea how much a dishpan of sand would weigh?

I saw dirt yards full of roosters, each in their own wicker cage, looking for a fight. And their handlers baiting them, shoving them into other rooster's faces. And wiping their wounds with bright green liquid.

I saw countless stray dogs, much of their hair gone, scrawny and scratching and diseased, slinking around looking for food. Some were nursing a litter. One was dragging its back legs on the road behind it.

I saw a kitten so malnourished and probably born of a malnourished kitten that it hardly looked like a kitten - all belly and eyeballs.

I saw the underside of Paradise and smelled the garbage.

SOCIOLOGY TURNED ON ITS EAR

The hardest working children were rewarded in Koh Samui. They were given the best chance to better themselves. They inherited the rich, coconut growing land in the interior. The lay-about siblings only got the beach land — good for growing nothing and uninhabitable during monsoons.

Then the tourists came.

And now the lay-abouts drive Mercedes Benz cars and wear designer clothes and make big deals with developers. And the hard working siblings work long, hard hours trying to scratch out a living growing coconut.

In Koh Samui there are halves of families that do not talk to other halves of families. Haven't for years. Won't for years. (When I told my sister this story she said, So what the hell is the lesson in that?)

WATCHING FOR THE BATS

If you stay at The Simple Life, on the southeast coast of Koh Samui, stroll north along the beach just before sunset and out to the point that faces a large, offshore island. Then watch the sun set. Sit on the rocks and watch the whole, glorious, silent, sinking process.

Then look straight up over your head.

Above you will be thousands of bats from the island, silhouetted, silently winging their way inland to hunt insects for the night. You see the scalloped bat wing shape but they don't make a sound. Just silent shadows gliding in to start their night.

A privilege to witness.

BUTTERFLIES

I had never seen so many colours and patterns and just plain so many butterflies. Big ones and little ones wafting around me. Black, yellow, blue, orange and pure white. A butterfly farm was popular with tourists. I didn't have the heart to go. Framed sets of mounted butterflies were for sale in the markets. Heartbreakingly beautiful. Something lovely to own. You could show your friends. In a frame, you have control.

TALISMEN

They kept me company and kept me grounded.

When I asked," Why am I doing this? What am I trying to accomplish here?" I could re-read my quotation from a strange little spiritual book written in the 40's: Your own individual, spiritual, consciously recognized and gallantly guarded evolution is the only gift you can give to the world and your only value of any genuine significance to the world or to yourself.

Ah yes - that's what this journey was all about.

When I forgot why I had gone out into the world I could look at the picture of the beckoning road between two rows of trees and feel the pull to go down it and down all the roads that waited to be explored.

When feeling self-doubt I could look at the Levi's ad Sonia had given me. It was a drawing of people running off the page to the left and alone, bounding off the page in the opposite direction, one woman. Woman trusting her instincts the headline read. Yes.

When I wanted to remind myself that I wasn't abandoned by the world, wandering homelessly without connection to other people, I could look at my little picture album. In there I could see my daughter; my sister Kath and I, apres cross-country skiing; my Mom in her yard with her arm around me and a look of glee on her face; my nephew Andrew shot while in Thailand; my beloved cat and my beautiful little sunshine house and garden. My home, my sanctuary.

When I doubted my capabilities I could read my sendoff card from Andrew, stuck into my album: I'm so glad that you could make all of this happen! and from Kath: You're a winner.

I could read notes of support and encouragement that I received as I traveled and had tucked in with the others, such as Sonia's first fax after I left home: Everyone misses you but knows you are going to have the time of your life. May the wind be at your back. Love you.

When I needed to feel loved and cared for, I could look at the card from my wonderful friend Maureen and see a painting of two little girls in giant-brimmed mommy-hats and dressups having a tea party at their little table in a garden. A garden party. Then I remembered all the love and joy and humour that we share. The history. The values. The comfort of complete trust and respect for each other. Love.

I could visualize all of my team sounding just like they do at home, encouraging, advising, supporting, being their wonderful selves and treating me like they always do with generous hearts.

And as I rode along or lay in a bed somewhere in the dark I could hear the gentle click and feel the dangling reminders from Sonia of we-are-all-here-with-you: a tiny, gold, St Christopher's medal and beside it a tiny amber heart hanging from my watchstrap. The St Christopher's medal was never blessed by a church but it was given with my daughter's love and blessing. It was her way of sending her protection along with me. The amber heart, a gentle golden, piece of the world, transformed by time. And there they were, always on my wrist, gentling tapping as I moved, always loved.

SNOW LEOPARD

I had found an old copy of Snow Leopard in a used book stall in Koh Samui and it felt timely to read of Peter Matthiessen's journey with its underlying spiritual quest at the same time that I was ending mine. Would he reveal the secret that would help me take back what I had learned? The secret of coping with re-entry? I approached the ending of his journey with anticipation. As he came down from the Tibetan mountains he only saw the parts of himself that had not changed. He asked in desperation: "Have I learned nothing?"

Yes. There it is. The secret. A gently, unassuming little kernel. Have I learned nothing? We always feel that. It is part of being alive. We always want to be closer to enlightenment, freer of fear and doubt, we want to find greater peace and feel a failure when we aren't there.

If this pilgrim, seeking so earnestly, watching and listening so openly had been disappointed in his growth, I guess we all would be.

It's okay. Maybe the wise traveler only sees his shortfall. I would too. And that was fine.

THE END, THE EVERYTHING

THE END OF THE RAINBOW

I was thinking ending. I was thinking returning home. It had me reflect on the pivotal point of the trip. The middle of the teeter totter. The gift that was so purely golden, so perfectly magic that it would nurture me forever.

It had been a hard days riding. I had climbed many New Zealand hills. I was in the saddle for thirteen hours. Up through the Gorge, gusty wind and rain on and off. I had another hour to go to get to Dargaville, my first chance for a place to stay.

It was late in the day. There were fields around me and mountains behind them. Thank goodness it was fairly flat from here on, just more riding than I would choose. And here was coming yet another little squall through the golden evening light. I could see the rain had already reached the field on my right.

That was fine. I knew these little rainstorms now and they didn't last long enough to soak my clothes and they made a gentle sound, a calm, patting sound - pat, pat, pat. I was patted by the cosmos.

After seeing the little rainstorm coming, I turned to my left, and there, in the grass at the edge of the road, was the rainbow. Just here. It started right in the grass. I could see the blades of grass behind it, through the colours. I stopped and stared. That was really a rainbow and it was really right there in the grass beside the road. Beside me.

I looked straight up the pillar of rainbow climbing up into the sky. The hair stood up all over my body. The other half of the rainbow wasn't even in my field of vision. This is happening now — this thing that doesn't happen. I leaned on my handle bars and drank it in.

Rainbows are elusive. People have chased them, trying to get to the end. And I was there. Here. Now. This was it. The secret place. It had come to me and I had pedaled around the world to get to it. And I had arrived. And the moment of meeting was so gentle that I could have missed it. I could have ridden by without turning my head that way. Eight more feet and it would have been behind me.

I knew this would only be a moment. I held my breath. I didn't need a picture. This was outside time and outside place. This would be magically mine forever.

I turned back to the west where the sky was filled with millions of drops of rain falling down on me already. A golden blessing dropped gently on my face as I looked up. They mixed with my tears so softly that we were crying together, this world and I.

Now the rainbow was whisking away across the field on my left. I watched it become distant. It was traveling away fast and had doubled itself. Across the field and into the place where rainbows are supposed to be, over a distant hill. Now I could take a picture. A picture of the rainbow that had come and touched me.

Every frustration from five months of traveling, every ache, pain and weariness was melted away. I had put myself out here, I had been blown off the road by wind, I had cursed yet another steep hill, I had felt cold and sorry for myself — then — a gift.

That's why I did it. To be there, exposed, available, so that when the gift came, I was there to receive it. I had ridden to the end of the rainbow. And the end of the rainbow was where I was. I didn't need to look any further. Wherever I was, was the end of the rainbow. The magic place. We are the magic place. The pot of gold at the end of the rainbow is me.

A gentle gift from the universe to take home with me. Now home and the end of the rainbow are wherever I am.

YOUR CHAKRAS ARE IN ORDER

I don't know much about chakras. I know there are seven. They are in different places in your body. They seem to have something to do with your energy and ultimately your health. Attitudes affect chakras, chakras affect attitudes. That's what I know about chakras.

But I had a spare afternoon just before leaving Thailand and heading home. The resort offered meditation lessons, group meditation, massage, reflexology and chakra reading. Chakra reading. Hmm. That sounded good. I wondered how my chakras were doing. I wondered if I could learn lessons to take home with me, such as how to make the transition from riding around on my bike in other countries to being back in Canada and finishing the edit of my new cycling guidebook. Let's do a chakras reading.

My cabana had an open rooftop penthouse. There were two chairs up there, a hammock, a chesterfield and a cat. There was a grass roof on top. Our fantasy of tropical living.

Sutra was Italian. She had a lovely lilting voice that I won't try to reproduce and was hard to understand sometimes but that didn't seem to matter. We sat in the roof penthouse. Both of us had our eyes closed and she talked slowly to me about what she saw. It took half an hour but the ideas she voiced are captured here.

YOUR CHAKRAS ARE HEALTHY AND STRONG.

Your courage chakra is very strong and that makes it possible for you to be encouraging to others. You are good at that. You can give them courage.

You are in very good touch with your feelings and intuitions. To protect that you must retreat regularly to restore yourself. You can end up doing too much and keep on going too long and then you are like a force-fed baby that does not have time to digest. It prevents you from realizing your potential. (Yes, I had seen this happen.) You need plenty of time to reflect and be still. If you can get the retreats and peacefulness you need you are entering a period of enormous creativity and explosive growth.

Your power chakra is excellent but sometimes it sounds like you can dilute your power. It is important that you be clear when there is something you do not like. If you put up with something that you do not like without speaking out, you are diminished.

You have a tiny tear, like a piece of damage, like worn fabric or overused tissue on your chakra about your sexuality. You have been disappointed and it has left you cynical. You have given up on it but you shouldn't. Talk to your face in the mirror like you are seeing yourself on a video and see your face saying that even though many of your sexual experiences have been discouraging, you shouldn't fear that they will all be. Without healing that you will be held back fulfilling other parts of yourself.

Another chakra with a tiny tear, I see a bit of old defiance from long past that is hard on you. It is minor but worth being aware of and attending to when you have a chance. It connects to two people. If you can resolve it, you will have a chance to influence those people.

And your last chakra is very shining and beautiful and whole. Inside it I see your guardian angel. She is shimmering in light. This wise woman will always be there for you. She has been with you for your whole trip and has guided and protected you. She is guiding me through this reading. She will always look after you.

I don't believe it. She's found Granny.

CARRYING MY LESSONS HOME

Other long-distance travelers that I met in airports, in customs, in hostels, spoke sadly of the end of the trip. It was the end of a magic time. The old stuff waited for them at home. They weren't sure how long they could last there. Friends reported it to be a long struggle, sometimes months trying to accept that the trip was over while feeling same old, same old. I wondered how I would cope with that. I was smiling as I rode. I was ready to find out.

My journey was ending. When my Other Traveler and I began riding back up toward the airport on Koh Samui we were starting home. I was at peace. I had accomplished what I set out to do. I had found what I wanted to find. The world had been my teacher.

I had been in pain when I had long ago asked my journal: what it is all about? I get no answer. I have mortgaged my house and now I go out there into the unknown. To return to greater unknown. And empty coffers. And no prospects of making money. And an aging body that loses market value every day. And a loss of drive to solve any of these any more. I am alone.

I couldn't imagine then how I could earn a living and enjoy myself at the same time. Now I knew I was going home to start a new adventure writing cycling guidebooks, continuing to see the world from a bicycle and helping other people do so too.

I had wondered where I fit into this newly shrinking world. I wondered how I would behave, alone, out there. I had dared to hope that I would, somewhere, somehow, learn to connect with my instincts, my inner wisdom, intuition. I wanted to find a way to live life guided by some grounded truths. To be at peace with myself and the forces of the universe.

I longed to find a way to be in the world at fifty-one and ninety-one that transcended fading looks and gave me confidence in my other qualities and the momentum to move forward based on fresh priorities.

And here I was on the other side of the world, three quarters of the way around it. And I knew new things that had gently unfolded to me. The Other Traveler had become part of my daily life. The choices I faced were now made a new way. The nurturing I felt came from all around me. I saw it, felt it and drew comfort from it. I knew there would be new lessons, new challenges ahead and the nurturing would be there too.

While I traveled I was still singing Around the world I searched for you; I traveled on when hope was gone to keep a rendezvous; I knew somewhere, sometime, somehow, I'd look at you and I would see the smile you're smiling now... tum de tum de tum tum tum and so on ...I found my world in you." I never decided to sing it. I would catch myself singing it. I smiled when I caught that coming from somewhere at the back of my head. I wasn't singing it to my yet-to-be-found lover or life partner. I knew I was singing that song to my soul, to me and the Other Traveler who now saw with my eyes, heard with my ears and was right beside me as we went around each bend in the road together. I sang around the world and grinned. Yes I had found what I was looking for.

I had learned that home was wherever I was. That I have within me the open arms that greet and nurture and welcome and love. And they travel with me. Coming home I looked forward to seeing the faces I love, hearing the voices that I had carried within me around the world. And knowing that wherever I was, love and comfort were with me.

Now I was beginning a great new adventure. The next journey.

Let the journey begin.

The End.

The Beginning.

Thank you Everythingness.

AFTER WORDS

WE'RE GOING HOME TOGETHER

The Koh Samui airport was outside. Everything happened in the open air: check-in, baggage tagging, flight changes, waiting for the plane, boarding announcements. You sat under the grass roof and watched the plane come in. You watched the new tourists clamor down the door-stairwell, get on the little open air bus and get wheeled over to the "terminal" where they milled around waiting for their bags to be unloaded, found the driver to their hotel, relished the inevitable sun and believed that the rest of Koh Samui would be as clean and manicured as the airport.

We, on the other had, were leaving. Paradise about to be lost.

The airport guards were reluctant to let me cycle in. They were used to waving through busloads of people from hotels. They were used to taxis. What was this person on a bicycle? No category. I was waved on to the next gate. Someone else's problem. The next gate was to staff parking. I went through the parking lot and got within ten meters of the "terminal," just around the hedge, when I was stopped again. I showed the guard my ticket, I made signs of my bike and I, together, going up in an airplane. No. No. No. No bicycle is going around the hedge. No.

So I leaned my bike on the hedge and started around it on foot just as one of the "airline" guys noticed the scene and came over. "Okay. Okay. Okay." Waving his arms, talking fast to the security guard in that way that seems like they are arguing. Protests from the guard, animated Thai discussion while the new guy tugged my arm and waved me and my bike through. I'm in. I'm going home.

The baggage wagon was pulled up behind the check-in counter. As I stood under the grass roof I watched the baggage handlers load my bike onto their wagon. I felt teary eyed. She was once again in other people's hands and they didn't know that she deserved to be treated with respect. Strangers would grab her. Toss her onto a pile. Jam things on top of her. My friend. My trusty stead. My bike and Brenda made me feel protective. I'm coming Brenda. Peace be with you. I'm coming home.

INTO THE CHAOS

A week after returning to Canada I felt all the old fear and hopelessness as I struggled with the accumulated weight of my financial crisis and what I was trying to make happen: buy a laptop and software, negotiate map production, get winter clothes out of storage, pay bills, connect with clients — the mountain of personal re-organizing and business administration. All done at fast forward so that I could get Brenda out of boarding and relocate to my mother's house in BC.

In the midst of this whirlwind I squeezed in a journey's-end visit to my astrologer, Deanna. She said: Your struggle of many years, maybe your whole life, is over. To reap the rewards of this trip, especially December and January, you should let things sift and settle. Your journals will be goldmines. The changes in you have been deep and profound and when they start manifesting themselves externally they will change the way you relate to people, particularly around the issues of power and giving it up. Some people will try to stop this change in you. You will choose to not be around people that drain you. Take Brenda and go up to your Mom's and write.

I was staying with friends who were allergic to cats so I wasn't yet able to re-claim Brenda but I visited her where she was boarding. Iris had been wonderful to Brenda. She had given her free run of her house along with her own cat. She brushed Brenda every day and knew the things Brenda liked. She had let Brenda take over a little window-sill bed where she lay and looked out the window all day long.

Brenda was furious. She wouldn't let me touch her. She wouldn't look at me. She hated Iris's cat with every nerve in her body.

I went back to my friends' house, climbed into bed, plugged in my Walkman and played Conquest of Paradise. I sobbed. Brenda I have betrayed you. I have abandoned you. How could I have left you to pay for my adventure this way? There were no answers. There was no resolution. It just was.

It took me another week to finish what needed doing in Calgary and take the bus up to my mother's. Brenda followed on the plane, much to the amusement of all my friends. In minutes we were settled in, safe and united. Buddies. Brenda would run ahead of me up the stairs and stop and turn and reach her paw out in the air to me. And I would sit on the stair below and we would put our foreheads together and make little noises to each other.

Then I started to write.

CYCLING INTO YOUR SOUL

TRY YOUR OWN SOUL JOURNEY
These travel stories have their own lessons. Take them for yourself. For those of you who like stepping stones to begin your own journey, I humbly offer a few.

FIND ANSWERS TO YOUR QUESTIONS
Going to work every day gives you specific and tangible rewards. But it can leave you starved for life's purpose and spiritual nourishment. If you are asking:

Is this what I want to be doing?

Isn't there more than this?

What should I do instead?

How do I get in touch with my instincts?

...it's time to cycle into your soul.

A cycling spirit quest can help you make contact with your inner guide and teach you how to make decisions that support something natural inside you, something that's bigger, more fulfilling than the goals you have imposed on yourself.

Going out into the world, alone, gives you a chance to meet your mythical monsters, renew yourself and return with what First Nations People call a spirit guide.

START WITH THE PRACTICAL STUFF
Get all the practical stuff out of the way. For your own peace of mind, as well as out of consideration for everyone else in your life, get your affairs in order.

Get travel medical insurance that truly covers worst case scenarios.

Have an up-to-date will in the hands of someone you trust.

Get enough life insurance so that you can be buried and your bills paid and affairs closed off.

Set up your house/condo/apartment/farm to be self-sustaining if possible. Renting furnished is an option. Storage at a friend's is another.

Get a loan or mortgage, draw from savings, do what you have to do to get some money together to finance the trip. Talk to other travelers about current costs. Think about how well it works for you to "go native," which is the cheapest way to travel. Be realistic about how often you need hot showers, clean beds, western food. You learn some of these things as you go but bear in mind that few of us can sustain life happily at the rock bottom level lived by much of the world.

Establish someone you trust to look after your affairs on the home front. Leave several photocopies of your passport and credit cards with them so they can send a copy to you if yours get lost or stolen. They will also move money around in your bank account, pay your credit card bills, deal with sending you things you forgot, receive the things you send home because you just can't carry all that stuff and hassle your financial institution when you can't withdraw money on any of your cards.

Get a range of credit and bank machine cards. There are many countries with bank machines now but these often have problems with their lines. Having a second and third card to draw on increases your options. Get an American Express card because their travelers' services can help you out in a pinch. Take personal cheques along. Oddly enough, there are places overseas that will give you cash for a personal cheque when you have a credit card with you.

Gather the medical supplies and bicycle tools that you will need. Think small and efficient but arm yourself for everything you can imagine occurring.

Don't over plan what is going to happen when you return. Have a financial cushion and a place to stay the first few weeks you are back. But you will change while you are on this journey and you don't want to be locked into dated decisions.

KEEP THE PLAN OPEN

When you travel with a fully planned itinerary you continue to follow external forces, even if they are of your own making. There you are, on the other side of the world, doing what the list tells you to do next. What you want to do is to loosen the hold of outside schedules and rules so that you can tune your ear to another kind of guide. It will cost more but to make choices out there, on your own, as you travel, is one of the ways that this kind of journey helps you find your inner guide.

Start with a ticket to someplace.

There is nothing wrong with having the odd bit of structure in there: meeting friends somewhere for example or even doing a business transaction. That can add to your reflections of being untethered and alone. Just don't lock yourself in to several of them. And observe how you feel about these commitments/breaks as you travel.

Then think in generalities. Be aware of political hot spots. There is plenty of world to see and you don't need to risk getting caught in the crossfire of someone else's squabble. Do think about the weather you are willing to deal with and find out what to expect in the places you are considering. There are weather guides in libraries and Internet is undoubtedly crammed with weather data. Ask other travelers. Contact your local meteorologist.

Try to hear your whims about what you want to have happen on this trip, even before you leave. Don't worry if they are vague. You aren't out there yet.

Go for as long as you can afford.

REMEMBER THE SPIRIT QUEST

It is easy to get bogged down with all the things you want to accomplish on a major trip: see the world, enjoy nature, test your ability to cope on your own, build your fitness, explore business opportunities and see specific things. It helps you keep your focus at this feast to have one thing written out that inspires you, that feels like it keeps you going toward the quest that matters to you. I used the quote from "I Say Sunrise":

Your own, individual, spiritual, consciously recognized and gallantly guarded evolution is the only gift you can give to the world and your only value of any genuine significance to the world or to yourself.

Over and over this sentence brought me back to listening to my soul and following its murmuring. I credit this quote with ensuring that my journey felt like a success at the end.

TAKE ALONG YOUR TALISMEN

Pack as little as possible. But when you pack, think of your spiritual needs as well as your physical ones. Spiritual? What are spiritual needs? I don't really know. Maybe think of emotional needs, helping yourself feel centered and balanced and healthy. Maybe think about what helps with self-exploration. Listen to what other people say about finding their soul path and think about what would work for you. Not a suitcase of stuff, just some nice things. Your talismen.

Prepare a mini-album like the kind grandmothers carry in their purses. Include in it photos of people and things you love, illustrations and quotes that inspire you, notes and letters from friends that convey love and support and encouragement. These will remind you of your value system and nurture you when you feel adrift. Take a piece of jewelry that has emotional significance and keep that close to your body all the time.

EXPERIMENT

Years ago I read an article on creativity. It said that when you change a habit, even a habit as simple as dressing before brushing your teeth instead of after, you break out of a pattern that you don't think about and thereby unleash creativity. On the road many of your habits are shot. What happens when you dabble in others?

Try getting up much earlier or lying in bed long after you waken. How does that feel? What about eating before you ride? Riding before you eat?

Eliminating sugar? Doubling the water you drink? Getting a haircut from someone who doesn't know your hair, doesn't know your language and, for all you know, doesn't know anything? Eating in a truly local restaurant, just you and the locals?

Your experiments can be brief, just enough to see what happens. Do you want to try the next step? Or an alternative? Or go back to what you did before? Or talk to someone about it? Or write in your journal?

When your experiments feel driven, return to old habits for a while. You've learned where your comfort zone drops over the edge of the world.

ACCESS WHAT IS IN THERE

You are trying to reverse years of shutting off the little voice that tried to tell you it was tired or lonely or afraid. You had work to get done, goddammit. And goals to get to. That whiny voice just held you back. Put your head down and keep going. Better to listen to that motivation tape in the car. Now there's a voice worth listening to.

You've been successful. The little voice is now shut off. So how do you get it back? You don't know where to find it any more. I didn't either. So you need some excavation tools, some techniques that give access to what's going on behind the conscious mind. Some that have worked for others are: writing, drawing, meditating, observing dreams, visualizing and giving yourself the time to ponder whatever thoughts come into your head.

If you explore them openly, these approaches help you re-find that inner voice. They don't work like looking up a phone number or surfing the Net. They work in a quieter more indirect way. One of the things you learn is to appreciate and trust the strange, soft way that they do work. Try them. Approach this as if everything counts. Hear what you say to others. Read what you write down. Look at the pictures you choose to take.

Writing - Try writing in a journal. If this is new to you beware of trying to do it right when there is no right. Jot down whatever comes to mind. That's the sneaky part about this. You are looking for the ends of innocuous threads hanging out. They don't look significant these little thoughts, recollections of dreams, ideas, perceptions. They just feel like useless stuff. Get it down and look at it. See where the next thought goes. Try writing when you are really tired. Dog tired. The brain isn't working. Ah good. Lets see what the stuff behind it has to say.

Eventually these turn into ruminations, observations, questions and insights that open layers of other stuff, recall long forgotten memories and get you moving down and in and along those threads to interesting things. Looking back you will see that they inch you along on the inner part of your journey.

Drawing - For some people sketching, doodling, drawing comes easily and naturally. For all of us it comes from a place inside that is more whole brain and therefore more whole us, than the writing part of the brain. Even if this isn't something you do well or spontaneously it might be fun to experiment with what comes up. We've all seen enough "modern" art to know that accurate representation isn't the only game in town.

Visualizing - You can visualize situations that will give you access to your subconscious. It works well as a tool to explore something that is worrying you or seems to hold you back or you are afraid of and don't know why. When you want to figure out what is really going on in there, try visualizing. Here are a couple of visualization scenarios that gave me access to inner information.

After getting comfortable and relaxed, close your eyes, slow your breathing and conjure up a forest in your mind. Let it emerge before you, out of your imagination. See it in vivid detail: colours, shapes, sounds, smells, textures and temperatures. Go into it. What do you find? Spend time in there and learn its secrets. What do you feel?

Another setting for inner exploration is to imagine a cave. Where is it? What is it like there? Go inside. What do you find?

Think up your own situations that will set the stage for you to explore images from inside your subconscious. Create a door. See it in detail. Open it and walk through. What's there? Afterwards write down what happened. Sometimes it takes a few days for the significance of these to dawn on you. Let them unfold.

Meditating - Breathing is the easiest meditation focus for me. It's always there. It feels like my mind can take a little rest, lolling on top of the giant, black globe of my breathe. Up and down, up and down.

It was Jack Kornfeldt in Path with Heart who said that maybe meditating is just the act of over and over and over bringing your focus back to your breathing. That was a relief. I had almost given up to the mind-babble that swamps my attempts at meditation. Jack took the pressure off to do this meditation thing properly. Now I can shift my focus back to my breathing without seeing it as yet another meditation failure. That is meditation.

I don't know if meditation has been a direct source of insights for me but I do know it gives me distance and, a chance to see how persistently my mind barges in when I decide that it's okay to think of nothing for a while.

So just keep turning back from the babble to that resting place. Set aside time. See what happens.

Body meditating - Learn what your body can teach you about yourself. Doing yoga, I have learned that my fear lives in my back. I get cramps in my back when I am holding on to something I'm afraid of losing. Not something immediate, like a contract, something older and deeper that feels more like dread, such as my daughter moving away. Painful and restricting back pain. Now I know that my body is telling me something when my back tightens. Instead of trying to eliminate the symptoms, now I listen. I follow them like a thread back to the feelings. I let them teach me what is going on inside. What does your body tell you about the inside your heart?

Yoga has also taught me to feel the energy in my body. When I end a pose and the muscles and nerves are still returning to their unflexed position, the waves of energy are rebounding inside like the ebb of an orgasm. I lie still and feel it. Delicious. It tells me that there is something aside from tissue and bones and nerves and impulses and blood in there. There is my life force rolling around.

Explore yoga or Tai Chi or some other form of physical meditation. Take a tiny book with you or learn just enough before leaving to practice it on the road. Listen to what your body says. Give it what it wants.

FIND YOUR SPIRIT GUIDE

Consider finding your own wise guide to consult with on the road. I don't know why my advisor chose Granny. I cannot give you a formula. It feels important to find one. Think about family members, friends, historical figures. Ask other people who know you well to explore ideas.

Choose your guide and start "meeting" together before you leave. Sit quietly twice a day, relax and conjure up that person in your mind's eye. See them in detail and feel their presence. Ask them questions and confide your thoughts and feelings to them. Just imagine them being themselves. Watch them respond. Let them evolve.

At the end of each visit, thank them for being with you. Granny and I reach out and take each other's hands, both hands. Then we kiss each other on each cheek, like she always did, being French. It is a little blessing we give each other. Thank you Granny. and Go in peace my little traveler.

At first, as in many of these gentle things, you will wonder if your are doing this right. It is fun to watch that change and the relationship take on a life of its own. You no longer wonder if it is what it should be. It just is.

DRINK WATER

This was another guideline from my advisor that worked well for me. The stresses of travel are huge: the emotional uncertainty, changes in food, water, sleeping schedule, virtually everything in your life. You are also exposed to diseases that you haven't encountered at home.

Bottled water is available nearly everywhere. When you feel overtired, run down or have that tell-tale warm place at the back of your throat, go out and get an arm full of bottled water, go back to where you are staying, lie low and drink and drink and drink. Read, lie around, write in your journal, listen to your Walkman, doze. And when you start feeling better, taper off the water intake gradually. And contemplate your landscape from this little resting place. Things have changed. You have healed yourself in that little bubble of time. What would you like to do next?

ACCEPT KINDNESS

Be careful of the natural tendency to fear the unknown. North Americans watch too much TV and it teaches them that the world is a dangerous place.

I do not believe the world is dangerous. I believe you can come to danger anywhere - including in your own house. After all, you live in this world-where else will you encounter danger?

But I do not believe that there are malevolent forces out there waiting to pounce on you. In fact I believe most people are interested in you and quickly come to care about you. Over and over you will see people reach out to help you, express their well-wishes, try to make a difference. Watch this safety net. Let yourself be supported by it, deflected by it. New doors open.

Each day, for a few minutes, send out Peace be with you from your heart to the foreheads of people you encounter. Feel peace in your heart, softly, going out to them. Feel yourself give them peace. Particularly do it when you feel uncertain or nervous. It prevents you from shutting down and sending out bad signals.

When your sensors pick up danger, listen to them. When they are stroked by kindness, let them be. Expect that other people will help you in spite of those who don't. When you go into a new situation, assume you will be treated well. Watch strangers rise to the occasion.

LISTEN

Watch, listen to the world, notice. Find the things that nurture you. Give yourself the time to absorb them. Open to it all. Don't discount what happens in urban and even industrial settings.

Hear your body. Give it rest. Give it exercise. Give it the food it wants. Let it teach you.

Feel your body and mind and spirit strive for balance. After a few days of pushing hard and fast and long, respect your body and spirit when they ask for rest, a change. It may come out as an appetite that cannot be satisfied or crabby-ness or craving conversation with someone who knows you. You see that ebb and flow of your energy, sometimes for no apparent reason. Respect those life rhythms. Seasons, tides, weather patterns and you. Ebbing and flowing together.

Watch your reactions to beauty, fun, joy and see the ripples of that through you and others.

Watch that non-cognitive part of yourself that emerges and let yourself learn respect for it. Learn what happens even when you don't understand or influence it.

Phone home and waste time and money when you want to. Learning to deliver to your needs is part of the unfolding that will open your inner world.

Accept that, like all life, there will be days when it is just tiresome hard work. And then be ready to be touched by magic at unexpected moments.

WATCH THE MYTHICAL FORCES

The struggles of mythical characters against the forces of evil and human weakness are being played out around you. You can't see that at home. It is hard to step back far enough to see those symbolic forces. On the road you can see yourself as a player in those dramas. You are dealing with timeless, basic stuff: finding food, places to sleep, water. Symbols are in your face, teaching life lessons.

The forces that you cannot influence seem to take on mythical power: weather, plane/train/boat schedules and bureaucrats. Experiment with approaching them from a new place of acceptance. In case you missed the point, watch other travelers railing in frustration at officials, to no effect at all.

You will see the power of believing in your ability to — make it over the mountains, manage in a village where no-one speaks your language, scale walls, tame dragons, cross gorges. You see yourself creating your future each day. You see how much power you have as the director of your own movie.

You see beauty, that you could easily have missed, in surprising places and you are reminded that noticing beauty anywhere requires something from you. Mary Jean Irion, an American writer, asks: Normal day, let me be aware of the treasure you are. Let me not pass you by in quest of some rare and perfect tomorrow. Ah yes.

As you watch the mythical kinds of obstacles that you encounter you learn to see the challenges at home in a mythical way.

GAIN CONFIDENCE IN YOUR OWN GUIDE

Forget should, forget need, forget everything you have read here. Turn inward and do what you want. That's where your guide is. Learn what you like and do that, however odd. This is your self-discovery, your journey into your own soul. This book can only start you. Once you have the tools to travel your inner avenue, stay true to what you find there.

CONTINUE THE JOURNEY AT HOME

Your return home is a new kind of journey. At no other time will you be so challenged. This is when you need to protect yourself from slipping back into old patterns, being driven by external forces. You know where that leads you. When you try to find a new way to earn a living, a new way to be at home, it is important to keep in touch with yourself, with your spirit guide.

You went out there looking for ways to live differently at home. Protect what you learned. This may mean you change some things about your living circumstances and the way you earn a living. You may spend time with different people, doing different things.

It's easy to panic when you feel your out-there lessons don't apply back here. There will be periods of doubt and feeling down and believing you are lost. Did I learn nothing? There always will be. That's part of the ebb and flow that you saw while you were on the road. Do what you did when you panicked on the road. Stop. Listen. Feel. Step sideways and watch. This is a useful time to experiment. The answers come travelling on the back of your own creativity and through your body.

Create protected time for yourself to process and ponder. Easy to say. Hard to do. Your ability to apply your life lessons back at home probably depends on this. You need time to hear and feel. Review life back home. What matters to you now? What should you choose? What draws you? Well, you have the tools now to ask those questions and go inside looking for answers and to know when answers are not yet ready to emerge. It is like waiting for bread to rise or seeds to germinate - a gentle, loving process. Soft trust.

And when they do emerge, as gentle as flowers unfolding, you see them for what they are: your guides, your beacons, your answers. Now you trust them, these gentle messages from the underground, these insights, this knowing what matters to you. Now you know how to live your life so that you integrate inner and outer forces. You know how to be nurtured by all of it.

FLOATING

The ornithologist and I warmed ourselves in the morning sun while we watched baby ducks in a pink plastic dishpan. They were swimming frantically. The two of us giggled as they zigzagged around the minute pond.

"They're so busy. Zig zag, dash, dart. You'd think they had somewhere to go."

"Yeah. The funny thing is that they don't know that they can float. Up to a certain age they really are paddling for dear life. They think they'll sink if they stop. And then, one day, they know. They figure out that they float. After that they just sit there — floating."

New Journey Unfolds
Many unknowns.
You're going in.

AROUND THE WORLD

THE ROUTE THAT UNFOLDED

The map on the following pages traces the route I followed. I started the trip knowing that I would circumnavigate the world, move to the Southern Hemisphere for their summer and make all other choices intuitively, on the road. The inefficiency of route-choices based on weather shows up around the Mediterranean area.

The map shows general location but not detail. I would happily help anyone who wants more information.

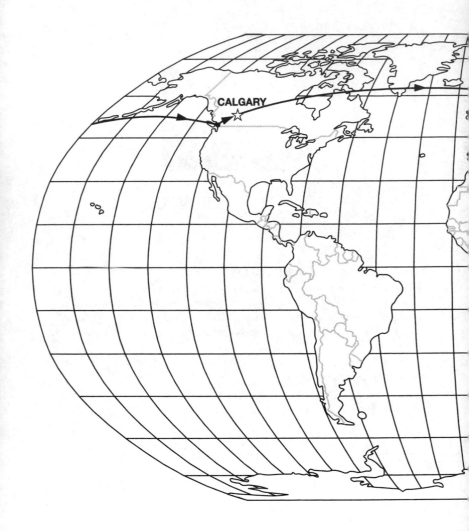

JOURNEY AT A GLANCE

Nice
Corsica:
Bastia
Saint-Florent
L'Ile-Rousse
Calvi
Flight: Calvi to Paris
Flight: Paris, Istanbul, Antalya
Antalya
Cycling east on the south coast of Turkey:
Aspendos
Side
Monaugat
Alanya
Gazipasa
Anamur
Tasucu
Oct Ferry: Tasucu to Girne, Cyprus
Cycling Cyprus
Girne
Kaplica
Kantara
Bogaztepe
Gazimagusa
Flight: Cyprus to Izmer
Cycling south down the west coast of Turkey:
Gumuldur
Ephesus
Kusadasi
Soke
Didim
Bodrum
Torba
Marmaris
Kedreia
Ferry: Bodrum to Rhodes (Rodos)
Rodos Town
Cycling Rhodes:
Lachania Beach
Kemasti
Ferry back to Bodrum
Bus: Bodrum, Bursa, Ankara
Ankara
Flight: Istanbul, Abu Dhabi, Singapore
Singapore
Flight: Singapore to Auckland

Nov Auckland
    Cycling the North Island of New Zealand:
    Whangerei
    Russell
    Paihia
    Kerikeri
    Kaeo
    Whangaroa
    Coopers Beach
    Karikari Peninsula
    Cape Reinga
    Kaitaia and the Gorge
    Rawene
    Opononi
    Dargaville
    Matakohekauri Museum
    Paparoa
    Bus: Auckland, Hamilton, Urenui
    Cycling the southwest coast of the North Island
    Waitara
    Inglewood, Stratford
    Eltham
    Hawera
    Patea
    Wanganui
    Bus to Wellington
    Wellington
    Ferry: Wellington to Picton on South Island
    Cycling Northeast coast of South Island
    Picton and Blenheim
    Kaikoura
    Cheviot
    Waipara
    Christchurch
    Flight: Christchurch to Auckland
Dec Flight: Auckland to Seoul Korea
    Namyangju,a small town outside Seoul
    Train and bus around South Korea
    Kyonju
    Pusan
    Mokpo
    Cheju-do
    Seoul
Jan Flights: Seoul, Hong Kong, Bangkok, Koh Samui
    Nara Gardens, Koh Samui
    Cycling around Koh Samui
    Chaweng

Simple Life, southeast corner
Cocacabana Beach Club - southwest side
Nathon - west
Axolotl Village - northwest
Ziggy Stardust - north
Nara Gardens
Feb   Flights home: Koh Samui, Bangkok, Kuala Lumpur, Vancouver, Calgary

READING AND RESOURCES

I Say Sunrise; full title: What is beyond the darkness? Some say chaos and darker night. I say sunrise. Talbot Mundy De Vorss & Co. 1947. This is a strange book. It suggests, for example, that it is hopeless to attempt sitting quietly and emptying your mind to meditate. Talbot favours keeping yourself busy with something automatic like knitting or walking and letting your mind become still while you are otherwise occupied. Has merit. I wasn't quite sure where he stood regarding Nazis, that was ambiguous. But the quote I use from it about our responsibility to nurture our spiritual development was my pole star throughout my journey and continues to be today.

Marg Archibald's Excellent Cycling Adventures in Niagara; Marg Archibald, The Monday Communications Group Ltd, 1999

Marg Archibald's Excellent Cycling Adventures in Southern Alberta; Marg Archibald, The Monday Communications Group Ltd, 1997

Path with Heart: Jack Kornfield, Bantam Books, 1993

Seven Spiritual Laws of Success, The: Deepak Chopra, AmberiAllen Publishing and new World Library, 1993. This is a tiny book that teaches you how to keep your life focussed on your spiritual evolution. It is invaluable when you return to the pressures of everyday life and want to remain true to the things you have learned intuitively as your traveled.

Snow Leopard, The; Peter Matthiessen, Chatto & Windus, originally printed in 1979 but recently reprinted.

CREDIT & THANKS

PHOTOGRAPHS

I shot most of the photographs myself. Sometimes I handed the camera to a bystander to shoot. The exception is the photograph of my Grandmother on the cover. This photo has stood on my mantelpiece for years. When I sent it to Lynn Rennie for cover consideration, she said, "I opened the package and picked it up. It seemed like more than light and shadow and emulsion on paper. It had a life of its own. This is an amazing photograph. My hands shook when I held it. She looks like an angel." Sonia heard about this conversation and she said, "When I was little I always thought that I was an angel."

Riding into the Void: I shot with my remote on an isolated road inside The Golden Ring in Russia

Into the World through Russia: This concrete pillar stood in the middle of nowhere, surrounded by empty fields, beside a road through the Golden Ring.

Chasing the Sun South: an astrological clock in the old town square in Prague. My astrologer, Deanna, can look at this and tell the day, year and time that the photo was shot.

Benim Gogia Turk: was shot by a bystander while I strolled the waterfront at touristic Didim in Turkey.

Into the War Zone: was shot by a cooperative crew member at the back of the high-speed ferry between Turkey and Cyprus.

Turkey Re-Visited: captures part of the ruin of the library of Celsus at Ephesus, Turkey.

The She-Colossus of Rhodes: was shot by British tourists in a rental car as I struggled over the mountains in western Rhodes.

In Transit: is in the bar in Raffles Hotel, Singapore.

Home on the other side of the World: catches me boarding the ferry that runs from the North to the South Island in New Zealand.

A New Playground: is my sister at a women's monastry isolated in the hills above Namyangju, Korea.

Paradise Found: is shot on the main road, around the perimeter of Koh Samui, an island in the Gulf of Thailand

The End, The Everything: catches a glimpse of the retreating rainbow which, a few moments before, had risen from the side of the road I was cycling. The road was the deserted highway, north of Dargaville, New Zealand.

After words: shows a delightful little cat in an outdoor restaurant in Rhodes, however the chapter is mainly about my own cat - Brenda.

Cycling into Your Soul: catches the narrow road from Whangaroa on the northeast corner of New Zealand's north island. Anywhere you find a overhanging tree it beckons you to cycle under it, invites you to cycle into your soul.

Around the World: was shot by my Mom, in her den, as we traced the route I followed, after the fact.

Journey at a Glance: shows me on an isolated beach in Koh Samui, shot by the only other people there.

Reading and Resources: shows part of the amazing mosaic church in Russia, outside Jaroslavl. It's there because I love the picture.

Credit & Thanks: captures the statue and offerings at the outdoor airport in Koh Samui, Thailand.

Outside back cover photo is at the Moscow Cityport as I prepare to board the cruise ship that will carry me away from Moscow traffic to Jaroslavl where I began cycling.

THANKS

Sue Dutton sat in a restaurant with me as I recounted some of my travel adventures and insights. She said, "You have to write the book, Marg." She kept saying that until it was written.

Ian and Linda Dallas read the first draft and the second and third. Their conviction that this was a story well told carried me through doubts and fears. Later they checked the last copy. This saved me the embarrassment of obvious mistakes getting into print. Throughout, they cared for me and the journey I told. They protected it from the challenges of well-meaning critics who envisioned a different story. I am grateful for their generosity and their perspective. We gave birth to this story together.

Lynne Rennie, a highly regarded graphic artist and a special friend, loved the story and offered to create its visual presentation. Our gleeful collaboration was one of the most rewarding parts of the journey. She has done an amazing job and given me the chance to see the journey anew.

Our thanks to MapMedia Corporation for providing the base map.